RECALIBRATE

Praise for the book

N.K. Singh, with contributions from his distinguished co-author Dr P.K. Mishra, has written a book that outlines the reforms that could transform the Indian economy at this critical time. *Recalibrate: Changing Paradigms* constitutes the most penetrating commentary on the Indian economy today.

—**Jagdish N. Bhagwati**, University Professor (Economics, Law, and International Relations), Columbia University

N.K. Singh's new book comes at a time of global uncertainty. The combination of challenges—of recurring pandemics, geopolitical conflict and hurdles to sustainability and economic development—requires fresh domestic and multilateral responses. Together with Dr. P.K. Mishra, N.K. Singh shines a light on the new thinking required and possible solutions, drawing on his leadership in policymaking. We ought to heed the book's call for a recalibration of social contracts and mutual obligations within and among nations.

—**Tharman Shanmugaratnam,** Senior Minister, Singapore and Chairman, Group of Thirty

In *Recalibrate: Changing Paradigms*, N.K. Singh, wisely and rightly, calls for a sustainable, resilient and innovative approach to growth and development. He is informed and positive about the ways forward to a productive economy and society and he applies his wealth of practical experience to how they can be delivered. In so doing, he also draws on the great experience and thoughtfulness of Dr P.K. Mishra. These ideas are already shaping India's future. The world should listen.

—**Lord Nicholas Stern**, CH, Kt, FBA, FRS, IG Patel Professor of Economics and Government, London School of Economics

The more the world changes, the more experience is needed to chart a course forward. In this important volume, N.K. Singh and P.K. Mishra draw on their vast wisdom gained while helping policy actors think and thinkers act to provide guidance on the main issues of the day. India's issues are the world's concern and this book deserves a global audience.

—**Lawrence H. Summers**, Charles W. Eliot University Professor and President Emeritus at Harvard University

RECALIBRATE

CHANGING PARADIGMS

N.K. SINGH

WITH SELECT INSIGHTS FROM

P.K. MISHRA

RUPA

Published by
Rupa Publications India Pvt. Ltd 2022
7/16, Ansari Road, Daryaganj
New Delhi 110002

Sales Centres:

Allahabad Bengaluru Chennai
Hyderabad Jaipur Kathmandu
Kolkata Mumbai

Illustrations: Mohit Suneja

ISBN: 978-93-5520-280-2

Third impression 2023

10 9 8 7 6 5 4 3

Printed in India

CONTENTS

SECTION 3
FISCAL MATRIX AND BEYOND

Introduction

THE NEW INESCAPABLE IMPERATIVE

This decade commenced on a somewhat optimistic note, seeking to address one of our key challenges—creating a development process in consonance with our environmental compulsions. The three landmark framework agreements adopted by the international community in 2015 on global warming and climate change—the Sendai Framework for Disaster Risk Reduction 2015–2030, the Sustainable Development Goals (SDGs) and the Paris Agreement—gained renewed momentum.[1]

---

[1] The Sendai Framework for Disaster Risk Reduction 2015–2030 (United Nations Office for Disaster Risk Reduction, 2015) adopted by the UN member states in Sendai, Japan, on 18 March 2015, sets a 15-year non-binding and voluntary pathway aimed at achieving 'the substantial reduction of disaster risk and losses in lives, livelihoods and health and in the economic, physical, social, cultural and environmental assets of persons, businesses, communities and countries over the next 15 years.' The SDGs, adopted on 27 September 2015, at a special UN Summit, envisage an Agenda 2030 for Sustainable Development as a commitment to eradicate poverty and achieve sustainable development by 2030 worldwide. The Paris Agreement, adopted at the 2015 United Nations Climate Change Conference (COP21), on 12 December 2015, came into effect on 4 November 2016. It aims to strengthen the global response to the threat of climate change by keeping global warming to well below 2°C above pre-industrial levels and pursue efforts to limit warming to 1.5°C.

Though there is no formal link between the three international processes and each was negotiated separately, the elements of these agreements overlap. It is well-accepted that climate change, sustainable development and disaster risk agendas are interlinked. The three distinct agreements, each with its own goals and review mechanisms, had the common objective of setting the world on a path towards a sustainable and climate-resilient future.

In a sense, the United Nations (UN) got off to an early and eloquent start to this new decade while setting the 2030 Agenda for SDGs:

> [...] We are resolved to free the human race from the tyranny of poverty and want and to heal and secure our planet. We are determined to take the bold and transformative steps which are urgently needed to shift the world on to a sustainable and resilient path. As we embark on this collective journey, we pledge that no one will be left behind.[2]

National governments, in pursuance of the UN SDGs, have designed and implemented policies in conjunction with business associations and civil society groups. January 2020 looked like a time of multiple new beginnings. It was clear that we needed to face certain daunting challenges but some comfort could be drawn from the fact that beyond the vision, purposive implementation and action had commenced.

However, by March 2020 it was clear that the world was irretrievably changing, although it took some time for that awarenesses to sink in. Covid-19 arrived and disrupted not only lives and livelihoods but also the functioning of the global

[2] 'Resolution adopted by the General Assembly on 25 September 2015: 70/1. Transforming our world: the 2030 Agenda for Sustainable Development', United Nations, https://bit.ly/3xuYb5E. Accessed on 18 April 2022.

social and economic order. The ripple effects of our varying responses to the pandemic have potentially threatened and risked our current way of life and our social and economic fabric.

The pandemic has shown us that we are all connected, irrespective of our preferences or predilections. We rely on supply chains—spanning cities, countries and regions—for the most mundane components of the most everyday products, from swabs to solar panels to chips. These connections may fray in the future, as interdependence is exploited in new arenas of war, including information and cyber warfare. However, these connections run deep and cannot entirely be severed.

The pandemic has highlighted the movement that makes modern labour markets, economies and, in some cases, families function. We travel for work, pleasure and our families. So, it is not practical to remain in a lockdown forever. We also cannot ignore proximity and geography—people under duress move. It is the most primal form of adaptation to change.

It has changed the way we meet—opening up new possibilities via the virtual and online sphere while closing down the formation of valuable relationships that build durable social capital. Much of our economy is built around enabling such meeting and leveraging these opportunities for in situ collaboration and joint work. We have had to adjust to the modification of these opportunities during the last few years.

These far-reaching changes were not part of the usual ebb and flow of the world. It resembled a point of no return—a tipping point in the language of complex systems. Is it good for us? Will it foster trust and collaboration, including the social capabilities we need, more than ever? Only time will tell.

The first two years of the pandemic have also shone a spotlight on the vast inequities across and within countries, as well as the stubborn, sometimes irrational and often self-reinforcing roots of this inequality. On the one hand, the crisis has promoted unprecedented partnerships, where various companies, universities and others joined forces to develop diagnostics, therapeutics, possible vaccines and testing centres. On the other hand, access to these vaccines and treatments has remained highly unequal. We have seen a stark divide in the fortunes between those who could work remotely and those who depended on society functioning in a constant flow of people, gatherings and movement.

The pandemic was not the only major disruption of the decade. In 2021, the Sixth Assessment Report of the Intergovernmental Panel on Climate Change (IPCC) summarized the worsening news from the scientific community on climate change. An alarm was raised to undertake rapid action to avert even worse damages to the 'operating environment' that sustains us.[3] Further, in 2022, the IPCC has sought to focus on three working group reports, which will be finalized by September 2022. The report of Working Group I on *The Physical Science Basis* was published in August 2021 to provide the latest data on, and physical understanding of, climate change.[4] The report of the Working Group II on *Impacts, Adaptation and Vulnerability,* published in March 2022, focuses particularly on energy transitions in terms of land and ocean ecosystems; urban and rural infrastructure; and industry and society.[5] The report of Working Group III on *Mitigation of Climate Change,* published in April 2022, provides a global assessment of the climate change mitigation progress as well as sources of global emissions.[6] We have seen

---

[3]'Sixth Assessment Report', IPCC, https://bit.ly/3uQZRob. Accessed on 18 April 2022.

[4]'Climate Change 2021: The Physical Science Basis', IPCC, https://bit.ly/3LXxyL5. Accessed on 8 May 2022.

[5]'Climate Change 2022: Impacts, Adaptation and Vulnerability', IPCC, https://bit.ly/39LTTgo. Accessed on 8 May 2022.

[6]'Climate Change 2022: Mitigation of Climate Change', IPCC, https://bit.

that the future of climate change is here, for some much more than others.

The rise and fall of Covid-19 and its variants, the increasing concerns about environmental news and the shifting sands of geopolitics in the digital era have forced us to reckon with certain realities that could have been ignored in the past. The armed conflict in Ukraine and the weaponization of the international financial system in 2022—by way of freezing the voluntary dollar reserves—will undoubtedly have far-reaching consequences for the global order. Further, an opaque mix of truths, lies and selective representation—amplified by the very same technologies that drive the global currents of friendship, ideas, art and so much of the best of humanity—has affected our understanding of where war ends and peace begins.

The Great Renewal

Covid-19 and the 2021–22 updates to the global climate and environmental assessments have forced us to recognize that we are changing the earth faster than we, or other species, can adapt. Whatever one believes about the origins of Covid-19, it is impossible to ignore the background rate of new zoonotic diseases that come from the increasing overlaps between habitats and homes. In more ways than one, we have become unproductively unequal, fractious and fragmented as societies. The basic trust and sense of security needed to support social collaboration is weak—and Covid-19 highlighted this in spades.

Further, as geopolitical configurations change more rapidly than ever before in these unprecedentedly uncertain times, the international structures developed in the aftermath of World War II, which we have inherited, will need transformative

---

ly/3LX6DyK. Accessed on 8 May 2022.

changes. The fallout of the ongoing Russia–Ukraine war will force us to seek a new world order—a multipolar world with groups of countries and regions that provide leadership to foster trade, pursue benefits of the value-added chains and seek patterns of cooperation beyond the known structure, with a greater tilt towards multipolarity and a hybrid mix of self-sufficiency.

What we do with this reckoning and how we harness the conclusions drawn from these emerging insights for the longer road is, in some ways, more of a Great Renewal. Our approach to these questions will be telling and consequential. There is no escape: we have to get it together to be a team!

Planning for this recalibration is a historical necessity and will shape our thinking in 2022 and beyond. In fact, there are many who insist on going beyond just restarting to build more resilience into the post-Covid-19 economy. In an article on global economic recovery and the Herculean task of restoring the household and business balance sheets that comprise its foundation, economist Joseph E. Stiglitz wrote, 'In managing these effects, an ounce of prevention would be worth a pound of cure.'[7] We must take care to avoid our vulnerabilities from 2019. Kristalina Georgieva, managing director of the International Monetary Fund (IMF), called for the issuance of $500 billion Special Drawing Rights (SDR), and urged for strong G20 policies to prevent 'dangerous divergence.'[8] This would be enormously helpful in restarting the economy, particularly as several rich countries have also committed to donating or lending their allocations to countries that need

[7]Stiglitz, Joseph E., 'A Global Recovery's Leading Variables', *Project Syndicate*, 4 January 2021, https://bit.ly/3EqAzjO. Accessed on 18 April 2022.

[8]'Strong G20 action to reverse "dangerous divergence" in global economy: IMF chief', *Hindustan Times*, 24 February 2021, https://bit.ly/3MerddK. Accessed on 18 April 2022.

them the most. In India, similar sentiments were echoed by Prime Minister (PM) Narendra Modi, who mentioned that 'India is ready to do whatever it can to further global good and prosperity. This is an India that is reforming, performing and transforming.'[9]

It is, therefore, no surprise that in the business world, the 50th annual meeting of the World Economic Forum (WEF), in January 2020, brought economic and political domain experts and leaders together to discuss ways to rebuild society more sustainably. The theme continued for the 2021 Davos summit, and will undoubtedly shape things in 2022 and beyond. Among policymakers, variants of the Build Back Better framework have become rallying cries for capital budgets and innovative missions among national governments. The World Bank and IMF's spring meeting agenda for 2021 was peppered with panels on 'A Peoples' Recovery', 'Green Recovery' and other similar statements of intent. The spring meeting agenda for 2022 maintained the idea of building back better with panels on 'Finance for an Equitable Recovery' and 'Boosting Resilience in Turbulent Times' with an emphasis on the global supply chain.

Broad contours of solutions are taking shape. There is a growing consensus for what has been described as the acceleration of the stakeholder economy. This could steer the market towards changes to wealth taxes, the withdrawal of fossil-fuel subsidies and the new rules governing intellectual property, trade and competition. The need to shift metrics to encourage governments and businesses to incorporate and fund more green and sustainable infrastructure projects is inescapable. As part of the recalibration, the harnessing of technological innovations of the Fourth Industrial Revolution

---

[9]'PM Modi addresses India Global Week 2020 in the UK via video conferencing', Narendra Modi, 9 July 2020, https://bit.ly/3wciHWl. Accessed on 8 May 2022.

in every sector is inevitable to address the lacunae in all the sectors of society.

However, acting on these ideas and implementing these plans is easier said than done. The turbulence seems to be accelerating with successive waves of Covid-19 and the intersecting physical, digital and financial wars that shape the underlying channels and flows of an economy already under stress. Systems also change slowly, and efforts to move quickly to the new have raised the spectre of inflation.

Rewriting the Social Contract

True transformation will require a deliberate, shared attempt to break away from the patterns of the past. It will also require a conscious, collective shift towards a new social contract between and within nations. In 1762, French philosopher Jean-Jacques Rousseau published *The Social Contract,* in which he explains that the only legitimate governance rubric is one that is consented to by people for the sake of mutual preservation.

Redefining this social contract—between citizens and the State—constitutes an integral part of recalibration. With the challenges of Covid-19 and the rise of technology, the social contract needs to be rewritten in the following ways.

- First, we must address issues of climate change, energy use and overall consumption patterns.
- Second, we must simultaneously increase agricultural productivity without expanding its climatic and environmental impact.
- Third, the government must upgrade its basic investments in its citizens, which includes healthcare and education, for more robust human and social capital.

- Fourth, the broader concerns of the governance architecture, which ought to combine the virtues of stability and change, are continuing issues that must be addressed.

These four challenges together—advancing human development and well-being for a growing population within a tightening envelope of carbon space, natural resources and ecosystem services—form the greatest innovation challenge we have had to grapple with. Closer home, we are already strengthening our ability to rise to the occasion. We have attempted to redefine the fiscal architecture of the Indian governance matrix, manage complex geopolitics and continue to refine India's growth potential in its economic and fiscal policies.

Even as we look to the future to envision a better tomorrow, the realities of implementation require close attention to the past, particularly to understand why it has taken a drawn-out pandemic for us to focus on long-standing problems. In this context, *Recalibrate: Changing Paradigms* contains essays on various aspects of the challenges described above. These essays, compiled over a period of three years, are broadly classified into groups corresponding to the critical elements of the recalibration outlined above.

This book, written by me, contains select insights from the principal secretary to PM Modi, Dr P.K. Mishra, who has authored five chapters. The views, opinions and analyses in all the other chapters are entirely mine and, hopefully, will be as engaging to the readers as they have been for me.

The first section explores the function of governance. Even before the pandemic, the world was experiencing a shift in governance from a Westminster model to a more presidential model, in the context of dominant world leaders. Chapter 1 seeks to understand how the pandemic will affect all this, including the increasing need for a shift in the social contract.

Chapter 2, written by Mishra, recounts his years working in Gujarat as a young Indian Administrative Service (IAS) officer. He narrates some personal experiences and anecdotes to analyse how the constructive (and mostly harmonious) relationship between politicians and bureaucrats, and peoples' active participation and involvement contributed to Gujarat's rapid development, especially during the early decades after its formation, and even in recent decades. The chapter brings out micro-level issues and challenges of implementing development policies and programmes at the grassroots level.

Chapter 3 deals with federalism and Centre–state relations. It broadly discusses India's fiscal architecture in the federal context. The dialogue on long-term fiscal issues was somewhat interrupted due to the pandemic. We now have to consider how it can return to an upward trajectory.

Chapter 4 looks at the emergence of urban local bodies (ULBs) and rural panchayats in what is called the third tier of governance. These local bodies have emerged as important entities in these challenging times.

Section two gives insight into a people-first policy approach. Given his rich experience in agriculture and related sectors, Mishra deals with several pertinent issues regarding agriculture in India in Chapter 5. Going beyond the issues of productivity, modern inputs, infrastructure and marketing, he delves into four basic ideas impacting agricultural development. First, although it is known that agricultural activity is riskier than other economic activities, the problem of risk has not been addressed effectively. Second, agricultural development depends a great deal on what happens in the sectors other than agriculture. Third, the role of the rural non-farm sector, though recognized by experts, has historically not been integrated with our agricultural policy and programmes. Fourth, non-agricultural sectors, particularly industry, have not been able to divert and absorb the agricultural workforce to a degree commensurate with the decline in the share of agriculture in the Gross Domestic Product (GDP). Mishra then describes how a holistic strategy has been adopted in recent years to address these challenges.

Chapter 6, written by Mishra, focuses on technology and its role in the future of education. This chapter looks at recent initiatives undertaken in the school ecosystem, including DIKSHA (Digital Infrastructure for Knowledge Sharing), one class with a dedicated TV channel and the use of other digital media such as podcasts and radio, to mention a few.

Chapters 7 and 8, written by me and Mishra, respectively, focus on the health sector in pre- and post-Covid-19 India. The part written by me covers the evolution and architecture of our health policy over a longer period of time. Mishra's chapter focuses particularly on the key initiatives taken by the government to address the pandemic as well as the futuristic changes, reforms and use of technology in this context.

Chapter 9 has been authored by Mishra, who is internationally recognized for his contributions to the field of disaster risk management. This chapter looks at how the practice of disaster risk management in India has evolved over the last two decades. While outlining some of India's key successes, particularly in protecting lives, it highlights emerging challenges and suggests strategies for tackling them. It reflects on the lessons from the ongoing pandemic, described by some as a Black Swan event, and its implications for the future.

Climate change is the theme of Chapter 10. In fact, even before the emergence of the unforeseen global pandemic, climate change and issues of sustainability were being discussed in light of the Anthropocene. Climate goals are also directly aligned with problems of clean air and carbon dioxide emissions.

The third section of the book analyses the fiscal matrix and beyond. In this, Chapter 11 outlines issues of competition in the corporate and financial domain, as well as issues of market dominance, and what the role of regulators must be in the post-pandemic world.

Chapter 12 continues the discussion of India's fiscal policies with regard to the Fiscal Responsibility and Budget Management (FRBM) Review Committee (2016), which I chaired. It also looks at the issue of state finances, contextualizing it with Budget 2022–23 and Economic Survey 2021–22.

Chapter 13 discusses the Finance Commission (FC) of India, which I have chaired. The workings of the FC are important to the federal architecture of India. There are issues that each of the FCs—from the first to the fifteenth—sought to address in the contemporary context, particularly against the backdrop of the pandemic.

These are essays from the 'before time' on the need for reform. These were written when the status quo felt more comfortable and seeking change looked more daunting. But now that we've been pushed to the edge of a new wave of choices, we need to recount and remember the lessons in these essays. The need for change is obvious. Paradigms of the past need to be recalibrated. This is an inescapable imperative. We hope that bringing these essays into the public domain can be an opportunity for triggering wider discussion. It will also help create broader awareness of the need for a global recalibration in the social, political and economic spheres.

Section 1

MATTERS OF GOVERNANCE

1

STABILITY AND CHANGE

Achieving complementarity between the PMO and Cabinet Secretariat

The fulcrum of governance in the Westminster model is the PM. He is supported by the Cabinet Office and, invariably, all PMs have a Prime Minister's Office (PMO). In a democracy, the parliament, as the law-making body, has a separate role assigned under its constitution, and the judiciary works within its own domain. In the Indian governance architecture, the PM is the head of the executive branch. So, in this architecture, the PM, the Cabinet Secretariat and the various ministries and entitled organizations constitute the executive branch. In the overall pyramid of governance, the relationship between the PM, the Cabinet Secretariat and the PMO plays a central role.

However, there was a time when neither the Cabinet Secretariat nor the PMO existed. Prior to Independence, the Viceroy's Executive Council was established under the Indian Councils Act, 1861. This Council had a secretariat, which was a precursor to the Cabinet Secretariat. The Viceroy's secretariat was headed by his private secretary, who did not attend the Council meetings. Much later, the private secretary's role increased in importance, as he was made responsible for coordinating the work of the departments when the portfolio system commenced. Members of the Viceroy's Executive Council were assigned different departments. It was only in 1935 that the Viceroy's private secretary came to be known as the secretary to the Viceroy's Executive Council.

This Executive Council's secretariat became the Cabinet Secretariat during the period of the interim government in September 1946. Article 77(3) of the Constitution of India, 1949 says, 'The President shall make rules for the more convenient transaction of the business of the Government of India, and for the allocation among Ministers of the said business.' The work of the Cabinet Secretariat, therefore, inter alia, includes the administration of the Government of India (Transaction of Business) Rules, 1961 (ToB Rules), and the Government of India (Allocation of Business) Rules, 1961 (AoB Rules), to facilitate the smooth transaction of business in ministries and departments.

The PMO was first established as the Prime Minister's Secretariat (PMS) in 1947, during the time of Independence. The PMS was created for the immediate purpose of taking over the functions performed till then by the private secretary to the Viceroy because the PM took over the functions which the Viceroy performed as the executive head of the government.

The PMO is an extra-constitutional body, which finds no mention in the Constitution. However, it was given the status of a 'department' under the AoB Rules, which briefly explain the PMO and the Cabinet Secretariat as such:

- Prime Minister's Office: To provide secretarial assistance to the Prime Minister.
- Cabinet Secretariat: (i) Secretarial assistance to

the Cabinet and Cabinet Committees; (ii) Rules of Business.

The PMS, during the tenure of PM Jawaharlal Nehru, had some joint secretaries and was assisted by a small secretarial staff. M.O. Mathai recounts, 'The staff of the PM's secretariat is not responsible for advising on policy or for executive [*sic*] the Prime Minister's decisions on policy. They are only gatherers and conveyors and, in short, mechanics men.'[1]

This tradition continued till 13 July 1964. On that day, PM Lal Bahadur Shastri appointed L.K. Jha, my father's batch mate, fondly known as LK, who had been the secretary of economic affairs, as the secretary to the PM. Thus, for the first time, the PMS did not have a joint secretary but a full-fledged secretary to the Government of India. At LK's insistence, I believe, there was a new insertion in the AoB Rules, which said that the function of the PMO was 'to provide secretarial assistance to the Prime Minister.'[2]

With this new insertion in the AoB Rules, the role of the cabinet secretary, who earlier had the vital responsibility of being the last advisor to the PM, got diluted. This had far-reaching consequences, which we all know. It made a qualitative and structural difference in the rubric of governance but this was in a world that thought mainly about hierarchy and the 'last word.'

---

[1]Mathai, M.O., *Reminiscences of the Nehru Age*, Vikas Publishing House, 2008.

[2]I had accompanied my father to congratulate L.K. Jha on his appointment as the secretary to the PM, who was at the time living in 36, Aurangzeb Road. My father made the jocular remark that, 'Congratulations, LK, for two things: first, for the high office you now occupy; and second, for this remarkable coup, which has now permanently destroyed the traditional ethos of the Civil Services establishment.' What he meant was that LK's note as principal secretary would now be the last note the PM would read. That position, indeed, has been writ in stone.

Of Hierarchy and the Last Word

After PM Shastri's passing away, LK continued as the secretary to Indira Gandhi. However, his somewhat liberal views became an increasing irritant to the more Left-minded members of the establishment. This was also a time when Mrs Gandhi began to increasingly lean on the Left parties to purge the Congress by either removing or downgrading those who were perceived as her political challengers, like Morarji Desai. In a certain sense, an era of a relatively liberal economic policy was beginning to wane.

With the arrival of P.N. Haksar to replace LK, there were other changes. Haksar's ideological bias soon gave rise to micro-scrutiny from the PMO, along with meritocracy becoming increasingly irrelevant. This undermined the basic philosophy of respecting institutional responsibilities and, in some way, brought out the worst aspects of the power of having the last word.

Creating structures upon structures generates its own dynamic, as everyone starts looking for an enlarged turf. The PMS soon acquired several joint secretaries, who were reporting to the new secretary to the PM. Multiple layers of decision-making were formed that disintegrated the chain for responsibility/accountability and led to the usual jostling for power and attention.

This weakened the Cabinet Secretariat. The PMS started mirroring a parallel government. The PM did not see files directly sent to him either by the Cabinet Secretariat or by relevant ministers. Files were marked down to the joint secretaries concerned, who would then obtain orders from the principal secretary, depending on their importance and the allocative functions assigned between them. The PM would see the shadow notes recorded by the officials of the PMO, suggesting a decision or a course of action, beneath which the original file also used to be kept. This gave the PM the option to either read the full file or its more succinct version, along with a proposed course of action from the senior officials of the PMO.

Clearly, things were never going to be the same, as we learnt from the succession of events. Even as PMs came and went, the concentration of power in the hands of the PMS was often an electoral issue. It figured in the electoral campaign of 1977, and unsurprisingly, when Morarji Desai succeeded Mrs Gandhi on 24 March 1977, true to his electoral commitment, he took decisive steps to circumscribe the powers of the PMS. For one, the 'Prime Minister's Secretariat' was rechristened the 'Prime Minister's Office', signalling that it would not yield the same degree of interference as had been prevalent during Mrs Gandhi's time. This change in nomenclature was, indeed, strange since, immediately after Independence, the name 'PMS' had been retained.

In today's more complex, fast-moving and, in many ways, more informed world, this way of looking at the Cabinet Secretariat and the PMO, as a matter of which office has the last word on what reaches the PM, is outdated and ineffective. We need to find a way of managing the head of the State that offers a path to agility, adaptability and innovation, while leveraging our strengths and capabilities across agencies and levels of government. The PM is entitled to the best advice available on key policy issues and the new frontiers of access that technology can offer.

In the UK, the PMO (10 Downing Street) currently includes a policy and implementation unit, a research and analytics unit as well as other functions. It retains a focus on a number of areas across government, especially those that reflect the PM's priorities. On the other hand, the Cabinet Office supports the Prime Minister and Cabinet (PM&C) of the UK, working via departments to coordinate the efficient execution of governance.

Similarly, in Australia, the PMO contains units to advise the PM on policy, strategy, media and their parliamentary duties. It also performs administrative functions. The PM&C acts as both the Cabinet Secretariat and the PM's source of non-partisan advice to government. It also undertakes longer-term strategic policy projects and monitors the implementation of government priorities. In a certain sense, therefore, in Australia, the sharp distinction between the Cabinet Office and the PMO seems to be somewhat blurred.

In Canada, this opaqueness is confounded because the PM's immediate office is separate from the Privy Council Office (PCO). The PMO is a partisan organization intended to serve the PM exclusively. The PCO is headed by the clerk of the Privy Council and secretary to the Cabinet, a public servant chosen in practice by the PM. This PCO is, thus, both the Cabinet Secretariat and the PM's source of non-partisan civil service advice across the policy spectrum.

So, how do the dynamics between the Cabinet Secretariat and the PMO work in India? I was privileged to work in the PMO as Secretary to PM Atal Bihari Vajpayee from 19 August 1998 to 1 May 2001. I learnt a lot during my tenure and some of these abiding lessons have, in some ways, been narrated in my autobiography, *Portraits of Power*.[3]

In retrospect, I believe the primary function of the Cabinet Secretariat is to be the fulcrum of stability. Particularly in times of frequent change of government, or an era of coalition, it ensures compliance to the institutional framework of rules and procedures prescribed under Article 77(3) of the Constitution. An example of this can be seen between 1989 and 1991, when there were three successive PMs—V.P. Singh, Chandra Shekhar and P.V. Narasimha Rao. This was also a

---

[3]Singh, N.K, *Portraits of Power: Half a Century of Being at Ringside*, Rupa Publications India, 19 October 2020.

period of great economic crisis during which the initiatives of V.C. Pande (cabinet secretary from December 1989 to December 1990) and Naresh Chandra (cabinet secretary from December 1990 to July 1992) ensured that the economic reforms and programmes remained intact. During this period, for understandable reasons, the PMO took the backstage, so to say, and the responsibility of the orderly conduct of important economic and policy issues rested with the Cabinet Secretariat.

The Cabinet Secretariat is also the fulcrum of stability because, in a democratic government, like India, it protects the integrity of the AoB and ToB Rules. In a parliamentary government, the PMO may be occupied by a PM who has scant respect for the rules of business.

The PMO will only mirror the personal predilections of the PM himself. Therefore, what can be done to protect the broader national interest in the spirit of the Constitution? In such moments, this responsibility inevitably rests with the Cabinet Secretariat and the cabinet secretary. Ironically, this brings me to what Viceroy Archibald Wavell had written in his letter to Frederick Pethick-Lawrence on 10 September 1946, '[Nehru's] Private Secretariat will be integrated with the Cabinet Secretariat and I think it will be easier for Nehru and also limit the occasions on which he goes off at a tangent.'[4] Nehru may or may not have gone astray, but there is no guarantee that no one in the future will. The Cabinet Secretariat, therefore, remains the protector of the overall constitutional framework, acting in pursuance of Article 77 to ensure that the procedures and processes are carried out with the integrity of their purpose.

As the head of the Indian Civil Services, the Cabinet

---

[4]Mansergh, Nicholas and Penderel Moon, *The Transfer of Power, 1942-7. Vol. 8, The interim government, 3 July-1 November 1946*, Her Majesty's Stationery Office, London, 1979.

Secretariat is also responsible for the coordinative functions of sorting out differences between departmental secretaries and ensuring that the points of view of the departments are reconciled with others who feel differently. The former UK Cabinet Secretary Gus O'Donnell, who managed the responsibility of the transition from the Gordon Brown government to the coalition with David Cameron and Nick Clegg, is a classic example of managing these differences. It is said that his authority as cabinet secretary was so absolute that he was affectionately given the nickname of 'GOD' since his initials appeared as such in government papers.[5]

The cabinet secretary also services not only the Cabinet but also the eight important permanent cabinet committees: Appointments Committee of the Cabinet, Cabinet Committee on Accommodation, Cabinet Committee on Economic Affairs, Cabinet Committee on Parliamentary Affairs, Cabinet Committee on Political Affairs, Cabinet Committee on Security, Cabinet Committee on Investment and Growth and Cabinet Committee on Skill Development. Heading these is an awesome and tiring responsibility. This, therefore, answers the question of whether the Cabinet Secretariat and PMO should be merged into one entity. I think the two institutions should remain apart and have an arm's-length relationship.

Lastly, one of the prime functions of the Cabinet Secretary is also recording the minutes of the Cabinet meetings. This is, by no stretch of imagination, a mere mechanical exercise. Crafting the intent of the Cabinet and interpreting it in a manner that the PM, as the chairman of the council, intended the outcome to be needs skills, domain understanding, innovation and often, imagination. In the popular UK television show *Yes, Prime Minister,* there is a hilarious scene involving

---

[5]White, Lesley, 'Gus O'Donnell: the man they call GOD', *The Times*, 6 December 2009, https://bit.ly/3FbJshQ. Accessed on 13 April 2022.

a Cabinet meeting. While the fictional PM Jim Hacker insists that there are no divisions in Cabinet, a dissenting member objects repeatedly about the happenings of the previous Cabinet meeting. In response, the PM's permanent secretary, Sir Humphrey Appleby, insists that,

> It is characteristic of all committee discussions and decisions that every member has a vivid recollection of them and that every member's recollection of them differs violently from every other member's recollection. Consequently, we accept the convention that the official decisions are those, and only those, which have been officially recorded in the minutes by the officials, from which it emerges, with an elegant inevitability, that any decision, which has been officially reached will have been officially recorded in the minutes by the officials and any decision, which is not recorded in the minutes has not been officially reached, even if one or more members believe they can recollect it. So, in this particular case, if the decision had been officially reached it would have been officially recorded in the minutes by the officials. And it isn't, so it wasn't.[6]

Unlike the Cabinet Secretariat, the PMO must be the fulcrum of change. This is so because the PMO is the principal vehicle through which all new initiatives of the PM are to be implemented. The PMO must also be a catalyst for change. In addition, it must be the final problem-solver. It can do so because it seeks to carry out orders at the behest of the chief executive, so to say.

For instance, when the far-reaching economic reforms

---

[6]Officially Official | Yes, Prime Minister | BBC Comedy Greats, YouTube, https://bit.ly/3sxIasv. Accessed on 04 may 2022.

of 1991 were undertaken, Dr Manmohan Singh was quite perplexed about how these were to be crafted and implemented. First, the economic reforms themselves were not entirely home-made, but the result of arduous interactions between multilateral lending institutions and the Government of India. Their implementation would not have been possible without the then Principal Secretary Amar Nath Verma, who called for innumerable interdepartmental meetings to ensure the implementation of the reform programmes articulated in the Budget. In the process, of course, he may have trampled over the conventional wisdom of many other departments, whose thoughts had remained embedded in times that were not relevant to deal with the crisis of that period.

In addition, the creation of the Foreign Investment Promotion Board (FIPB) under Principal Secretary Verma's chairmanship signalled to the world an important message—India was welcoming foreign investments. This represented a radical change from the old mindset, where we were grudgingly accepting foreign investments. The PMO played an important role in managing the Balance of Payment (BoP) crisis of 1991.

When I joined PM Vajpayee's office in 1998, my allocation of duties remained somewhat opaque. When I asked him what my responsibilities were, he gave me a classic, cryptic answer, 'Sab kuch', which meant 'Everything'. His response really made me wonder whether I was empowered to undertake initiatives that I couldn't have conceived of as a departmental secretary, in areas like telecom and roads, to mention a few. For instance, the PMO played a key role in moving over to a revenue-sharing agreement through innumerable meetings with the attorney general, the telecom ministry and the concerned minister. This enabled us to put the telecom sector on track. There were several other instances when the PMO played a leading role in getting the PM's big ideas implemented, which I have recounted in my autobiography.

On an aside, the leading role of the PMO sometimes has hilarious outcomes as well. During the corporatization of the Bharat Sanchar Nigam Limited (BSNL), the then Telecom Minister Ram Vilas Paswan suddenly announced a populist policy, known as freebies, to provide free telephones to 3.2 lakh employees of the telecom department. The finance minister (FM) objected to it and the PM was wary of Paswan's populist measures. Additionally, the corporatization of the BSNL needed a firm timeline. However, Paswan was anxious for his announcement to be implemented quickly.

In the midst of this situation, in June 2000, Vajpayee was about to leave on a tour of Italy and Portugal. I recall that before the plane took off, there were hectic negotiations on the telephone with Paswan, with us insisting that a firm date for the corporatization must be announced alongside the freebies. Paswan realized the broader benefits of improving the productivity of BSNL by making it a corporate entity, thereby benefitting the overall productivity of the economy. Besides, he was willing to agree to the privatization of BSNL in order to implement the freebies he had already announced. After hectic negotiations, the successively postponed corporatization of BSNL was implemented from 1 October 2000.

Another example is Vajpayee's announcement of the Golden Quadrilateral in October 1998. Frankly speaking, when I entered his room with his speech to be delivered before the Federation of Indian Chambers of Commerce & Industry (FICCI), he asked me if it contained anything worthwhile. When I stammered, he told me, 'What is the use of wasting everybody's and my time? Think of a big idea.' The big idea evolved into the Golden Quadrilateral, which was announced during a FICCI meeting. Two months after this speech, he said in his characteristic Hindi, '*Maharaj, aap logo ne ghoshna karwa di, ab banwa bhi dijiye*.' This translates to, 'You all have made me announce it, now make sure you actually build it.' This was a quintessentially

Vajpayee statement—short and pithy.

However, the financing of the Golden Quadrilateral remained problematic. The government announced a cess of ₹1 per litre on the consumption of petrol and diesel. There was a yawning gap between the revenue available and the likely expenditure. Having considered various alternatives, I asked the Ministry of Finance whether the proceeds of the cess could go into a non-lapsable pool, and since the cess would be in perpetuity, if large borrowings could be contracted and the debt paid through the securitization of the future annual accrual from the non-lapsable fund. Understandably, the Ministry of Finance had strong reservations. In fact, in one of the meetings during that period, the then finance secretary asked me if I would recommend the creation of a fund outside the Consolidated Fund of India had I been working in that ministry. Without hesitation, I said, 'Of course not,' but added that you look at things depending on not what you may have believed but where you sit. I was now sitting in the PMO and had been assigned the task of getting the PM's 'big idea' implemented. It was agreed that they would send this proposal back, opposing it, for the PM's consideration. Again, it was the job of the PMO to overrule.

The PMO does not do business as usual, but is in the business of overruling. It is the business of the ministries to put forward their point of view as cogently as they can, but it is the business of the PMO to overrule and ensure such outcomes, as would be consistent with the final objective that the PM may have in mind for the broader national interest.

The PMO must not only be a problem-solver but an agent for change, as is evident from the events preceding the constitution of the FRBM Act. With PM Vajpayee's approval, a committee was set up to draft India's future fiscal policy. This committe was headed by Dr L. Vijay Kelkar, with Urjit Patel as a member. The committee concluded that, notwithstanding past pronouncements on fiscal behaviour, there were no legislation or stipulated targets and little accountability. It also suggested that an FRBM Act must be passed by Parliament. This Act was to stipulate the levels of permissible fiscal deficit as a percentage of the GDP. Based on this committee's report, Vajpayee decided to enact legislation on fiscal laws, called the FRBM Act, which was approved by Parliament in August 2003. It was a major change in the area adhering to fiscal targets. It was also a departure from the past belief that containing fiscal deficit was not necessarily an unmitigated virtue.

The Next-Gen PMO's Approach

As we move into the twenty-first century, we face a plethora of complex challenges. In addition to the scope to innovate and create, we also need to be grounded and use the full capabilities that we have across various levels of the government and ministries. We need to build our powers of anticipation amid the uncertainties of interdependence while remaining connected with our realities to respond to challenges.

In such an evolving scenario, how can we shift from a mindset of hierarchy to one of complementarity and equality between the PMO and the Cabinet Secretariat? How do we update the rules and the basic structure of balance across these two complementary capabilities—stability and change—given that we need both but there is an inherent tension between them?

Is refining the AoB Rules, if not redrafting them, the only answer? How do we strengthen the role of the Cabinet Secretariat in providing the key linkage between the various ministries, ministers and the PM while creating space for expertise in new ideas to meet emerging challenges? How do we adjust the coordinative functions between different ministries and departments to balance the remainder of the present while answering the call of the future? In such a scenario, how does the shift in the Cabinet Secretariat vis-à-vis the PMO redefine the role of the ministers in charge of their respective departments, as enshrined in the Constitution, and does the restructuring in the balance of power between the Cabinet Secretariat and the PMO impact their functions as well? Most importantly, which of these models or hybrids, lead(s) to faster, sound decision-making and more effective implementation?

To all these questions that I have posed for myself, my answer is a cryptic one: strategic ambiguity, let us say.

The AoB Rules, which define the role of the PMO and the Cabinet Secretariat, have been drafted with precision. They clearly demarcate the functions of these two bodies.[7] We do not need to change but we need to evolve with time. Therefore, we need to ask different questions. What are the key areas the PMO needs to focus on over the next decade or so? I would shortlist eight areas in which, I believe, the PMO is well placed to undertake new initiatives.

First and foremost, the issue of changing the matrix and architecture of governance for the institutional rationalization of departments and ministries. This is a neglected area and no entity other than the PMO is capable of undertaking this challenge. In fact, there are some obvious entities in the government that require far-reaching reforms. The first is a ministry where I worked for long—the Ministry of Finance. When Dr Singh was taking his leave as FM, he asked me, 'What do you think honestly has been my failing?' I was rather perplexed and said that I couldn't think of any. He

[7]The functions of the Cabinet Secretariat, as stated in the AoB, 1961, include secretarial assistance to the Cabinet and Cabinet Committees and the Rules of Business. The function of the PMO, as stated in the AoB, 1961, includes providing secretarial assistance to the PM.

said, 'I will tell you. The two entities which remained totally unreformed are the Ministry of Finance and the RBI.' He added in a tongue-in-cheek manner, 'Regrettably, I have headed both these institutions.'

About the finance ministry, there is no doubt that the monolithic structure needs a fundamental change in two important areas. First, with the abolition of the Planning Commission, the working of the department of expenditure has become increasingly untenable. I remember since the days when my late father was the expenditure secretary, the office of the financial advisors (FAs) did not exist and every small financial proposal needed the approval of the expenditure secretary. This was clearly untenable.

When the Planning Commission existed, the expenditure secretary had the benefit of adversarial advice from the advisor concerned in the Planning Commission. So, he could evaluate both the advice of the FAs as well as the expert advice from the Planning Commission. In the absence of these inputs, he is largely left with his advisor, any such consultant as he may choose and others who may wish to bring in their domain knowledge.

We need to, therefore, look at what other countries have done. Similar to the US, we may need to create an Office of Management and Budget (OMB), headed by a cabinet minister. The UK also has a similar entity called the National Audit Office. I also believe that the public debate on expenditure initiatives and outcomes should be undertaken in a consultative process rather than the way we undertake large public expenditures. In the current set-up, this is not possible.

There is no raison d'être for expenditure proposals to be integral to the treasury functioning. The treasury secretaries, so to say, or the secretaries of treasury in many parliamentary countries, including the UK (the Chancellor of the Exchequer), are not necessarily burdened with the responsibility of expenditure proposals. Instead, they weigh in on larger issues of the management of the economy as a whole.

Similarly, while the Department of Economic Affairs remains at the heart of economic reforms within the ambit of the government, I am unable to understand why, out of the best international practices, having an independent fiscal council has eluded successive FMs. Fifty-four countries have now adopted independent fiscal councils and that is an area where I think our institutional structure is deficient in comparison with other peer group countries. Few PMs have believed in fiscal norms more doggedly than PM Modi. So, this lacuna is difficult to wish away and could be rectified easily.

The Reserve Bank of India (RBI) has too many inherent conflicts of interest as not only the principal banking supervisor but also the principal debt manager of the government. Another instance is the working of the Ministry of Commerce and Industry (MoCI). Earlier, we could not change it because the Ministry of Commerce and the Ministry of Industry were separate entities. But with the merger of these two, why can't they function in the same spirit as the Ministry of International Trade and Industry (MITI) of Japan, which actively enables private investment to be catalysed? Fortunately, now that we have crossed the hurdle of deep suspicions with private capital, I think an MITI-like structure would be more appropriate for the MoCI.

Clearly, governance reform must be an important area of attention for the PM because these changes will require overruling departmental prejudices, uncertainties and turf protection.

Equally important is the need to improve the matrix of governance of trust between the Centre and states. Previously, the Planning Commission was one such entity and, even now, the NITI Aayog does this, to some extent, but there is a requirement for a different institutional framework for dealing with ongoing Centre–state relations. The Ministry of Finance's views are not trusted by the states, thus requiring an arm's-length relationship.

The nature of the federal compact prompts us to rethink the most appropriate mechanism for a continuing dialogue with the states that goes beyond fiduciary obligations of the type that the FC concentrates on, or the sort of functions currently being undertaken by the NITI Aayog. Of course, the closest in the mechanism so far is the FC. The states have traditionally relied on this body, and it is respected for its non-partisan approach—equidistant not only between the Union and states but also between the states by the application of quantifiable and monitorable normative standards. Thus, having the FC mediate a continuing dialogue with the states is a possibility.

Yet another important area that needs to be prioritized by the PMO is the issue of Centre–state relations. One possibility is rejuvenating the Inter-State Council, which is a constitutional body, but has remained by and large dysfunctional. This council could be restructured as an entity of the PMO—with the PM as the chairman and an independent vice chairman, with a small secretariat. It could become a useful instrument for continuing dialogue with the states. Over time, it could also acquire credibility and domain knowledge. One area the Council could take up is procedural and other reforms for catalysing private investment in states, particularly in relation to their cooperation on factors of production, some of which have remained in the domain of the states.

The fourth area is the reform of the criminal justice administration. We know that the Ministry of Law and Justice, which deals with the judiciary, has met with limited success. Yet, we realize that our judicial system, while being respected for fair play, is not regarded as one in which business can be transacted with ease due to the tardiness of this form of alternative dispute resolution.

The fifth important area is a nascent one—the creation of a risk perception and management unit within the PMO. In this regard, one wonders: why was it not anticipated that India was likely to face the consequence of a global financial meltdown? Or of the systemic weakness of the healthcare system? Or the weakness created by the lack of disaster-resilient infrastructure? Anticipating risk and preparing for events is an activity that only the PMO is well-positioned to undertake. Developing expertise with domain understanding on disaster management will have multiplier benefits.

The sixth important area involves the environment and technology. The adoption of technology dramatically improves the distribution of entitlements, like irrigation and the right mix of fertilizers. This is a positive step towards sustainable development, particularly for the environment. It also entails greater economy in the use of fossil fuels in agricultural practices. These examples can be replicated in other areas, like changing transportation systems to utilize renewable fuels and efficiently delivering health or educational services. The issues with embracing cutting-edge technology are being prioritized by the current political leadership. The use of 5G technology enhancing total factor productivity across different sectors and spheres from agriculture to health is well known.

In the recent Budget 2022–23, the use of technology in governance was emphasized with the launch of Ease of Doing Business (EoDB) 2.0 and Ease of Living. As a result of the Modi government's commitment to 'minimum government and maximum governance', over 25,000 compliances have been reduced and 1,486 Union laws have been repealed. The FM said,

> This new phase will be guided by an active involvement of the states, digitisation of manual processes and interventions, integration of the central and state-level

> systems through IT bridges, a single point access for all citizen-centric services, and a standardization and removal of assessment of the impact with active involvement of citizens and businesses will be encouraged.[8]

The seventh area is that of external affairs. Successive PMs have been concerned, and rightly so, with maintaining foreign relations. In fact, for a long time, it was joked that the PM is invariably his own foreign minister. With increasing global interdependence, and India playing a more critical role in the global arena, understandably, PM Modi has prioritized issues of global interdependence and India's role as an emerging economic power within the global framework. For a long time, the assignment of the National Security Advisor (NSA) was integrated with the functions of the principal secretary. These have, since, been segregated. This is to allow the NSA to focus on broader issues of geopolitics, defence and foreign policy.

There are, however, the more pressing issues of mainstreaming and aligning the approach of important economic ministries with the working of the Ministry of External Affairs (MEA). The economic ministries, understandably, feel that diplomats who work on missions abroad have scant understanding of complex economic issues. On the contrary, diplomats serving in key positions abroad often feel that their voices and suggestions on aligning some of our economic policies to further our economic interests often remain unheeded or inadequately addressed. How does one better align the conduct of our relations with the economic policies of key economic ministries? This is another area that must by prioritized by the PMO.

Finally, the eighth area is revitalizing public–private

---

[8]'Budget 2022–2023: Speech of Nirmala Sitharaman, Minister of Finance', Union Budget, 1 February 2022, https://tinyurl.com/4ccrt9kj. Accessed on 19 March 2022.

partnerships (PPPs). In the public perception, this has meant the private sector palming off risks to public-sector entities without bringing capital and managerial skills. The private sector has managed to create an impression that the governmental approval process is riddled with interminable delays. This important area of harnessing PPPs and harmonizing them with technology has remained elusive. We have a robust infrastructure programme, and without PPPs, it will have a very halting start. This is another area where, I believe, the PMO has an important role to play.

The Cabinet Secretariat and PMO functioning in close symmetry and synchronization will enable India to improve the matrix of its governance. In this process, the Cabinet Secretariat plays an exceedingly vital role for reasons mentioned above. However, stability cannot be an end in itself nor can change be guaranteed without stability. Therefore, the PMO needs to develop an adaptive, next-generation approach. The benefits of such an approach are promising, including increased stakeholder consultations that ensure their satisfaction, effective policy management that is responsive to the developmental need for speed, agility and innovation and, ultimately, better outcomes.

As Harold Wilson once said, 'He who rejects change is the architect of decay.' The PMO should be a force multiplier by enabling, facilitating, connecting and bridging the existing gaps to reduce disconnection and seek opportunities to add value. After all, as Plato said, 'The wisest have the most authority.'

An authoritative PMO, not an accommodative one, is in consonance with the needs and challenges of our times.

∞

This chapter has been extracted from N.K. Singh's closed-door lecture at the PMO on 8 December 2020.

2

PEOPLE, POLITICIANS AND BUREAUCRATS

Mapping Gujarat's development administration

Four years ago, H.R. Patankar and Dr Kirit Shelat, former civil servants, asked me to write an article for an edited volume *Developing Gujarat: My Memories.*[9] I was reluctant in the beginning. I thought about the value I would be able to add just by describing my experiences of various assignments and highlighting my work and contributions. Several others also would have done so. The development of Gujarat, as with any other place, is multidimensional. There are many factors that help determine the speed, spread and scope of such a process. Numerous individuals and institutions contribute to a development process. Nevertheless, they prevailed upon me, and I decided to focus on one aspect of Gujarat's journey to becoming a progressive state during the early decades after its formation, based on an analysis of my experiences over the years.

---

[9]Patankar, H.R. and Kirit Shelat, *Developing Gujarat: My Memories,* Sahitya Mudranalaya, Ahmedabad, India, 2018.

Sociopolitical Milieu

I propose a hypothesis that Gujarat's sociopolitical milieu contributed significantly to its rapid development, especially during the early decades after its formation, and even in recent decades. It is not easy to test this hypothesis based on quantitative or empirical data. Therefore, I would like to examine the postulate with the help of some personal experiences and anecdotes.

For the present analysis, the expression sociopolitical milieu comprises three aspects: people's awareness and proactive participation, voluntary/non-governmental efforts and the nature of the relationship between politicians and bureaucrats. There are, undoubtedly, several other factors (e.g. the entrepreneurial spirit in the state and the policy focus on industry) that influenced development in Gujarat. However, the three factors mentioned above possibly distinguished Gujarat from many other states and have played a significant role in its rapid and multifaceted development.

One marked difference between Gujarat and many other states is people's awareness and proactive participation. For instance, whether in the relatively less developed Tharad subdivision or Kutch district or the more developed Surat district, there were frequent interactions between the people and the administration. It was a two-way process. Elected personnel from urban areas, and even those from remote villages, did not hesitate to visit government offices at taluka and district levels seeking redress of their problems and grievances. People had a great degree of awareness and the administrative system provided access. For example, every Monday, known as 'Janata Day', was dedicated to hearing the grievances of common citizens. Officers had to prioritize meeting people over official work. Even on other days, people would visit the various offices, and meeting people during official tours was an important part of administration. Consequently, there was more effective and people-oriented formulation and implementation of development programmes.

Voluntary agencies—this term was more common than non-governmental organizations (NGOs) during the early decades after the formation of Gujarat—played a significant role in rural development activities, and in providing relief to drought- and flood-prone areas, which were very common those days. They worked at the grassroots level and understood ground realities. The government facilitated their work by coordinating with them. Those days, NGOs were known more for their work with rural people than for participating in national and international conferences and seminar circuits.

The nature of the relationship between politicians and bureaucrats impacts administration at all levels—village, taluka, district and state. In the 1970s and 1980s, when I worked at the subdivision and district levels, people respected political leaders as well as senior officials for their commitment to public interest and welfare. My impression is that the majority of political leaders were known for their selfless service and honesty, possibly because the legacy of the freedom struggle still had its imprint on them. Senior officers, particularly those in the IAS, were known to be honest, even though some of them did not have a reputation for competence and effectiveness. In other words, people, at times, doubted their capability but never their probity.

Unlike several other states, both political executives and senior officers in Gujarat were accessible to the people. The relationship between politicians and bureaucrats was generally respectful and cordial, though there were instances of clash and conflict. Officials generally were not known to be identified with a political disposition, regime or leader, unlike other states. Interestingly, some officers (although their number was small) who were close to some politicians when a political party was in power could continue to be similarly aligned, even when another party came to power. There were no large-scale transfers with a change in government. There was hardly any transfer based on the whims of political executives. However, this is a moot point since people's perception of political leaders and senior officials changed after the 1990s.

Reflections from the Field

My first experience of Gujarat was in Surat, during my district training. Most of my time there was devoted to law and order because of the Navnirman Andolan. It was there that I became familiar with how common people and prominent citizens interacted with the district administration. I worked in Tharad and Palanpur subdivisions as the assistant collector, in Kutch as the district development officer (DDO) and in Banaskantha as the collector and district magistrate during 1974–78. Subsequently, I worked in the remote tribal areas of Odisha for about five years. On returning to Gujarat, I worked in Mehsana district, which was one of the largest districts in those days, as the collector and district magistrate till 1985. Thus, for over a decade, I had field assignments, mostly in less developed areas with harsh geo-climatic environments. However, I enjoyed working at the grassroots level, interacting with people and their representatives from village to district levels. In the Gujarat secretariat, I worked in the departments of agriculture and rural development and revenue, all of which focused mostly on rural people. Never did I feel that I was in the wrong place.

I have described below several experiences and anecdotes that illustrate some of the dimensions of development administration in field-level organizations.

Subdivision Level

I began my career as the assistant collector of Tharad subdivision of Banaskantha district in the middle of 1974. At the time, Tharad was a village with a gram panchayat. Other villages were even smaller, with water scarcity because of low rainfall and proximity to the desert areas bordering Pakistan. There was no electricity substation around the villages in those days. Sometimes, there was no electricity for days on end, at times even for a week. So, even when there was a dust storm during peak summer, one could not close the windows, either in the office or at home, as the electric fans would not work because of frequent power failures. The drinking water sourced from deep tube wells was very saline. There was no other alternative because water from the ponds, as Ajim Khan, who cooked my meals, informed me, would have guinea worms. In several villages, people were infected with the guinea-worm disease, which used to cause worms to come out of the infected person's feet some months after the infection.

My first year in Tharad was a drought year. People and their representatives clamoured and argued with officials for more relief work. As the assistant collector, I chaired the taluka-level committee that sanctioned relief work. In its weekly meetings, non-official members, such as the taluka panchayat president, would have heated arguments with the mamlatdar, who was in his fifties and would lose his temper quite often. I found it difficult to calm them down because I was new and just in my twenties.

Relief work was started in many places to provide employment and income for sustenance. NGOs used to distribute relief materials, including food items such as *sukhdi*, made from wheat flour, jaggery and ghee, even in remote areas.

Four years later, in December 1978, while working in a remote tribal district of Sundargarh, Odisha, I witnessed a huge contrast in the attitudes and the relationship between people and the administration. Once, I visited a block office, similar to the Taluka Development Office in Gujarat. As I came out after a meeting, I saw five or six people standing outside at a distance. I asked the block development officer (BDO), who was seeing me off, why they were standing there. He replied that they were visiting the block office for some work but were too scared to come inside!

Gujarat summers are very harsh in areas closer to the desert, like Vav and Suigam. To inspect the drought relief work, we travelled long hours in cars. My driver, Raib Khan, would hang a thick jute bag with drinking water on one side of the vehicle to keep the water cool in the midst of strong, dusty, hot and dry summer winds. As the months passed, people from several areas complained of the shortage of dry grass/straw, which was used as fodder for cattle. I grew worried.

At the suggestion of a smart awal karkun (senior clerk), and against the advice of the sheristadar (senior-most official of the subdivision office), who was a seasoned and cautious person, I passed an order prohibiting the movement of fodder out of Tharad. This adversely affected the supply to a neighbouring district; the district collector of this area got concerned and wrote a strongly worded letter to his counterpart at Palanpur, pointing out that I had issued an illegal order and that I had no power to issue the said order. The latter accorded post facto approval on the grounds that there was an acute shortage of fodder and that I had been unable to take his prior approval because the telephone line had not been working, which was a common occurrence in those areas for days on end. Thus, even though I had committed a procedural lapse, because of people's complaints and pressure, a fodder crisis was averted.

In the Palanpur subdivision, particularly in the Deesa area, the riverbed land would be auctioned for potato farming every year. Over the years, vested interests developed and a few companies and individuals would collude to ensure that the same parties were allotted the same land every year at a low rent. Some people brought this practice to my attention and I changed the auction parameters to encourage competition and much higher bidding, resulting in increased revenue for the government. This caused uproar and representations by those who could no longer collude. The district collector, though somewhat displeased by the disruption, approved of the change, as did his successor.

Years later, when I visited Tharad, the experience was different. The electricity supply was regular and households were getting drinking water through a regional water supply scheme. In recent years, potable water is available to the people from the Narmada canal. The gram panchayat, which had become a nagar panchayat, is now a municipality. On the way to Deesa town from Tharad, I came across large tracts of land being used for potato farming through micro-irrigation. Clearly, potato farming is no longer confined to the riverbed land. Some farmers have also taken up horticulture and have set up processing and packaging facilities to support it.

After working for two years as the assistant collector in two prants, or subdivisions, I was appointed DDO, Kutch district, in 1976. Those days, Gujarat and Maharashtra were pioneers in introducing the Panchayati Raj system of local government for development administration. In fact, almost all development activities at the district level and below were transferred to the Panchayati Raj Institutions (PRIs) in Gujarat. Gujarat was ahead of Maharashtra, possibly because Balwantrai Mehta, who served as the second chief minister (CM) of Gujarat, had chaired a Government of India committee that had recommended the establishment of the Panchayati Raj system to better implement the Community Development (CD) Programme of the 1950s. The idea was democratic decentralization to address local problems locally and to make people politically conscious.

The district panchayat, with an elected president and DDO, as the chief executive officer (CEO), was to oversee all development activities related to education, health, agriculture, irrigation, rural development, drinking water supply, social justice, land revenue and so on. Those days, people looked upon the new system with great expectation. In the IAS, at times, the DDO was senior to the collector. In fact, a senior political leader had envisioned that in the not-too-distant future, the colonial institution of district collector would be replaced by district panchayat. In time, however, the scenario has changed.

For me, as the DDO, it was interesting, though quite often overwhelming, to coordinate such a wide range of activities—from dealing with divergent groups of officials to interacting with political persons as an integral part of the organizational structure—unlike my earlier assignment as the assistant collector. There were several functionaries to interact with—district panchayat members, chairpersons of various committees of the district panchayat, particularly the district education committee (which had a distinct role and was relatively autonomous), taluka panchayat presidents and members and, of course, the sarpanchs at the village level.

I frequently interacted with voluntary agencies, panchayat functionaries and people in both villages and small towns. Working with and in the midst of panchayat members was—though demanding and unpleasant or even conflicting, at times—indeed productive and useful. I gained some interesting experiences during this time.

The district education committee, headed by a non-official chairman, had autonomy in matters relating to primary schools. It followed a good practice of issuing transfer orders only during summer vacations. The downside to this was that hundreds of such orders were issued within a short period of time. A large number of teachers would request a transfer to towns and other nearby areas. A few weeks after joining, I learnt that there was widespread corruption and favouritism and, as a result, there were many complaints against officials and non-officials. When I took up the matter with the district primary education officer, R.H. Shah, he informed me that decisions were taken by the chairman, mostly on the advice of non-officials. I suggested to him that there should be some objective criteria and each case should be decided on merit. Since he sounded helpless, I discussed the matter with Bhimjibhai Valjibhai Chande, the chairman of the committee, a reasonable person in his early sixties. After some persuasion, Bhimjibhai agreed with me, and we went about listing definite criteria for screening and prioritizing applications. Since there were thousands of applications requesting transfers, I suggested that we visit the taluka headquarters for two weeks with prior publicity, so that applicants could come and present their cases.

At every taluka meeting, a large number of teachers—men and women—would come to present their cases. We heard each one of them. Some were facing genuine challenges, some were exaggerating their problems and some others were even trying to mislead us. Interesting facts emerged through these meetings, and we gained ideas and insights to improve the screening mechanism.

At one of the meetings, five young women stood up and vehemently criticized the transfer process. Their grievance was that married couples working as teachers were prioritized and preferred over unmarried women, which was unfair and unreasonable because the latter remained single and had to earn to support their families under difficult circumstances. Two of the women were bold enough to say, in the presence of so many people, that any unmarried man present should come forward to marry them. We were stunned. Bhimjibhai looked at me—I was unmarried then—visibly embarrassed. Suddenly, he lost his cool, which was very unusual for him, and chided the women for their misdemeanour, asking them to leave the meeting. Afterwards, we felt that the women's grievance had been genuine. Subsequently, we modified the criteria to include a preference for single women who had dependent family members.

When the final list was announced, it was highly appreciated for its fairness and objectivity by most stakeholders. However, some people who had been managing the system earlier with their networking and connections, and had lost out this time, started agitating. Although a majority of the teachers were satisfied, a minority, which was very vocal and politically connected, put tremendous pressure at all levels and created chaos for months. The role of Bhimjibhai in the entire process was noteworthy.

Without his cooperation, it would have been difficult to change the system. On 22 May 1978, a few days after I had left for Kutch to take up a new assignment as the collector and district magistrate of Banaskantha, an article in *Sandesh* newspaper from Ahmedabad stated,

> In the history of the District Panchayat and Education Committee, and particularly in view of the extremely corrupt administration of the Education Committee of the district, it was felt that it was impossible to have annual transfer of teachers free of corruption and favouritism. However, with the cooperation of Shri Bhimjibhai, Chairman of the Education Committee, Shri Mishra made it possible. There were tremendous protests and uproar. However, with the principle of giving justice and satisfaction to 90 percent of the peace-loving employees, even ignoring the 10 percent vocal and manipulative employees, Shri Mishra stuck to his decision, ignoring the protests, which strengthened his image as a strong administrator.[10]

---

[10]Translated from an article in the Gujarati newspaper *Sandesh*, 22 May 1978.

My experience with Jethmalbhai V. Madaiyar, the president of the district panchayat of Kutch, was somewhat different. He had a reputation of being a difficult person to work with. He could not speak Gujarati with ease. In fact, in most public meetings, some people from the audience would, as soon as he stood up to speak, demand that he should speak in Kachchhi; he would smile and then oblige the audience.

Two adjoining bungalows were reserved for the district panchayat president and the DDO. On a Sunday, a few days after I had joined as the DDO, someone came to my residence in the afternoon to inform me that the president wanted to discuss some matter with me. I was in a dilemma: should I go to his residence or not? I told the person that I was busy and would see him the next day. This event, which may have hurt his feelings, coupled with some differences over administrative issues later on, resulted in a strained working relationship between us.

The interpretation of a provision relating to the power of the DDO in the Gujarat Panchayats Act, 1961, in the matter of transfer of officials, became contentious. Jethmalbhai insisted that all decisions on the appointment and transfer of officials should have his prior approval. Since I did not agree with him, he introduced it as an agenda item in a meeting of the district panchayat general body. I explained my views in the meeting and the item was not approved. In a subsequent meeting, when I was not present, it was approved. I did not implement the district panchayat resolution and made a detailed reference with a comprehensive analysis of the legal provisions to the competent authority in the government, which upheld my view. This led to increased bitterness. In subsequent years, because of political developments and court intervention, the approach possibly changed.

In this context, a news item in *Sandesh* on 22 May 1978, inter alia, stated,

> In the context of the issue of transfer of some of the powers of DDO to presidents of Zilla Panchayats, when other senior IAS officers yielded to political pressures, he [Dr Mishra], in spite of such powerful pressures, stuck to his stand consistent with the legal provisions, and finally, the competent authority had to ensure the re-establishment of the original legal framework. This episode will form a milestone when the history of modern Gujarat is written.[11]

Despite our official differences, Jethmalbhai and I maintained good communication and cordial personal relations. When my father was being treated for cancer, a few weeks before he breathed his last at Bhuj, I was with him for about a month in a hospital at Ahmedabad. Jethmalbhai travelled all the way from Bhuj to Ahmedabad to enquire about his health. I still remember his consoling words: not many people are fortunate enough to take care of their parents in such trying times.

The Minister of Panchayat, Government of Gujarat, whom I had never met earlier, visited Kutch district for three days in 1977, addressed several gatherings in villages and heard their grievances. In his last public function at Bhachau, towards the end of his speech, to my utter surprise, he appreciated my work and even said that wherever he went, he heard only good things about me. His appreciation was in response to complaints of the district panchayat and a few taluka panchayat presidents, with whom I had some differences regarding administrative issues.

Kundanlal Dholakia, in his late sixties, was the Speaker of the Gujarat Legislative Assembly in the second half of the 1970s. He belonged to Kutch and used to visit Bhuj almost every fortnight. Usually, he visited some villages and insisted

---

[11]Translated from an article in the Gujarati newspaper *Sandesh*, 22 May 1978.

on reviewing the progress of the development schemes with the local people in the presence of the officers concerned. I accompanied him quite often. He was very knowledgeable, articulate and committed to people's welfare. At times, he felt that people in the villages did not realize his seniority in the state-level hierarchy simply because he was a local person. In many of the meetings with the villagers, he would first say that he had come from Gandhinagar and that he was one of the three highest constitutional functionaries of the state: the governor, Speaker and chief justice of the high court.

It was very interesting to interact with him. Once Dholakia told me that whenever he visited Bhuj, the collector and superintendent of police (SP) received him at his residence. I replied that I was not aware of that and would join them the next time. I did so when he came after some days—he was thrilled. He invited me to visit the State Assembly when it was in session. He arranged a visitor's pass for me and was extremely happy that I could witness him in his role as the Speaker.

Thus, it was in Kutch that I had, during the early days of my career, a real feel of the dynamics of development administration in a democratic structure at the local level. More than two decades later, I had another opportunity to be associated with Kutch's arduous journey in the aftermath of the devastating earthquake of 26 January 2001.

Banaskantha District

I worked as the district collector of Banaskantha, headquartered at Palanpur, for a few months before leaving for Odisha on an interstate deputation. It was a familiar place. Babubhai Jashbhai Patel was the CM of Gujarat those days. During his earlier term as the CM, I had been the assistant collector of Palanpur. Babubhai was a simple, unassuming and frugal person, who would travel only with a small jhola, which he carried himself. Whenever he came to a district, he did not expect too many officers to meet him, unless there was some official work.

The practice those days was that the collector and the SP would receive only the CM, not any other minister. One of the cabinet ministers from Palanpur sent a message, a few days after I had joined, that he would like to see me at the Circuit House the next day. I enquired with his office what the subject of our discussion might be but did not receive a response. On the day of his visit, I did not go to the Circuit House. I received a message that the minister would come to the collectorate. At my suggestion, the resident deputy collector (RDC) received the minister and escorted him to my chambers. Extending the usual courtesy, I stood up, offered him a seat on the left side of my office table, as was the practice those days, since there was no sofa set in my office. We had a good discussion and I accompanied him to his car to see him off. Later, the RDC told me disapprovingly that I should have offered my chair to the minister. I reminded him that while visiting a subdivision or a taluka office, I did not occupy the officer's chair, despite the latter's insistence. Fortunately, the minister did not mind my not meeting him at the Circuit House and we continued to enjoy a good relationship.

Mehsana District

In 1983, when I came back to Gujarat from Odisha, I was appointed the collector and district magistrate of Mehsana, which included two police districts—Mehsana and Patan. Within a few days of joining, communal riots broke out in Sidhpur, which continued for about six months and included a few days of violent incidents, some peaceful days and then, again, incidents of stabbing, setting houses on fire, etc. I became more familiar with Sidhpur and its police chowki than with the collectorate. Prior to the annual Sidhpur mela (fair), for which thousands of people congregate, the Patan SP wrote to me saying that the mela should not be allowed in view of the law-and-order situation. I reported this to the state government. R.V. Chandramouli, the then home secretary, called me from Gandhinagar, expressed his displeasure and told me that we should not deprive people of their fundamental right to congregate and continue with their tradition because of our inefficiency. The mela was hosted successfully and peacefully, though it was held on an alternative site close to the usual one.

Strangely, a few days after peace had been restored, some residents of Sidhpur threatened to leave and go to a neighbouring country! On a particular day, people started gathering at a central area of the town and, by noon, the numbers had increased to thousands. We were stationed at a nearby location, monitoring the situation continuously. This situation was volatile and could have resulted in violence and police action. The agitating leaders demanded that the SP and I should come and address them, which, we felt, was totally unwarranted and unreasonable. Some local political leaders were of immense help in keeping the communication channel open. On their assurance, the SP and I took the risk of going near the crowd, standing on a makeshift platform and saying a few words. In a few minutes, we left the venue. Fortunately, the mob gradually dispersed and a crisis was averted, thanks to the intervention of people and politicians.

Some months later, there were communal riots in some other talukas of the district. One day, violent incidents were reported from six or seven talukas. As riots continued for several days, many people were detained under the National Security Act of 1980. We received a proposal from the district SP for detaining a Member of the Legislative Assembly (MLA). I scrutinized the papers carefully and found that there were valid grounds for the arrest. I was, however, in a dilemma because of the possible political ramifications of such a step. Some of the senior officers of the collectorate advised caution. I could not decide on what course of action to take for two or three days. I eventually decided to stick to the facts of the case and my conscience, and take the plunge! I approved the proposal. It created a huge uproar in the Legislative Assembly, which had been in session. Opposition members alleged a political motive, even though there had been none. The home minister, for his part, replied that he had not given any such instruction to the district magistrate. An opposition member retorted that the home minister never gave instructions, he only gave indications!

The MLA was detained for over a month. A year later, he was elected Member of Parliament (MP). As returning officer, I signed the certificate of his having been elected and congratulated him. Three years later, I was travelling to Mathura/Haridwar with my mother, a few months before she passed away. The MP, who was in the same train compartment, spotted me. We had a long chat on many subjects. My mother thought he must be an old friend; she was astonished when the MP told her about the Mehsana days.

A decade later, when I was member (finance) of the Gujarat Electricity Board (GEB), Haribhai Patel, who had worked with me in Mehsana as the assistant collector, informed me that Keshubhai Patel, who had just become the CM, wanted to see me the next day. While waiting to meet him, I met the same MP, who had been called inside before me. Later, Haribhai told me that the same MP had spoken very highly of me when he had met Keshubhai that day.

I found the people of Mehsana, when compared with those of other districts, to be relatively more educated, progressive and assertive. MPs, MLAs and others would come to government offices with issues and argue for hours. If they were not satisfied, they would immediately go to Gandhinagar, the state capital, which was not very far. The district panchayat president, Atmarambhai Patel, was not from the ruling party at the state level and there were frequent clashes between the president and members of the district panchayat, who belonged to the other party, with both sides being very aggressive. The president perceived that the DDO was aligned with those opposed to him. In district-level meetings, there were frequent altercations between the president, the DDO and others. I kept a safe distance from all these groups and tried my best, though quite often unsuccessfully, to defuse the tension.

The Mehsana municipality permitted the construction of a shopping complex very close to the road passing through the central areas of the town and leading to the collectorate. When this was brought to my notice by some citizens, I advised the president of the municipality to either not go ahead or to keep an adequate margin from the road. However, my advice was not heeded and work began. I took recourse to an unusual step of prohibiting the construction under Section 144 of the Code of Criminal Procedure.

One day, out of the blue, I received a phone call from the CM for the first time during my tenure; he was annoyed and pointed out that development works were being obstructed. As I was explaining my position, he disconnected the phone. Needless to say, this perturbed me. Despite this awkward situation, I did not withdraw the prohibitory order, although the president of the municipality continued his campaign, even castigating me at a public meeting, where I had been present. After a few months, I was transferred to the State Secretariat as joint secretary of the Department of Agriculture. The municipality proceeded with the shopping complex. People faced tremendous hardship due to congestion and chaotic traffic. They talked about the unreasonable approach of the president of the municipality for years afterwards.

An Insightful Understanding

Today, when I look back at my days in the three districts of Gujarat, I am filled with a sense of nostalgia and disbelief, coupled with an insightful understanding of the development of Gujarat. The nostalgia comes from an attachment to the people and the places during those early years. I never felt deprived when in Tharad, even without electricity or the telephone for days on end. In retrospect, when I think about my responses while interacting with some of the politicians, maybe I was not reasonable. More importantly, when I recall and analyse, in hindsight, the events and experiences of those days, I realize that today, I have more insight and a better understanding of the dynamics of development administration at district and subdistrict levels: the interplay of people, politicians and bureaucrats in real-life situations. I would like to narrate a few more experiences of my later years before I draw some inferences in the context of the hypothesis stated at the beginning of the chapter.

Experiences at the State Level

I worked as the joint secretary in the Department of Agriculture for over three years. Little did I realize then that the subject of agriculture policy will continue to fascinate me for years to come. I worked as the agriculture secretary in Gujarat and later with the Government of India. Indeed, my interest in the conceptual and analytical aspects of crop insurance dates back to my days as joint secretary. After years of experimental and pilot schemes, the Government of India introduced a nationwide scheme—the Comprehensive Crop Insurance Scheme (CCIS)—in 1985. As joint secretary, I had to address some issues related to the implementation of the scheme in Gujarat. Farmers and cooperative banks in Gujarat were ahead of their counterparts from other parts of the country in quickly comprehending the potential of a scheme and deriving the maximum possible benefits from it. During the initial years, the highest numbers of claims were from Gujarat, particularly the Saurashtra area, although it led to more disputes and controversies.[12] It is another example of the awareness and proactive approach of the people in accepting, adopting and utilizing development initiatives. Some years later, early adoption of hybrid and even genetically modified varieties of cotton by Gujarat farmers resulted in high agricultural growth.

The Gujarat Electricity Board, Vadodara

When I worked as member (finance) of the GEB, after completing my PhD in the UK, one of the major issues was related to negotiating power purchase agreements (PPAs). It was a new approach for the country—no electricity board had the experience and expertise for this. At the time, PPAs were being negotiated with two well-established companies. I was assisted by two very hard-working, dedicated and competent officers—an executive and a deputy engineer—in addition to the chief engineer. The teams deployed by the companies were formidable, comprising national and foreign consultants and legal experts, well-dressed in suits, armed with voluminous and complicated draft documents to be negotiated. We used to discuss each and every line for days.

We took over six months to settle on one PPA, as our disagreements persisted. In the interim, the developer company repeatedly complained to the government that the delay was being caused by us, and that we had not been interested in the development of the state. S.J. Coelho, Chairman, GEB,

[12]Based on my PhD research, I have documented some of the issues in a book titled *Agricultural Risk, Insurance and Income: A Study of the Impact and Design of India's Comprehensive Crop Insurance Scheme*, Avebury, Aldershot, UK, 1996.

was under tremendous pressure. A distinguished civil servant, Coelho had been conferred the Padma Shri for his outstanding work as district collector of Kutch during the Indo-Pak War of 1965. He had vast experience in the power sector, particularly after his voluntary retirement from the IAS.

In the case of another PPA, we could not reach any conclusion for a much longer period. In the meantime, there were several other smaller proposals for barge-mounted power plants and other such projects. Frequent meetings were convened by senior officers at short notices in Ahmedabad. I could not attend some of the meetings because of non-receipt of notices on time, as one had to travel from Vadodara.

One day, Coelho was invited to Gandhinagar for a discussion on these issues. It was a small meeting in the CM's chambers. The Minister of Power, two senior officers and two senior functionaries of a company were also present. The Minister of Power, who was not known to be polite, said that power projects were not being finalized because of abnormal delays in the GEB and that the chairman was not allowing the member (finance) and other officials to even attend important meetings. Even the CM used some strong words. Coelho had never asked me not to attend any meeting, but he did not want to say that I had decided to not attend these meetings.

Seeing his precarious situation, I intervened. I presented the details of the meeting notices, some of which had reached me around midnight, indicating a meeting time as early as the next morning, and how it would have been impossible to attend such meetings. I mentioned that the chairman never asked me or any other officer not to attend the meetings. I argued that if the minister wanted to immediately finalize the PPA, as he said, it could be done in two weeks or even in a week, provided we agreed to whatever the developer wanted. That would imply an outgo of ₹20,000 crore from the consumers of Gujarat over the PPA period. Everyone in the meeting was stunned. The meeting concluded without any decision.

Coelho asked me to travel with him in his car on our way back to Vadodara. He admired my bold statements and said he had never seen me so 'angry' and using such strong words. Some days later, Coelho resigned. The proposed project in question—and many proposals for small thermal and barge-mounted power projects—never saw the light of day, saving the state economy from adverse consequences.

Secretariat, Gandhinagar

When I worked as the secretary to the government, in the Revenue Department, Government of Gujarat, which oversees the work of district collectors and manages the cadre of the Gujarat Administrative Service, there were complaints relating to bias and favouritism in transfers and posting. Although, initially, Vajubhai R. Vala, the Minister of Revenue, was not very keen to introduce any change in the existing system, being a reasonable person, he finally agreed to it, once all the aspects had been presented to him. In later years, he was very appreciative of what had happened.

Vala is an intelligent, friendly and light-hearted individual. Once, while having a general conversation on some development issues in Gujarat Bhawan, while I was visiting Delhi for a meeting in 1999, I mentioned to him that education should be prioritized, citing some results of a cross-country and econometric analysis on the role of primary education in economic development. Being a businessman, he strongly disagreed, arguing that incentives to industry and business should be prioritized. It was a very casual conversation, which I totally forgot over time. A few years later, I was surprised when he referred to our discussion and said that he had later realized how important the role of education is. I admired his willingness to accept new ideas.

Once, a senior minister suggested the transfer of a senior revenue department officer to a particular assignment. Even though I explained that it was not feasible, he repeatedly asked for it. One day, he called me late in the evening about the same issue and I again told him politely that it would not be feasible. He wrote a letter to CM Keshubhai Patel, complaining and asking that disciplinary action be taken against me, as I had been rude and misbehaved. As usual, the letter reached the general administration department. It was passed up the official hierarchy, travelling for several months through many levels, without any officers recording their views, so as not to antagonize the minister. Finally, CM Patel himself wrote on the file that the matter was to be closed right away, as he did not find the complaint against me credible.

Gujarat pioneered rural feeder segregation, i.e. separating feeders for rural farm and non-farm consumers. It improved both the availability and the quality of power supply in rural areas. It led to better load management and increased the power supply for rural households and small industries. Other states followed Gujarat's example, which is now well-accepted nationally. In Gujarat, this path-breaking initiative owes its origin to the vision and persistence of a politician.

A few months after Narendra Modi became CM, he asked, as there were numerous complaints of irregular power supply to villages, if there could be separate feeders for farm and non-farm consumers. The answer from both engineers and bureaucrats was negative. The GEB opposed it on the grounds that it would be infeasible and expensive. The departments of Energy and Finance were also against it, but they could not provide any alternative to improve rural power supply. As the principal secretary to the CM, I had several rounds of discussions with them, but could not convince them.

Finally, the CM decided to go ahead and ask all the stakeholders concerned to prepare a scheme for approval.

The file was submitted but none of them recommended the proposal—they all felt that the CM, being new to the position, was unable to appreciate the problems and consequences of his proposition. I was perplexed. I discussed the issue with the concerned engineers in the GEB, whom I knew personally since my days as a member (finance) of the GEB. We discussed some alternatives, such as a pilot project in a few villages, an evaluation after a few months, etc., and I assured them that I would not insist on any measure that would adversely affect the GEB. They finally agreed and, after initial hiccups, gradually the scheme took off. Given the proactive approach and determined efforts of CM Modi, the scheme was successfully accomplished. The rest is history.

The Kutch earthquake of 26 January 2001 was one of the most devastating events in recent decades. It caused the deaths of 13,805 persons and injured several thousand people. Over a million homes were damaged or destroyed. Thousands of artisans lost their livelihood. The damage to social and economic infrastructure, such as public buildings, roads, water supply, power system, telecommunications and health and education facilities, was enormous. The task of recovery and reconstruction was extremely complex.

In the aftermath of this earthquake, the Gujarat State Disaster Management Authority (GSDMA) was set up, with the CM as its chairman. I was appointed the CEO of this body, a position I occupied for over three-and-a-half years, till I was deputed to the Government of India. For most of this period, starting October 2001, I worked as the principal secretary to the CM of Gujarat, with the additional responsibility of the CEO of GSDMA.

A comprehensive reconstruction programme after the Kutch earthquake, comprising many sectors and a wide range of activities, was put in place. Even when the task of reconstruction appeared massive and challenging, medium-

and long-term aspects of disaster management were not ignored in the programme. There was particular emphasis on participation of people and NGOs.

- Each team for damage assessment at the village level included either a representative of an NGO or a teacher.
- Decisions regarding relocation or in situ construction were left to the gram sabha or village council.
- Even for urban reconstruction, there were public consultations for preparing development plans and town planning schemes. In many cases, the removal of debris was organized through village panchayats.
- Over 42,000 school rooms were repaired through village civil works committees, which included school teachers and elected representatives.
- The reconstruction of a large number of new school rooms and other infrastructural work was undertaken through PPPs, i.e. government agencies and NGOs/ private sector working together.
- A list of beneficiaries and details regarding financial assistance were displayed at public places and on the GSDMA website.
- Thousands of legal literacy camps were organized to educate people on their rights and the legal remedies available to them.
- Eminent citizens, academicians and people's representatives at state, district, taluka and village levels reviewed the reconstruction and rehabilitation work from time to time.
- A benefit monitoring study was undertaken by an international consultancy firm.
- There were committees at various levels for the redressal of people's grievances.
- District judges from the affected districts were declared as ombudsmen for the redressal of grievances.

At the political level, there was transparency, openness to ideas from outside (for e.g. from national and international organizations) and the involvement of people and civil society. There was maximum possible delegation of powers to the GSDMA and district officers for sanctioning infrastructure and housing projects to facilitate the speedy implementation of reconstruction work.

The then CM, Keshubhai Patel, devoted a great deal of his time and energy in laying down policies for recovery and reconstruction, along with schemes and guidelines, and creating and implementing an organizational structure at the state and district levels. CM Modi, who succeeded Patel, ensured further refinement, improvement and effective implementation of the programme. His meticulous planning, attention to detail and organizational capability activated and enthused the entire administration and other stakeholders.

The accomplishments of the GSDMA were acclaimed nationally and internationally. In October 2004, the GSDMA received a Gold Award of the Commonwealth Association for Public Administration and Management (CAPAM) for 'Innovation in Governance'. The award committee observed that the massive earthquake rehabilitation and reconstruction programme was a paradigmatic shift from the conventional approach. Each of its various initiatives, like the owner-driven reconstruction programme, the role and involvement of the community, the transparency and equity procedure and various capacity-building initiatives taken up during the programme, involved innovation in governance.[13]

After the Indian Ocean tsunami of December 2004, in April 2005, the Asian Development Bank (ADB), the Organisation

[13]I have documented the experiences of the Kutch earthquake in the form of a book *The Kutch Earthquake 2001: Recollection Lessons and Insights* (National Institute of Disaster Management, New Delhi, India, 2004).

for Economic Co-operation and Development (OECD) and Transparency International organized an expert meeting on corruption prevention in tsunami relief. On their invitation, I made a presentation on our experience in Gujarat, which was, by that time, widely known for its focus on transparency, accountability and people's participation.

The present institutional structures of disaster management in several states and at the national level owe their origin to the successful experience of Gujarat, particularly of the GSDMA. Gujarat was the first state in the country to enact a comprehensive legislation on disaster management, even before a national act had been passed. In recent times, possibly no other post-disaster reconstruction and recovery programme has been as influential as the Gujarat programme, in terms of its approach, organizational structure and disaster reduction initiatives.

A Harmonious Approach

What I have outlined above is, no doubt, time and situation-dependent. Maybe it is influenced by my subjectivity and nostalgia for my experiences in Gujarat. It may or may not reflect the experiences of others. The objective is to test a hypothesis or to analyse whether a certain postulate or idea can crystallize some distinctive factors that played a significant role in the development of Gujarat during its formative years. To that extent, the experiences and anecdotes, even if less relevant today, do help us draw some inferences.

The experiences I have described span over three decades, starting 1974, and are associated with many places—from remote villages to districts and the state capital. Some readers may feel that I have included too many unrelated events and anecdotes. The idea was to have a representative sample of adequate size for drawing inferences.

Witnessing and participating in the interplay of people, politicians and bureaucrats have been interesting, exciting and even challenging. On the one hand, whether in Tharad, Bhuj or Mehsana, people raised their voices, although the degree of awareness and assertiveness varied widely. On the other hand, their participation was facilitated by the administrative system. Civil society organizations worked at the grassroots level not only during natural calamities, such as droughts and floods, but also for rural development—they were known for selfless service in those days. The relationships between politicians and bureaucrats were certainly complex, depending a great deal on the personalities involved. Further, the existence of empowered PRIs in Gujarat, unlike in many other states, presented both challenges and opportunities for faster development.

Considering the empirical evidence based on the experiences I have described, the overall picture that emerges is that we cannot reject the following hypothesis: Gujarat's sociopolitical milieu contributed 'significantly' to its rapid development, especially during the early decades after its formation, and even in recent decades.

I generally had good working and professional relations with politicians, particularly as the DDO and district collector, and later in the Secretariat, though there were problems with some of them. In most cases, both at the district and state levels, they contributed immensely to the development process and in collaboration with bureaucrats, most of whom were committed to their duties and responsibilities. No doubt, there were differences and even conflicting views. Yet, politicians and bureaucrats respected each other in most cases. There was receptivity, tolerance and a broad-minded approach, as I have illustrated with some examples.

At times, civil servants lament that they could not perform well or achieve certain goals because of political pressure and interference. Similarly, politicians talk about bureaucratic inertia, rigidity and reluctance to change. Indeed, the words 'political' and 'bureaucratic' are very often used with a negative connotation. The fact remains that in a democratic polity, both politicians and bureaucrats are necessary participants. The question is: how should they play their roles so that the system can achieve its objective more comprehensively, optimally and effectively? Balwantrai Mehta, the former CM of Gujarat, had once said that the Panchayati Raj system would succeed if officials do not behave like non-officials and non-officials do not behave like officials. This is still relevant for a democratic system at any level.

Much of the tension and many a conflicting situation can be avoided if minor issues are accommodated, keeping basic principles intact. Yielding to political pressure leads to more such pressure. Political pressure is not insurmountable. If one is sincere, objective and open to the views of others, there will be less chance of political vengeance. Indeed, politicians, in most cases, respect a person and hold her or him in high esteem if they perceive that one is objective and without any bias.

Experience shows that there are few political constraints when undertaking development activities. Very often, conflicts arise in matters of transfer, posting and certain regulatory activities. The challenge is handling divergent views, perceptions and interests, as there are many differences among people and across jurisdictions. In some cases, there are clashes and conflicts, in some others, collusion—as summed up by the term—the 'politician–bureaucrat nexus'—and in many cases, there is a harmonious approach. My experiences in Gujarat indicate a predominance of the third alternative.

Political entities can provide flexibility to a rigid bureaucratic system, making it more responsive to people's needs. They can also bring in realism to a system that can be at a distance from those who it is meant to serve. A politician with a vision and commitment can take a state or a country to new heights.

In Gujarat, more prominently during the early decades after its formation, the relationship between politicians and bureaucrats was, in most cases, harmonious and constructive, less adversarial and much less collusive. This critical factor, along with people's active participation and the involvement of voluntary agencies, played a significant role in accelerating the pace of development in Gujarat.

This chapter has been extracted from P.K. Mishra's article from the book Developing Gujarat: My Memories.[14]

[14]Patankar, H.R. and Kirit Shelat, *Developing Gujarat: My Memories*, Sahitya Mudranalaya, Ahmedabad, India, 2018.

3

FEDERALISM IN A FLUX

New dimensions of intergovernmental relations

Federalism is integral to our governance architecture. It evolved over a period of time, much before Independence and its key features are embedded in our Constitution. These features are related to the various aspects of governance, the distribution of financial resources and the delineation of functions to different layers of the governance matrix. Its evolution, however, over a period of time, has become opaque in multiple ways. There is a need to understand the new context, both in its ideological moorings and in federal practices.

India is going through a transition in intergovernmental relations. State boundaries based on linguistic factors or administrative conveniences are getting blurred due to the impact of technology and migration. Socio-economic trends, such as technological change, rising mobility and market integration, have led to dynamic federalism.

There is, undoubtedly, a need to rethink and redesign the structure of credible fiscal partnership. This should not degenerate into a race to garner more resources. Instead, it should lead to innovative attempts to enhance growth capability at multiple layers of governance, address endemic backwardness of regions and territories, improve the overall competitiveness of the economy and contribute to the new dynamics of an Indian value-added chain. The current economic restructuring and sluggishness must be viewed anecdotally, as they are transitory in nature and do not impair our long-term growth potential. We need to recast our framework in a contemporary context. This will enable multiple aspects of governance to become more transparent, meaningful and conform to changing political and social dynamics.

Architecture and Adherence

The term 'fiscal federalism' was coined by the German-born American economist Richard Musgrave in 1959. Wallace E. Oates, in his writing in 1999, said that fiscal federalism is concerned with understanding which 'functions and instruments are best centralised and which are best placed in the sphere of decentralised levels of government.'[15] However, this concept applies to all forms of government: unitary, federal and confederal.

Fiscal federalism broadly considers the vertical structure of the public sector, fiscal policy institutions and their interdependence.

First, it needs to be determined to which level of government different expenditure responsibilities are assigned. The conventional starting point is that local governments are more sensitive to the needs and preferences of the citizens than the higher levels of government. In general, this suggests

[15]Oates, Wallace E., 'An Essay on Fiscal Federalism', *Journal of Economic Literature*, Vol. 37, No. 3, 1999, pp. 1120–1129.

that public goods and services should be provided by the lowest possible level of government. This consideration is also implicit in the European Union's (EU) subsidiarity principle and fiscal decentralization in most sovereign countries. However, according to the conventional view, policies concerning macroeconomic stabilization and redistribution, foreign policy, security and defence should be left to higher levels of government in any federal architecture. In addition, policies that induce significant spillover effects to other jurisdictions could justify assigning particular tasks to the central government.

Second, one needs to consider the approach and strategy for the financing of public goods and services at multiple levels of governance. The starting point is that the level of government responsible for the provision of a particular product or service should also be responsible for funding it and collecting the necessary revenue. If this is so, it is expected that the provider bears the full costs of a provision, consequently, limiting a moral hazard. As different types of tax instruments have heterogeneous characteristics, for instance, due to differences in the mobility of their tax base, they should be allocated to the level that is most effective in raising the revenue. Thus, tax instruments should be assigned such that each government could realistically collect sufficient tax revenues. In practice, different levels of government are only rarely self-sufficient in terms of financing their legal responsibilities.

Third, and as a consequence of the previous point, one needs to determine the appropriate instruments (and their degree) to equalize disparities in fiscal resources and fiscal needs, both over time and across jurisdictions. In most federal systems, there exist both vertical transfers, in which there are transfers from different levels of government to each other, and horizontal transfers, in which there are transfers within the same level of government. The differences between revenues and expenditures are called vertical and horizontal fiscal imbalances or fiscal gaps. Borrowing and different types of transfers (including tax sharing, conditional and unconditional grants and transfers based on demographic factors) are alternative instruments to stabilize the imbalances in revenues and government expenditures over time.

Fourth, and to the extent that the vertical design does not impose fiscal discipline to an adequate degree, one needs to adopt strategies to cap excessive spending and borrowing at each level of government. The logic is mainly to maintain intergenerational equity and avoid fiscal free-riding as well as moral hazard: given the interconnected area and fiscal framework, governments may implement policies that have negative spillover effects on other jurisdictions and regions. Governments may also aim to benefit from transfers from other regions. In all federal countries, some form of fiscal rules and governance exists with respect to budget deficits and borrowing but the strategies differ.

Finally, it needs to be noted that, in many respects, the allocation of responsibilities and instruments to different levels of governments is never so clear-cut, as there is always some degree of overlap. For example, many government responsibilities are either shared between the federal and state governments or their actions are coordinated. In addition, harmonization in tax bases and national standards imply that fiscal instruments are not always fully adjustable to regional preferences, even if the instruments are solely assigned for regional use.

Federalism means different things to different people. There are federal romantics who believe that the future of India lies in greater autonomy and power to the states and that the evolution of the polity has deprived the subnational governments of making a more meaningful contribution to our development process. They could also say so about the third tier of the government, namely panchayats (rural local bodies) and ULBs. There are others, however, who look at this issue in a more clinical way, broadly examining the architecture of fiscal federalism and its adherence to the original architecture. But as Charles Kennedy said, 'We have to win the vocabulary before we succeed in the vision'. The same holds true for fiscal federalism. And so, in this chapter, my focus will be on the changing landscape of Centre–state relations and the dynamic federal polity in India.

Federalism in the Colonial Era

The federal system is essentially a post-Industrial Revolution phenomenon. India as a federal system is about 70 years old, compared to more than two centuries of federalism in the US, Switzerland or Canada. There is a wide variety of international experiences in fiscal federalism on the basis of:

- the division of functions among different tiers of government;
- the design of fiscal transfers;
- the principles of assessment; and
- the institutional arrangements.[16]

Intergovernmental fiscal transfers are either constitutionally or legally mandated.

Many of the features of India's fiscal federalism are intertwined with the history of the East India Company and the British Crown. The East India Company was granted a charter of incorporation in 1600 CE by Queen Elizabeth, which gave the East India Company the exclusive right to trade

[16]Ma, Jun, *Intergovernmental Fiscal Transfers in Nine Countries: Lessons for Developing Countries*, The World Bank, Economic Development Institute, Macroeconomic Management and Policy Division, 1997.

with India. The East India Company then set up a number of factories and trading centres at different places in India. Bombay, Madras and Calcutta became the main settlements and were declared as presidencies. Under the Regulating Act of 1773, the Calcutta Presidency was given full powers over the other two presidencies of Madras and Bombay, which, for the first time, resembled the setting up of a government in the country. However, only in the Charter Act of 1833 was a central fiscal authority with the presidencies as integral constituents formed. This Act vested the financial and legislative powers in India solely in the Governor General of Bengal, who was designated as the Governor General of India, making the entire administration centralized. The current system of the financial year ending on 31 March along with the principles of the English budget system were adopted when the Crown took direct control in 1858. The Union, State and Concurrent Lists of the current Indian constitution have their genesis in the first Budget, which was presented in 1860–61 under the new system.

A system of diarchy, dividing the administrative subjects into central and provincial categories, was a result of the Montagu–Chelmsford Reforms enacted in the Government of India Act, 1919. Under the Act, provinces got power by way of delegation, whereas the Central Legislative Assembly retained the power to legislate for the entire country on any subject. The Act also divided the sources of revenue between the Centre and provinces.

The Government of India Act, 1935, established a federal system with provinces and Indian states as two distinct units. Under the Act, legislative powers were distributed under three lists: Federal List, Provincial List and the Concurrent List. This Act made the revenues and finances of the provincial government distinct from those of the federal government. The Act also provided for the collection and retention of levies by the federal government and spelled out details of the distribution of financial resources and grants-in-aids to provinces. As per the Act, such sums as prescribed by His Majesty in the Council were to be charged on the revenues of the federation. The Government of India Act, 1935 established the basic structure of fiscal federalism in India, one that survives even today.

The Constituent Assembly, formed in 1946, adopted a unitary form of government. However, the federal framework evolved indigenously over a period of time. The final shape of the federal government and federal finance was incorporated in the Government of India Act, 1935. It also had some features of a parliamentary system. However, the nature of the relationship between the proposed federal government and the provinces of British India relative to that of the princely states was resolved only after Independence but before the Constitution was adopted.

Constitutional Context and Beyond

At the time of Independence, in 1947, India had nine provinces and over 500 princely states. The princely states accounted for 40 per cent of the territory and 30 per cent of the population, and were diverse in size, character, systems and the nature of their relations with British India. They were integrated with India after Independence, and the Union of States came into existence on 26 January 1950.

However, there was no unanimity within the members of the Constituent Assembly with regard to the name of the country. While some members suggested the traditional name (Bharat), others advocated the modern name (India). Hence, the Constituent Assembly adopted a mix of both ('India, that is, Bharat'). Secondly, the country is described as a 'Union' although its Constitution has a federal structure.

On 4 November 1948, Dr B.R. Ambedkar, while moving the Draft Constitution in the Constituent Assembly responded to the question as to why India is a Union and not a federation of states,

> The Drafting Committee wanted to make it clear that though India was to be a federation, the federation was not the result of an agreement by the States to join in a federation and that the federation not being the result of an agreement no State has the right to secede from it. The Federation is a Union because it is indestructible.[17]

Broadly speaking, in the evolution of fiscal federalism, there has been marked stability in the processes and procedures. The annual budgetary processes of both the central and the state governments are independent exercises and have to go through Parliament or state legislature. For most of the post-Independence era, the existence of the Planning Commission injected a centralizing dependence in more ways than one. The Planning Commission became a parallel institution for the transfer of resources from the Union of States. While the focus of the FC, which was first constituted in 1951 under Article 280 of the Constitution, remained on the revenue account, the Planning Commission was predominantly concerned with the capital account. Successive FCs commented on this as being inconsistent with the spirit of the Constitution in the devolution of resources. There were other developments like the 73rd and 74th amendments of the Constitution in 1992, giving recognition to PRIs and ULBs with specific functions assigned to them under the 11th and 12th schedules of the Constitution.

Two key institutions have been the coordinating entities

---

[17] 'Motion *re.* Draft Constitution', Parliament of India, Lok Sabha, House of the People, https://bit.ly/3u3Rh3Z. Accessed on 16 March 2022.

between the Centre and the subnational governments. First, the National Development Council (NDC) constituted in 1952 to oversee the work of the Planning Commission to approve their five-year plans (FYPs) and midterm appraisals. Second, the Inter-State Council created by a constitutional amendment in 1990, based on the recommendations of the Sarkaria Commission Report.

Over time, India changed imperceptibly in its economic policies and governance rubric and it became incumbent for Centre–state relations and their dynamics to keep pace with the changing needs of the time.

Evolving Challenges

Indian federalism has faced several challenges for a long time. Some of these have been listed below.

Future of the Seventh Schedule

The Seventh Schedule of the Constitution broadly demarcates the functions of governance between three lists. It distributes the legislative and financial powers between the Union and the states. List I pertains to subjects of the Union, List II pertains to subjects of the states and List III includes subjects in a category called the Concurrent List, which pertain to both the Union and the states. In the event of conflicting legislation, the law passed by the Union prevails.

Over a period of time, the areas covered under the Concurrent List have increased. This is based on the 42nd Amendment of the Constitution in 1976, which shifted the subjects of forest and education from the State List to the Concurrent List. Furthermore, following the 42nd Amendment, a new entry, 20A 'population control and family planning', was added to the Concurrent List. This is the bedrock of the subsequent National Population Policy, which, anecdotally, is currently being debated in multiple forums. This transfer to the concurrent subjects means the principal obligation in relation to issues of family planning are in the domain of both the Centre and the states except, as mentioned earlier, any central legislation would override any laws made by the states.

While the changes discussed here were made through formal Acts and constitutional amendments, there are other ways in which the original demarcations have been whittled down and often metamorphosed. Take, for instance, the issue of entitlement-driven legislations. Some time ago, we entered an era of entitlement-based standalone legislation. The classic examples of such legislation are the Mahatma Gandhi National Rural Employment Guarantee Act (MGNREGA) of 2005, the Right of Children to Free and Compulsory Education Act, 2009 and the National Food Security Act, 2013. How do these standalone entitlement legislations mesh with the Seventh Schedule of the Constitution? Do they transgress the earmarked borders? And how is it that none of the states, at any stage, formally opposed the transgression of these limits? There were areas where the fiscal romantics should really have intervened, as employment, education and food were entirely intended to be in the domain of the states. I scarcely remember the issue of the states' autonomy ever coming up for serious analytical critiques. Political expediency pervaded Constitutional misgivings.

Incongruence of Article 282 with the Letter and Spirit of the Seventh Schedule

Article 282 of the Constitution says, 'The Union or a State may make any grants for any public purpose, notwithstanding that the purpose is not one with respect to which Parliament or the Legislature of the State, as the case may be, may make laws.'

Originally, in the Constitution, this was not expected to be an overarching provision but an extraordinary one to be used very sparingly. With regard to Article 282, K. Santhanam, chairman of the Second FC, had said:

> This was not intended to be one of the major provisions for making readjustments between the Union and the States, if that was the idea, then there was no purpose in evolving such a complicated set of relations of shares, assignments and grants. There is no purpose in having two Articles enabling the Centre to assist the States - one through the Finance Commission and the other by more executive discretion. In the latter case, even parliamentary legislation is not needed. Of course, it will have to be included in the Budget. But, beyond being an item in the Budget, no further sanction needs to be taken. Therefore, in my view, this Article was a residuary, a reserve Article, to enable the Union to deal with unforeseen contingencies. That was how this Article was used both by the British Government and, after transfer of power, before the first year of the First Five Year Plan. Under this Article, only some grow-more-food grants and some rehabilitation grants were given.[18]

In his opinion to the Ninth FC, constitutional expert Nani Palkhivala maintained,

> Art. 282 is not intended to enable the Union to make such grants as fall properly under Art. 275. Art. 282 embodies merely a residuary power which enables the Union or a State to make any grant for any purpose,

[18]Quoted in 'Speech of Shri N.K. Singh, Chairman, XVFC at the launch of the book "Indian Fiscal Federalism"', Press Information Bureau, 28 March 2019, https://bit.ly/3icusp6. Accessed on 16 March 2022.

> irrespective of the question whether the purpose is one over which the grantor has legislative power.[19]

GST and the Room to Manoeuvre

The above needs to be viewed along with the changes in Part XII of the Constitution, which resulted in the adoption of the Goods and Services Tax (GST), designed to make India a common market and entity. The GST Council, which is also a constitutional body, takes decisions through its fitment committee on the rates of the GST as both Parliament and state legislatures have assigned their financial powers to this empowered Committee. The states we visited as part of the 15th FC often complained that their fiscal autonomy and the room to manoeuvre on revenues had been greatly circumscribed by the GST. It is a case of pooled sovereignty for the betterment of common good. Nonetheless, the GST Council is still in its nascent phase and needs to revisit its design and decision-making process in a more fundamental way. The entire area of GST reforms is an ongoing dynamic. In the *Report of the 15th Finance Commission for 2021-26* which was submitted on 9 November 2020, these reforms have been extensively analysed, along with suggesting the changes necessary to fulfil their original purpose.

Fiscal Fraternity of the Centre and States

The most fundamental lesson from India's experience with the second wave of the Covid-19 pandemic is that managing a grave national crisis requires federalism by way of fiscal fraternity of the Centre and states. The federal government must inevitably take the anchor's role.

From a federal perspective, the Seventh Schedule of

---

[19]Ibid.

the Constitution gives states precedence over the Centre on health. Entry 81 of the Union List grants the legislative power for 'inter-state migration; inter-state quarantine' to the Centre. Meanwhile, entries 1, 2 and 6 of the State List give the legislative spheres of 'public order,' 'police' and, importantly, 'public health and sanitation; hospitals and dispensaries' to the states. However, entries 23 and 29 of the Concurrent List allocate the areas of 'social security and social insurance; employment and unemployment' and 'prevention of the extension from one state to another of infectious or contagious diseases or pests affecting men, animals or plants' to both the Centre and states. There is, thus, a significant overlap and opacity in the demarcation of roles, functions and responsibilities of the Centre and states.

The Constitution further states that under Articles 73 and 162, the executive power of the Union and states is 'coextensive with the legislative power.' Thus, from the constitutional scheme, the state governments are expected to play the primary role in the management of healthcare, as well as law and order, while the Centre is expected to provide the overarching national leadership, facilitate coordination among key federating units, monitor the overall pandemic situation and provide financial and other critical assistance to the states.

As the crisis loomed large in India in early March 2020, the Centre and the states invoked two available legal instruments to deal with the crisis. The Centre declared the pandemic as a 'notified disaster,' and cited the Disaster Management Act, 2005, in particular, to impose a nationwide lockdown on 24 March 2020. As the word 'disaster' is not included in the Seventh Schedule, the Centre used its residuary powers to invoke the law and issue various directives to the states as the pandemic situation aggravated.

The states, for their part, turned to the Epidemic Diseases Act, 1897, which empowers them to deal with an epidemic-like situation. Many state governments used this law to issue State Epidemic Diseases Covid-19 Regulations, 2020 for their jurisdictions, including restrictions on movement and closure of commercial establishments, offices and other public places. Various sections of the Indian Penal Code, 1860 were used by the states as a guide for laying down punishments for violators, much before the Centre started issuing its own guidelines.

Central Unilateralism and State Autonomy

The federal response to the pandemic has evolved in a number of ways. The first wave, in 2020, can be described as a play between central unilateralism and state autonomy. The constitutional provisions and existing legislations confer the primary responsibility for handling a situation like the Covid-19 pandemic to the state government. Nonetheless, the Centre inevitably assumed the role of an anchor and led from the front in managing the pandemic, particularly during the periods involving national lockdowns. As the pandemic threatened human lives and livelihoods, demanding swift action on a national scale, the Centre took over many responsibilities that otherwise fall within the domain of the states. Among many comprehensive measures, the Centre took a series of decisions to scale up vaccine procurement, knowledge enhancement for setting standards and guidelines for the state and local governments and the mitigation of interstate externalities.

Therefore, the pandemic necessitated the invocation of the wider powers of the Centre, especially during the early phase: it was the Centre that imposed the lockdown and the Centre monitored states responses, including physical distancing norms, regulation of economic activities and provision of financial packages.

Clearly, during the first wave, the Centre acted swiftly and decisively, as federal governments are expected to do during national emergencies. So, while the first wave of the pandemic was about a 'unitary' and, understandably, a centralized response by the Union, the second wave saw the opposite response. Louise Tillin, a known scholar on federalism, captures this trend succinctly when she says, 'India has moved from unilateral centralized decision-making in the first wave to something that approximates unilateral decentralized decision-making—by default—in the second wave.'[20]

The decentralization logic became more visible in the case of the vaccination policy. As the country faced acute vaccine shortages, many state governments called for autonomy to procure vaccines from international markets. The Centre acceded, as analysts found it impractical given the demand–supply mismatch and the competition for vaccines. Several states that went ahead with tenders for procuring vaccines found no prospective bidders. This, along with the varying pricing of vaccines, created an untenable situation. It soon became a contentious aspect of India's federal structure, as the Centre and states blamed each other for the confusion. It even required the intervention of the Supreme Court to seek an orderly approach.

Apart from issues of Centre–state coordination, various state governments were in conflict with each other over the availability of oxygen and essential medicines, and seeking access and supply chains. The intervention of the Supreme Court sought to resolve this deadlock between the states. Finally, order prevailed and today, the issue of vaccine procurement and supplies at the most optimum prices rests with the central government, as it should. Equally, the

---

[20]Tillin, Louise, 'Center and States Need to Coordinate, Not Compete', Center for the Advanced Study of India (CASI), 24 May 2021, https://bit.ly/3Ik6FOG. Accessed on 16 March 2022.

interplay between international diplomacy, foreign policy and encouraging new vaccine supplies in an orderly way is now the new approach that is being adopted for the ongoing pandemic. This would be equally applicable in case the pandemic lingers on or there is an emergence of another variant of concern.

Inherent Contradictions

Democracies all over the world have become leadership oriented and this is more de jure than de facto. In presidential governments, this is axiomatic, but this is also starting to be the case in democracies where votes are sought for the PM.

In a federation, the central leadership matters to a great extent. For example, India's electoral positions are significantly centred around the leadership of political parties. Votes are solicited or garnered based on the incumbent or potential PM or CM.

Fiscal federalism, thus, cannot remain warped in time exclusively to consider the domain of the central and subnational governments. In this sense, it is now increasingly felt that the Westminster model of parliamentary democracy may have outlived its utility even in the country of its origin. Since the expectations from the heads of the governance structures—PMs and CMs—influence the psyche of the electorate, the world may have de facto moved to a more presidential model. Undoubtedly, there will be a gap between de facto and de jure, and this is one of the inherent contradictions between precept and practice. Over time, the practice must adapt to bring about greater convergence and symmetry.

The nature of governance has changed fundamentally. For instance, while visiting a subnational government, it is not possible for the head of the central government to explain that he cannot provide any support for drinking water, improved power supply or enhanced agriculture because the subject does not fall under the purview of the central government but is in the domain of the states. This is not a practical proposition because the Constitution must serve and adapt these to the changing expectations of the people.

Reconciling the harmonious relations between the subnational and national entities must address this principal challenge of the changing dynamics of the electoral framework and the parliamentary democracy from which multiple mandates are secured.

An Abiding Theme

Even prior to the pandemic, federalism in India faced multiple challenges. Its fragility has been greatly compounded by the underfunded and neglected health system and weak state capacity. The spirit of cooperative federalism, in a broader sense of the term, has been an abiding theme of our federal polity. The most important lesson is one of flexibility—flexibility between unitary, federal and confederal forms of government. The evolving role of the central government as a principal anchor in extraordinary times like these is inescapable. The engagement of state governments in not only implementation but also in ameliorating relations, containing issues, rolling out plans and engaging with all stakeholders is a synergy, without which our responses would not be optimum. Furthermore, going beyond centralization or decentralization, the engagement of the third tier of government in the initiatives of both the central and the state governments would enhance their reach, coverage and awareness—an important bulwark in times like these.

Some challenges that need to be addressed to improve cooperative federalism have been listed below.

The substantive point is to relook at the Seventh Schedule in a contemporary context. Unless we redraw the contours of the Schedule, some of the incongruities between the contours of the Seventh Schedule, Article 282 of the Constitution and the standalone legislation on various subjects will remain cluttered and opaque. Both in theory and practice, many beliefs and principles which prompted our forefathers to give the Constitution its present shape may need some basic reconsideration. Long before I have said this, in a report submitted in 1971 by the Rajamannar Committee, formally known as the Centre–state Relations Inquiry Committee, said,

> The Committee is of the opinion that it is desirable to constitute a High Power Commission, consisting of eminent lawyers and jurists and elderly statesmen with administrative experience to examine the entries of Lists I and III in the Seventh Schedule to the Constitution and suggest redistribution of the entries.[21]

It is time to pay heed and act on this valuable recommendation.

In the past few months, the country has witnessed an interesting and remarkably coordinated effort by the Centre and states in addressing a collective challenge. These exigency responses will enhance the understanding of the Centre–state dynamics and mechanisms for improving federal governance and, more importantly, reinforcing federal trust. The experience offers an opportunity to revisit the recent debate around the federal organization of powers under the Seventh Schedule. It has been argued that such organization of powers is not cast in stone and the arrangement requires a review. Such an exercise is indeed necessary, but what should be its broad contours? The review should allow the carving out of the roles of the Centre and states to address hitherto disregarded and emerging

[21]Debroy, Bibek, 'The Seventh Schedule relook', *Financial Express*, 13 January 2022, https://bit.ly/3a3Vu19. Accessed on 16 March 2022.

concerns—for instance, a viral pandemic or climate change.

The asymmetry in the working of the GST Council and the FC deserves serious considerations. The FCs recommend the distribution of revenues between the Union and states, thereafter, among the states and also between states and their third tiers. After the 73rd and 74th Constitutional Amendments, all FCs have also been advised to recommend grants to the third tier. They are also expected to look at projections of expenditure and revenue. But the issues of GST rates, exemptions, changes and implementation of indirect taxes are now entirely within the domain of the GST Council. This leads to unsettled questions on the ways to monitor, scrutinize and optimize revenue outcomes. The fact that the GST Council is a permanent body while the FC is not—the FC makes awards for five year or six year spans—further complicates their dynamic. Since both the FC and the GST Council are constitutional bodies, a coordination mechanism between the two is now an inescapable necessity. The commonalities of issues and the absence of any recourse or course correction mechanism is an aspect that many states have highlighted when we visited them.

With the abolition of the Planning Commission, many economists and policymakers have argued about an institutional vacuum. While the NDC is performing an important function, the states have pleaded for a credible institution acting as a link for a policy dialogue with the Centre. In Australia, states came together in 2005 to set up the council for the federation of Australia to jointly represent their interests in Canberra. While we have an institutional entity like the Inter-state Council, it needs to be rejuvenated and restructured to be made more purposeful, given the current institutional vacuum. There needs to be serious consideration to build entities by way of a more permanent and credible consultative mechanism.

Reforms in the Public Finance Management System (PFMS) are a continuous process. Previous FCs made recommendations on various aspects of PFMS of both the Union and states with a focus on budgetary, accounting processes and financial reporting. These deserve to be acted upon, given the need for an integrated and cohesive response from both the Centre and the states.

The post-pandemic period required a reprioritization of expenditure to critical care needs. In light of the pandemic, the endemic neglect of the health infrastructure and the health sector as a whole needs redressal. This must be a high priority because we have become painfully aware that, given the multiplicity of factors, this may not be the last pandemic. At a national level, the healthcare infrastructure needs to be strengthened, based on the recommendations of the National Health Policy (NHP) 2002 and 2017, and public outlays need to be substantially augmented. We cannot get away from strengthening district hospitals and multi-specialty care, along with increasing the available manpower, which should be the case even in the normal course of our health programmes. Apart from strengthening district hospitals, primary health centres at the block level also need substantial strengthening.

Many of these regulatory and other changes have been outlined in the report of the 15th FC, which has devoted a special chapter to health. Among other things, these include a permanent national health service based on best international practices, other innovative changes like the Diplomate of National Board (DNB) courses or training of paramedics, which can have immediate multiplier effects. Further, the recommendations of the National Rural Health Mission (NRHM) and some notable examples of well-functioning decentralized health systems in some states would be worthy of replication. In this regard, the 15th FC recommended ₹70,051 crore for urban health and wellness centres (HWCs), building sub-centres, primary health centres and block-level public health units and for supporting the diagnostic infrastructure for primary healthcare activities. The financial awards for each of these individual states have been fully accepted by the government and their implementation has also commenced.

In many ways, the pandemic has also exposed the inadequacies of the existing constitutional and legal provisions in dealing with a pandemic or a pan-India health emergency. There are concerns about the vagueness of both the Disaster Management Act, 2005 and the Epidemic Diseases Act, 1897 in the context of a pandemic. While both these laws do not have provisions relating to health emergencies, both the Centre and states resorted to either expansive interpretation or ad hoc measures, such as issuing ordinances to protect frontline workers or ensuring implementation of physical distancing norms. This makes it imperative for the central government to initiate the drafting of a comprehensive national legislation that can effectively deal with pandemics, like Covid-19, and other national emergencies that India could face in the future. A comprehensive national legislation under the concurrent powers is clearly an inescapable priority.

There are extraordinary stories of success by many states strengthening the role of their third tier during the pandemic. For instance, the Odisha government delegating powers to the sarpanch, the Brihanmumbai Municipal Corporation (BMC) following certain protocols in coordination with the Mumbai Police, and the role of local bodies in Kerala and, indeed, in other states as well, are laudable.[22]

---

[22]The Odisha government vested the sarpanch with the powers of a magistrate to control the movement of migrants and oversee physical distancing norms. Similarly, the Kerala government allowed local bodies to do contact tracing, conduct health camps and sanitation drives and sensitize people on health protocols. To encourage sustainable agricultural activities, the local governments at the village level also ensured employment and critical food supply chains.

During the first wave, district-level interventions in Agra (Uttar Pradesh), Bhilwara (Rajasthan) and Pathanamthitta (Kerala) were exemplary in containing

Aligning the fiscal and debt paths of the Centre and the states is an arduous but inescapable task. A differentiated debt path for the states, which recognizes the present constraints and issues of legacy debt, must be handled with sagacity and sensitivity. This issue has been greatly aggravated during the pandemic. Many countries have amended their fiscal rules to provide for additional public spending to revive their economies that have been adversely affected by the Covid-19 pandemic. Fiscal rules provide a credible commitment to fiscal prudence. They set numerical limits on fiscal aggregates, such as the level of fiscal deficit, public debt or the growth of public expenditure. A key feature of all robust fiscal legislation is the escape clause, which allows for temporary deviation from fiscal targets in the event of unforeseen circumstances. The clause is in accordance with a limited number of well-defined exceptional circumstances and prescribes time limits for such deviation along with the path of reform to the original targets.

Among the Asian, middle-income emerging peers of India, Indonesia's fiscal rule provides for limiting the fiscal deficit to 3 per cent of the GDP in any given year. However, it decided to suspend its fiscal deficit cap of 3 per cent of GDP during 2020–22.

In 2018, comprehensive amendments were introduced to the Fiscal Responsibility and Budget Management (FRBM)

---

the spread of infections. Similarly, municipalities in states like Maharashtra, where the Covid-19 cases were steep, also made innovations in crisis management at different phases of the pandemic. The collaboration between the BMC and the Mumbai Police to supervise quarantine procedures and create public awareness in the Dharavi slums is worth mentioning. They succeeded in controlling the Covid-19 outbreak in the area. The BMC repeated the feat during the second wave by quickly innovating in contact tracing, testing and expanding medical support by creating 'ward-level war rooms'. In other words, decentralized responses bore fruits at the local level, wherever governments delegated powers and trusted these self-governing institutions.

Act, 2003 to incorporate some of the recommendations from the report of the FRBM Review Committee, chaired by me. Among other changes, the fiscal deficit target of 3 per cent was proposed to be achieved by 31 March 2021. Another key feature of the amendments was to prescribe a relatively more nuanced escape clause. The statutory escape clause permitted the central government to deviate from the annual fiscal deficit target on the grounds of national security, act of war, national calamity, collapse of agriculture severely affecting farm output and incomes, structural reforms in the economy with unanticipated fiscal implications or decline in real output growth of a quarter by at least 3 percentage points below its average of the previous four quarters. However, any deviation from the fiscal deficit target could not exceed 0.5 per cent of the GDP in a year. The escape clause also mandated that a statement explaining the reasons for the deviation and the path of return to fiscal deficit targets should be laid before both houses of Parliament.

Even before the pandemic, the escape clause was invoked to informally deviate from the fiscal deficit targets. While presenting Budget 2020–21, FM Nirmala Sitharaman used the escape clause to deviate from the fiscal deficit target of 3.3 per cent for 2019–20. This clause was also used to deviate from the target for the next financial year, i.e. 2020–21. The fiscal deficit was relaxed by 0.5 per cent to 3.8 per cent for the financial year ending 31 March 2020, and to 3.5 per cent for the financial year ending 31 March 2021. The achievement of 3 per cent of the fiscal deficit target was shifted to 31 March 2023.

On the same occasion, the FM mentioned the need to draw a fresh fiscal road map. This has become an inescapable necessity. Indeed, the 15th FC has made a pointed suggestion for the constitution of an intergovernmental group—intergovernmental because it must include the Centre and states to evolve a more realistic fiscal road map, given the ongoing pandemic and the attendant uncertainties. In the long run, no doubt, fiscal institutions, like a fiscal council, will be of enormous value.

Strengthening the federal compact is invariably an exercise in reinforcing trust. In the financial sphere, apart from intergovernmental transfers through the FC, the route of transfers through Centrally Sponsored Schemes (CSS) and benefits of central outlays are well established. These come out of the Consolidated Fund of India and are discretionary, subject to such conditions that may be imposed. They are in the category of grants. A somewhat innovative approach has been taken in the recent Budget of 2022–23, in which ₹1 lakh crore have been assigned to the states for augmenting their capital expenditure. This budgetary allocation is interest free and repayable in 40 years. In effect, based on inflation, these would really turn out to be grants. The use of the grants mechanism to improve the quality of expenditure in the states is innovative. Notwithstanding the end use restrictions, capital expenditure is purposive in enhancing overall productivity, creating greater employment and addressing local needs, particularly improving state-level infrastructure by way of rural roads, bridges and culverts, to mention a few.

Federalism is a philosophy that is inescapable for a complex country like India. However, it must go beyond partnership that is not embedded wholly in fiduciary obligations. The issues of national priority transcend boundaries because they are designed to address the basic tenets of growth multipliers benefitting every segment of society. They also address welfare tenets on health, housing and employment as inescapable national priorities. Swachh Bharat Mission (SBM), New Education Policy (NEP) and Ayushman Bharat Yojana (ABY), to mention a few, are some major initiatives that constitute an integral part of the changing nature of obligations between the Centre and states.

We must address the limitations of the written Constitution while never forgetting that it is a pillar of stability. As the American author Dan Millman writes in his novel *Way of the Peaceful Warrior*, 'The secret of change is to focus all of your energy not on fighting the old, but on building the new.'[23] I do believe that if the fresh initiatives implement some of the suggestions that I have made in this chapter, they could impart new dynamism to fiscal federalism. Federalism may be flexible. Trust is not; it needs constant nurturing and rejuvenation.

This chapter has been extracted from N.K. Singh's 17th L.K. Jha Memorial Lecture[24] *and the launch of the Indian Institute of Management Bangalore's (IIM) Policy Talk series.*[25]

---

[23]Millman, Dan, *Way of the Peaceful Warrior: A Book That Changes Lives*, Perseus Books Group; New edition, April 2006.

[24]Singh, N.K., 'Fiscal Federalism: Ideology and Practice', Reserve Bank of India, https://bit.ly/386NSKB. Accessed on 4 May 2022.

[25]PGPPM students at IIMB launch 2020–21 Policy Talk series with a lecture by Mr N.K. Singh, YouTube, https://bit.ly/38Rd73u. Accessed on 4 May 2022.

4

THE THIRD TIER

Embarking on a new era of governance

In his famous Gettysburg Address, delivered during the American Civil War, President Abraham Lincoln described democracy as a 'government of the people, by the people and for the people.' Lincoln's address continues to have an irresistible ethical, almost romantic appeal. Many, indeed, compare it with the nascent independent republics that existed in India, where people were the real rulers. However, beyond small city states with a few thousand people, its relevance was not immediately obvious in large countries.

What we accepted in India after Independence was not direct democracy, but a model of parliamentary democracy for the country, as well as its constituent states. In the resulting model, people elect representatives to make laws. An executive enforces those laws and the laws must respect the mandates of the Constitution.

However, Mahatma Gandhi viewed the self-sufficient and self-governing village panchayats as a way to go back to direct democracy. These bodies were essentially based on the principle of subsidiarity. This is the organizing principle of a federation that believes in dealing with economic, social and political issues at the most proximate (or local) level of governance that is consistent with their resolution. For example, subsidiarity is the general principle of devolution for delegating powers to different layers of government in the EU laws. Governmental functions are best carried out by the smallest unit of governance possible, which is closest to citizens, and delegated upwards when the local entities cannot perform the task efficiently.

The illustrious founding fathers of our Constitution had enshrined village panchayats in Article 40 of the Directive Principles of State Policy. It cast an obligation upon the states to take credible steps to organize village panchayats and endow them with such powers and authority as may be necessary to enable them to function as units of self-government. Nonetheless, this vision of our democracy was more meaningfully implemented 29 years after the Directive Principles had been formulated.

The conceptualization of the local self-government system in post-Independence India emanated from the reports of four important committees: the Balwant Rai Mehta Committee (Committee on Panchayati Raj Institutions, 1957), the Ashok Mehta Committee (1977–78), the G.V.K. Rao Committee (Committee on Administrative Arrangements for Rural Development and Poverty Alleviation Programmes, 1985) and the L.M. Singhvi Committee (1986). While the issue of empowering the third tier of government received support and sporadic action both from the Centre and the states, a coherent approach did not come about until the 73rd and 74th amendments to the Constitution. Under these amendments, these institutions were formalized in our governance architecture.

The recognition of the panchayats as 'institutions of self-government' also broadened the role of the FC through the insertion of the subclauses (bb) and (c) to the Clause (3) of Article 280 of the Constitution. Article 280(3)(bb) refers to the measures needed to augment the Consolidated Fund of a state to supplement the resources of the panchayats in the state on the basis of the recommendations made by the FC of that state. Since then, approximately 3 million representatives have been regularly elected to about 2.6 lakh rural local bodies across the country. Providing basic services at the grassroots level makes them the primary interface between citizens and the government.

The Constitutional Amendment Bill assigned functions, finances and responsibilities for the viable functioning of the PRIs. They ensured certainty, continuity and predictability. The 11th Schedule of the Constitution was added to delineate 29 functions to be entrusted to the panchayats and the 12th Schedule was added to delineate 18 functions to be entrusted to the municipalities. There was also the question of resources based on entry 5 of the State List in the Seventh Schedule of the Constitution, which entrusts the responsibility of the PRIs to the states:

> Local government, that is to say, the constitution and powers of municipal corporations, improvement trusts, districts boards, mining settlement authorities and other local authorities for the purpose of local self-government or village administration.

The states are obligated to delegate the well-known three Fs—functions, funds and functionaries—to the panchayats based on the recommendations of the state finance commissions (SFCs). The Ministry of Panchayati Raj at the Union level is expected to play a supplementary part in this overall scheme. PRIs also act as agents for implementing some of the flagship schemes of the Union Government covering basic needs such as the MGNREGA for employment, Pradhan Mantri Awas Yojana (PMAY) for housing, Jal Jeevan Mission (JJM) for drinking water and SBM for sanitation, to mention a few. The third tier also performs the agency function for many of the development programmes of the state governments.

Role of the Finance Commission

Following the 73rd and 74th Constitutional amendments, it became standard practice for FCs, starting from the 10th FC, to assign resources to the third tier, although the proportionality and break-up between conditional and unconditional grants varied. All these grants invariably came out of the Consolidated Fund of India and were essentially grants recommended by the FC and accepted by the government. The quantum of funds alloted by the FCs have been listed in Table 1 below.

Table 1: The quantum of funds allotted by each FC

S. No.	*Commission*	*Funds (in INR crores)*
1	10th FC	5,381
2	11th FC	10,000
3	12th FC	25,000
4	13th FC	87,519
5	14th FC	287,436
6	15th FC	436,361

Source: 'Finance Commissions: A Legacy of Trust', Finance Commission India, https://bit.ly/3MMAv0X. Accessed on 4 May 2022.

The 15th FC made a significant change by recommending grants of ₹436,361 crore from the Union Government to local bodies for 2021–26. It is an increase of 52 per cent over the corresponding grant of ₹287,436 crore by its predecessor for 2015–20. After careful consideration, we concluded that these bodies require substantially enhanced resources. The tax revenues or resource mobilization by these institutions for their overall budgetary requirements have remained grossly inadequate.

Furthermore, given the pandemic, in the aforesaid grant, the 15th FC also recommended a grant of ₹70,051 crore to plug critical gaps in primary healthcare. It has also recommended performance-based grants worth ₹8,000 crore for incubation of new cities and ₹450 crore for shared municipal services. The rural–urban distribution of the remaining ₹357,860 crore was incrementally enhanced in favour of the ULBs from 67:33 in 2021–22 to 65:35 by 2025–26. This tilt reflects India's ongoing rapid urbanization.

The FC's great dilemma in all this was the 'substitution effect'. Because the FC continues to provide funds for the third tier and the state governments know this, they more often than not decide to spend their money, which they would have otherwise given to the third tier to meet other revenue expenses. How does one ensure that our devolution is supplemental and results are in additionality, not substitution? This is an issue that needs further analysis.

Key Challenges

The third tier faces significant challenges. Some are legacy issues while others have been compounded by some recent developments.

First, how do we make each state government adhere and act in accordance with the constitutional provisions relating to the SFCs? The constitutional provision pertaining to the SFCs in Article 243I(1) states,

> The Governor of a State shall, as soon as may be within one year from the commencement of the Constitution (Seventy third Amendment) Act, 1992, and thereafter at the expiration of every fifth year, constitute a Finance Commission to review the financial position of the Panchayats and to make recommendations to the Governor.

As you would have noticed, these exactly mirror the provisions pertaining to the central FC. Given the pressures of the states and the anxiety of the Union Government to find out what resources would be left to them for their own planning and decision-making over a normal cycle of five-year awards, the central FC has been constituted with alacrity and firm timelines.

Furthermore, the constitution of SFCs is obligatory under Article 243I and 243Y. In practice, however, while the constitution of the Sixth SFC was expected to happen by 2019–20, only four states have done so: Assam, Bihar, Punjab and Rajasthan. Several states are still languishing in their second and third SFCs. The last SFCs constituted in each of the states have been listed in Table 2 below.

Table 2: The status of SFCs

State	*Last SFC Constituted*
Assam, Bihar, Punjab and Rajasthan	6th
Haryana, Himachal Pradesh, Kerala, Madhya Pradesh, Maharashtra, Odisha, Sikkim, Tamil Nadu, Tripura, Uttarakhand and Uttar Pradesh	5th
Andhra Pradesh, Karnataka and West Bengal	4th

Chhattisgarh, Goa, Gujarat, Jharkhand and Manipur	3rd
Arunachal Pradesh and Mizoram	2nd
Erstwhile Jammu and Kashmir and Telangana	1st

Source: Ministry of Panchayati Raj's presentations to the 15th FC.

This is an area where I believe that the only injured or adversely affected party is the third tier of the government. Unfortunately, given their somewhat weak financial position, they have never felt empowered enough to seek and enforce this constitutional obligation. Nonetheless, looking back, I think that this dereliction must be purposefully resolved. Beyond the third tier, the implementation of this constitutional obligation indeed affects the rubric of overall governance. This is a subject that certainly deserves attention to ensure the fullest compliance of these constitutional provisions in letter and spirit. Additionally, as part of the process of empowering the SFCs, one of the conditions is to ensure the devolution of functions as prescribed in the 11th Schedule of the 73rd Amendment.

Not constituting a central FC under Article 280 of the Constitution would have far-reaching consequences. It would upset the delicate equilibrium in the architecture of Centre–state relations. Adherence to constitutional provisions is the inescapable responsibility of both the Centre and the states. Thus, the Constitution enjoins on the President the obligation of constituting an FC every five years. Equally, it enjoins governors to constitute state FCs in accordance with Article 280. This symmetry of actions by both the Centre and the states is central to the architecture of credible, viable and orderly Centre–state relations. The implications of this failure constitute a deep malaise affecting the working of the third tier.

On our part, the 15th FC recognized the importance of constituting the SFCs as part of the constitutional obligation. In our recommendation number 26, we stipulated,

> We recommend that all States which have not done so, must constitute SFCs, act upon their recommendations and lay the explanatory memorandum as to the action taken thereon before the State legislature on or before March 2024. After March 2024, no grants should be released to a State that has not complied with the Constitutional provisions in respect of the SFC and these conditions. The Ministry of Panchayati Raj will certify the compliance of all Constitutional provisions by a State in this respect before the release of their share of grants for 2024–25 and 2025–26.[26]

This stipulation, which has a financial consequence, can be further reinforced by other directions from an appropriate judicial authority. The governors are reasonably expected to discharge their constitutional obligations.

Second, these adverse consequences result in the resources of the third tier invariably remaining scant. They remain hopelessly dependent on the awards of successive FCs even after the 73rd and 74th amendments. FCs are not obligated to make any financial awards. All that the Constitution enjoins upon them is to ensure that the Consolidated Fund of the State is augmented for meeting the obligations of the third tier. The last four FCs that have given financial awards have done so believing that these are transitional support mechanisms and cannot be a permanent feature. As for the 15th FC, we toyed with the option of abstaining from making awards in order

---

[26]"Finance Commission in COVID Times: Report for 2021-26', Finance Commission India, https://bit.ly/3Mt1xKR. Accessed on 4 May 2022.

for the SFCs to be constituted in a timely way. However, if we had done so, the finances of the third tier would have been in a state of disarray. We were also prompted by the fact that a substantial part of the resources of the third tier have been subsumed under the constitutional amendment that led to an all-embracing GST. If we also had abstained from making these awards, it would have made the working of the third tier totally unviable.

Third, the long-term financial viability of the third tier has been a persistent issue. Even though the transfer to the third tier from the Centre and the states has generally increased over time, the expenditures of the third tier have also crept up while revenues have remained stagnant at around 1 per cent of the GDP for over a decade. Even before the implementation of the GST, which subsumed many of these taxes of the third tier, the revenues of the third tier were decreasing over time, from 0.3 per cent of the GDP in 2010–11 to 0.25 per cent in 2017–18. Furthermore, many of their sources of revenue, like taxes on advertisement, entertainment and agricultural produce, building registration fee and common property resources, to name a few, were subsumed in the GST in 2017.

So, there are only three logical steps to be taken:

- Since what has been subsumed in the GST cannot be undone, because the GST was implemented through voluntary consent of all the state governments, a compensating mechanism should be put in place. Some state governments, such as Kerala, Maharashtra and Bihar, have enacted separate laws. Other states should consider setting up such necessary institutional mechanisms to compensate the local bodies in lieu of the revenues forgone due to the GST. This is an area where more empirical work needs to be done.
- Since the state GST subsumes all the taxes of the third

tier, it would be logical for a certain fixed fraction of the GST, either a percentage or in fixed terms, to be earmarked from out of the state GST to devolve to the third tier. There could be a compensation formula for the state GST to be made available to the third tier. This would be fair and equitable considering the fact that while the taxes are being subsumed, no compensating mechanism has been worked out. Unfortunately, the debates in Parliament in relation to the GST also did not discuss this issue.

- Most importantly, moving forward, is the area of additional revenue beyond the subsumed taxes? This relates to the issue of property tax. Property taxes are among the most important revenue sources for the third tier across the world. Compared to its OECD peers, India performs poorly in terms of generating revenues from the urban immovable property tax. The data shows that while the average collection from property taxes in the OECD group is about 1.1 per cent of the national GDP, the number for India is about 0.2 per cent of the GDP, which is just one-sixth of the OECD average. For some OECD countries, such as Canada, the UK and the US, property tax collections form the bedrock of local bodies' revenues, and constitute about 3 per cent of their GDPs.

Several factors lead to low property tax revenue in India, including undervaluation, incomplete registers, policy inadequacy and ineffective administration. Another big challenge for property tax administration is the lack of accurate property tax records in the jurisdiction of the third tier.

In the report of the 15th FC, we have made property taxes an entry-level condition to access the funds for ULBs while providing for a one-year window for states to notify the floor rates of property tax in two stages from 2022–23. For a state government, notifying minimum floor rates is now a necessary condition for availing FC grants. Once the floor is notified, the grants from 2023–24 onwards will be determined based on the condition that the growth in property tax collection should be at least as much as the simple average growth rate of the state's own Gross State Domestic Product (GSDP) in the last five years, which will be measured and taken into account.

India's experience with property tax has had a very mixed story so far. Needless to say, political economy factors and the recalcitrance of some states in imposing any property tax have been more than evident in our interactions with the states. Hopefully, with the recommendations of the FC now fully accepted, property taxes and their indexation in the GSDP will become an important source of revenue in the years ahead.

Fourth, the third tier faces issues of professional tax. The power of the state legislature is derived from Article 276 of the Constitution and entry 60 of the List 2 of the Seventh Schedule. Currently, the professional tax limit of ₹2,500 has been imposed by the 60th Amendment. At present, 21 states are collecting professional tax. It is curious that the recommendation of the 14th FC to raise this limit to ₹12,000 per annum has not resulted in any tangible action. The 14th FC had also recommended that Article 276(ii) of the Constitution be amended to increase the limit and stipulate that Parliament should have the power to impose limits with the caveat that it should adhere to the FC's recommendations. Apparently, its reason for giving Parliament the power to determine the tax limits was that states should not have unlimited power to raise a second income tax in the name of professional tax.

The substitution, diversion and consequences for direct tax realization have inhibited the central government from acting on the recommendation of the 14th FC. In the 15th FC, we have reiterated these suggestions and have sought to revise this ceiling, reckoning for the accumulated inflation over the intervening period, to protect the real value of the 1988 ceiling. This way, the upper ceiling turns out to be about ₹18,000, based on 1920 prices. Allowing ULBs to collect professional tax in India would be an important source of revenue, and its indexation would ensure a continuing source of revenue over a period of time. This is an area where I believe expeditious recourse to act on these recommendations would help improve the finances of ULBs.

Fifth, the third tier faces the issue of its electoral politics. Unfortunately, the electoral process has gotten warped because of the excessive politicization of elections in the third tier. While the electoral process has resulted in greater empowerment, particularly due to the women's reservation, there have been other adverse consequences. Elections to the third tier should account for local perception while selecting representatives that are most likely to meet the needs of the beneficiaries. Instead, it has become a needless pointer of whether these local elections represent a swing in the mandate of the ruling state governments and, strangely, are even considered to be straws in the wind for the popularity of the central government. Excessive politicization of elections to the third tier is avoidable, as it detracts from its broad objectives.

Sixth, connected to the issue of the electoral process in the third tier, is the broader issue of accountability by way of audit reports and performance criteria. The accountability of public funds is at the heart of sound public finance. Unfortunately, we have not progressed sufficiently in this area. In the twenty-first century, with a robust IT industry and increasing technical proficiency in the country, there is no reason why the accounts of every PRI, on a common classification scheme, should not be available on the internet for people to see and evaluate them right after the end of a financial year. Even the audit of such accounts and the duly audited account statements should be available with only a few months' lag. The 15th FC in its report for 2020–21 has pointed out that the timely availability of audited accounts, separately at the local body level and jointly at the state and national level, is a critical reform agenda. It has recommended that upgraded PRIASoft[27] needs to be integrated with the Integrated Financial Management Information System (IFMIS) of the state governments (wherever it exists) and the Public Financial Management System (PFMS) of the Controller General of Accounts (CGA) to generate online accounts of each rural local body, enable online auditing of such accounts and their consolidation at the state and national levels.

We have sought to address these suitably among the entry-level conditions and auditing of accounts. In the summary of our recommendations, we have stated,

> The entry level condition for rural and urban local bodies availing any grants due to them is having both provisional and audited accounts online in the public domain. States will receive grant for those rural and urban local bodies that have their provisional accounts for the previous year and audited accounts for the year before the previous, available online.[28]

Over a period of time, the digital penetration and connectivity in rural areas will significantly reduce the rural–urban information gap and enable the administration at the local level to function effectively.

Under the BharatNet project, 128,870 village panchayats were already connected with optical fibre by June 2019 and

[27]PRIASoft is a centralized accounting software to be used by all three levels of the Panchayati Raj—zilla, block and village panchayats.

[28]'Finance Commission in COVID Times: Report for 2021-26', Finance Commission India, https://bit.ly/3Mt1xKR. Accessed on 4 May 2022.

Wi-Fi spots were installed in 44,410 village panchayats as part of the last mile connectivity to all village panchayats. Phase-II of this project is being implemented, and all panchayats should be covered soon. The timelines for assured connectivity to all village panchayats, for which there is no dearth of resources, has been pushed back several times. I believe that its completion before the 75th year of our Independence will enable digital connectivity to harness the new frontiers of technology to the advantage of the third tier institutions.

The issue of performance criteria and financial resources linked to either inputs or outcomes has been a debatable one. After considering all points of view, the 15th FC adopted the following approach.

- Incentives should be outcome-based transfers.
- The outcome-based indicators should be fixed against each incentive through the use of credible and verifiable data, ideally with the attributes of being objective, reliable, universal, consistent, actionable, simple and not subject to manipulation.
- Incentives must be sufficient to induce desired outcomes.
- Incentives should reward a combination of both achievements in absolute terms as well as percentage changes in recent years to balance the efforts of advanced and laggard states.

There is a point of view that the binding characteristics of these performance criteria very often fail to achieve the desired objective. Untied resources enable the third tier to exercise flexibility to meet current and emerging challenges. At the same time, experience suggests that untied resources and their utilization, if unmonitored, can lead to systemic misuses. We have adopted a mixed approach in which, while a substantial part of the resources remains untied, others are linked to benchmarks that mirror the national objectives. A substantial part of these resources will be utilized to improve the health infrastructure at the cutting edge of the delivery system, particularly at the local level of panchayats and ULBs. These local bodies are closest to the people in rural areas, who will benefit from the improved health infrastructure.

Seventh, the third tier is plagued by the issue of its functions. Undoubtedly, the delegation of the functions of the third tier has been demarcated in the 11th Schedule. However, moving beyond notifying the devolution of these functions, for example, agriculture and agricultural extension, the states need to clearly demarcate the roles and responsibilities of which departments fall under the jurisdiction of the state government and which ones the PRIs are responsible for. Similarly, the roles of each of the three tiers of PRIs need to be elaborated. States like Bihar, Jharkhand, Uttar Pradesh, Punjab and Chhattisgarh can progress significantly in this regard. In any organization, there is a well-known and natural reluctance to devolve powers to the lower levels. However, this reluctance needs to be overcome for greater efficiency. The political struggle among the elected representatives to the Lok Sabha, Vidhan Sabha and PRIs from the area over turf issues should not become an obstacle in the path of PRI reform, hindering greater efficiency in the provision of public goods and services.

Eighth, the third tier faces the issue of capacity building. The problem of an adequate number and quality of functionaries at the PRIs needs to be resolved. There are few existing functionaries, who are mostly part-time and drawn largely from the state bureaucracy. While some challenges faced by the functionaries are genuine, others reflect a lack of will. The difficulties posed by the small size and huge number of PRIs can be circumvented through a rationalization of their number, and by using smart technology and off-site common resources. During our visits to the states, as part of the 15th FC, we recognized that, currently, without adequate resources, it would be difficult for the third tier and PRIs to employ either contractual or permanent engineers, planners or other talent needed for discharging their obligations on their payroll. Till such a time as some of the suggestions that I have outlined in my earlier comments are fully carried out, we expect the state governments to provide the requisite personnel support for enabling capacity building given the multiplicity of their inherent functions in the larger scheme of things.

Based on the analysis above, it would appear reasonable that in order to embark on a new era of governance by way of strengthening the architecture of the third tier of the government, there are some obvious steps forward. These would, inter alia, include the following suggestions.

- In terms of the architecture, the implementation of the constitutional provisions of Article 243I relating to the SFCs must be implemented and sequenced within the framework of the 15th FC's recommendations.
- To improve the scant finances of the third tier, necessary amendments should be made by the GST Council or through another constitutional amendment, which will enable a uniform compensating mechanism to ensure that a fixed percentage of the state GST is made available to the third tier.
- Property taxes must be indexed to the GSDP.
- A constitutional amendment also needs to be introduced for the collection of professional taxes at the level of the third tier, an important untapped source of revenue.
- The excessive politicization of elections needs to be obviated.

- Accountability through audit reports and adherence to performance criteria needs the fullest compliance. The use of IT and integration of PRIASoft with IFMS in order to generate online accounts for rural local bodies will ensure continued accountability.
- On capacity building, we need to not only enhance the resources of the third tier but also, during the transition, SFCs should ensure the availability of human resources from the state government by way of providing full- or part-time personnel from the state bureaucracy. This will enable the utilization of funds and implementation of projects.
- Harnessing digital technology to improve the integration of the third tier economy into the national mainstream.

As technology advances further, moving into the new internet era with the use of Internet of Things (IoT) and artificial intelligence (AI), the demarcation of outcomes and responsibilities will get fused in imperceptible ways. This will allow us to tap into the great potential of the third tier to contribute to the future of India. I look forward to this future with optimism. Continuing surveillance, awareness and efforts will enable the realization of our quest for, and unlock the potential of, the third tier. Not strength or intelligence but continuous effort is the key to unlocking our potential.

I believe that this is the moment for panchayats. Their time has truly come. Across the country, increasingly, educated youth are occupying positions of elected representatives in PRIs. The dynamism brought by young, educated female representatives is visibly felt in some panchayats, saying goodbye to the hitherto known Sarpanch Pati system. The state executive has been increasingly feeling the pressure from the people demanding efficient delivery of public goods. It can be effectively met only with deeper decentralization. The digital penetration and connectivity in rural areas is reducing the rural–urban information gap and pushing the administration at the local level to function effectively.

I believe that at no other point in post-Independence India has the need for empowerment of the third tier been a more urgent priority. Not because we are about to celebrate the 75th year of our Independence but because the ongoing pandemic has brought home one important message: our broken health infrastructure can only be rejuvenated with a deeper involvement, engagement and mainstreaming of the role of third tier institutions. During the course of our deliberations at the 15th FC, it was persuasively argued before us that the rejuvenation of our healthcare system is inextricably connected with the revival and robustness of both ULBs and rural local bodies. I hope that this pandemic, which has been a wake-up call, will enable us to restructure the third tier. As Franklin D. Roosevelt said, 'We have always held to the hope, the belief, the conviction that there is a better life, a better world, beyond the horizon.'

This chapter has been extracted from N.K. Singh's speeches at A.N. College, Patna on 8 January 2021, and the 14th V. Sankar Aiyar virtual memorial lecture on 22 October 2021.[29]

[29]Resetting Centre - State Finances: Rethinking the Third - Tier - 14th Sankar Aiyar memorial lecture, YouTube, https://bit.ly/384C4sr. Accessed on 4 May 2022.

Section 2

PEOPLE-FIRST POLICY

5

EMPOWERING HANDS THAT FEED US

Driving agriculture towards farmers' welfare

India has rapidly progressed in the recent decades. The Indian economy is undergoing structural transformations. The share of agriculture and allied sectors in the GDP has come down from nearly 52 per cent in the early decades after Independence to 18 per cent during 2019–20. However, the critical role of agriculture in the Indian economy has not diminished. Almost half of the labour force—about 45 per cent—is employed in agriculture, according to the Periodic Labour Force Survey (PLFS) 2019–20, and over 60 per cent of the rural population depends on agriculture for its livelihood. In other words, agriculture affects the life and livelihood of a large segment of the country's population. It meets the food and nutrition demands of over 1.3 billion people and contributes significantly to employment and demand generation in post-harvest activities that are not accounted for in the agricultural sector and the agri-input and agri-output industry. Agriculture also contributes to foreign exchange earnings in a big way with net exports (exports minus imports) of more than $15–20 billion. Another important aspect is that agricultural growth has a strong correlation with poverty reduction. In order to alleviate rural poverty and promote inclusive growth, we need to focus on agricultural productivity and farmers' income.

The role of the Green Revolution since the latter part of the 1960s, which initially focused on wheat in Punjab, Haryana and western Uttar Pradesh spread to more crops and more areas. Even beyond the Green Revolution period, efforts in developing new varieties, improved technology, agricultural extension and rural infrastructure resulted in increased productivity and production of several crops, livestock and fishery. In terms of numbers, production of food grains, oilseeds, commercial crops, milk, eggs, fish and, more recently, horticultural crops has increased multiple times.

Decade after decade, efforts have been made to diversify agriculture, promote high-value crop production, develop new technologies, disseminate new knowledge to farmers, strengthen institutional support to farmers, upgrade input delivery systems and improve agricultural and marketing infrastructure. Yet, during the last two decades, issues of farmer distress have posed new challenges for us all.

In the context of agricultural development, policymakers have been focusing on increasing productivity by developing high yielding crop varieties, using improved techniques and modern inputs, improving the system of agricultural extension, expanding irrigation infrastructure, agricultural marketing and so on. In spite of such efforts, why is there a perception that the condition of farmers has not improved, particularly when compared with other sectors such as industry and services?

No doubt, researchers have analysed the role of several agricultural and non-agricultural activities that directly and indirectly impact agricultural growth, such as power and rural roads. Yet, there are questions for all of us.

- It is widely discussed that the youth is not interested in agriculture. Nonetheless, why is it that close to half of the workforce is engaged in agriculture?
- How can we hasten the process of shifting people from agricultural to non-agricultural activities?
- Why has new knowledge not reached all farmers, and why do they continue to follow conventional methods of agriculture, which lead to poor returns?
- How do we modernize agriculture? Why are our yield levels languishing? Why is there a large yield gap between experimental farm research institutions and farmers' fields?
- India has now reached a stage where large surpluses of some commodities have emerged after meeting the domestic demand. What should be the policy for surplus management and export promotion?
- Why does farmer distress happen in areas where there is high agricultural growth?

Some of the questions listed above merit policy attention in the months and years to come.

Challenges for Today's Policymakers

In the context of the questions and issues mentioned above, I have put forward a few ideas to understand the prevailing situation of farmers and farming, followed by a deep dive into the risks they face, some of which have been listed below.

- Although it is known that any agricultural activity is riskier than other economic activities, the problem of risk has not been addressed effectively and adequately.

- Agricultural growth and development depend as much on the efforts that are put into agricultural activities, as on the sectors other than agriculture, and even on the efforts being invested in activities that are not directly related to agriculture.
- The role of the rural non-farm sector, though recognized by policy experts, has not been integrated with our agricultural policy and practice.
- The non-agricultural sectors, particularly industry, have failed to play a significant role in extracting and absorbing the agricultural workforce to keep pace with changes in their respective shares of the GDP.

The four aspects listed above are vital for transforming our agricultural ecosystem, but they have not been addressed effectively. This has possibly led to our efforts towards agricultural growth and development not being as successful as we expected them to be. This is a major challenge today for our policymakers.

Agricultural risk is broadly categorized into two types: yield risk and price/market risk. Yield risk arises due to weather conditions, like drought, flood, timing and distribution of rainfall, hailstorms, high-speed winds and temperature variation, as well as sudden insect and pest attacks. Price risk arises when the market price falls sharply and the farmer incurs a huge loss. This could be due to the domestic demand–supply imbalance or international commodity price movement. There are also frequent incidences of poor competition and price manipulation by buyers denying farmers the genuine price of the farm produce. Price and market risks assume greater importance with increasing commercialization of agriculture. Some other, less discussed risks include quality and timely availability of inputs, and background risks like those related to the health of the farmers.

Our conventional policy strategy for the agricultural sector has not focused adequately on an integrated and holistic approach. The institutional arrangements of various organizations and agencies tasked with agricultural development undertake their activities with a narrow, siloed perspective. For example, those in charge of agricultural extension guide farmers to increase production but do not consider the marketing aspect. Those who are in charge of agricultural marketing do not consider rural roads, storage and grading. Those who look after rural infrastructure care only about the physical aspect of the facility and overlook the services provided by the infrastructure, or the conduct and performance of the facility.

The biggest gap is in the integration of post-harvest activities, value chains and agri-food processing with raw produce and producers. Several studies show that a significant part of the income of farm households comes from rural, non-farm activities. This is clearly evidenced in the national-level survey titled the 'Situation Assessment of Agricultural Households and Land and Livestock Holdings of Households in Rural India, 2019'. These Survey reports are available for year 2003, 2012–13 and 2018–19. The first two reports were prepared by the National Sample Survey Office (NSSO) and the National Statistical Office (NSO), under the Ministry of Statistics and Programme Implementation, worked on the most recent one. The estimates of income derived from various non-agricultural and agricultural sources reported in the recent survey from the year 2018–19 have been presented in Table 1 on the next page. The contribution of the non-agricultural sector to the income of agricultural households is as high as 56 per cent. This is a significant jump over the year 2012–13, when the non-agriculture sector contributed to 40 per cent of agricultural households' incomes.

Table 1:
Average monthly income (in INR) from different sources per agricultural household between July 2018 and June 2019 for various size classes of land processed (in hectare) (where net receipt is obtained considering both the paid-out expenses and imputed expenses)

Size class of land possessed (in hectare)	*Farm size category*	*Total income (INR)*	*Share of various sources in total income (in percentage)*[30]		
			Crop and livestock	*Wages and salaries*	*Non-farm business*
<0.01		9,982	25.27	64.47	7.73
0.01–0.40	Sub-marginal	6,388	15.75	70.30	11.01
0.40–1.00	Marginal	6,951	34.50	56.19	8.20
1.01–2.00	Small	9,189	52.82	39.69	6.67
2.01–4.00	Semi-medium	12,997	65.75	27.30	5.83
4.01–10.00	Medium	22,453	76.85	19.03	2.10
10.00+	Large	50,412	88.72	7.82	2.31
All sizes		8,337	41.97	48.73	7.69

Source: National Statistical Office, 'Situation Assessment of Agricultural Households and Land Holdings in Rural India, 2019', Ministry of Statistics and Programme Implementation, Government of India, September 2021, https://bit.ly/3kvG7AB. Accessed on 2 May 2022.

30 The percentages in this table have been estimated by Professor Ramesh Chand, who is a member of the NITI Aayog, from the data in various parts of the SAS report.

It may be noted that agricultural households comprise a large number of agricultural labourers, and their wage earnings raise the share of non-agriculture income in the total household income. The 2019 report also provides detailed estimates of source-wise income by size and class of the land possessed. This helps analyse the sources of income based on various farm sizes. The first category in Table 1 may include households that are primarily labour based. The second and third categories comprise marginal land holding households and the fourth category represents the households with small farm sizes. Marginal farmers derived one-third of their income from agriculture (crop and livestock farming) and two-thirds from salaries, wages and non-farm businesses. Based on the estimates from Table 1, small farmers and semi-medium farm households earn 47 per cent and 34 per cent of their total household incomes from non-agricultural sources, respectively. These results show that the share of non-agricultural sources in the total household income is increasing—68 per cent farm households earn more income from non-agricultural sources as compared to the contribution of crops and livestock production, i.e. agriculture.

Another interesting finding is based on a study of Palanpur village, Moradabad district, Uttar Pradesh, over a period of seven decades—from the 1950s to recent years. The book *How Lives Change: Palanpur, India, and Development Economics* shows that, inter alia, the non-farm income of the households in Palanpur increased from 13.23 per cent in 1957–58 to 46.36 per cent in 2008–09.[31] Thus, both, macro- and micro- level evidence reveal the rising contribution of non-agricultural sources in the incomes of farm households. This change indicates that it is necessary to synchronize rural non-farm

[31]Himanshu, Peter Lanjouw and Nicholas Stern, *How Lives Change: Palanpur, India, and Development Economics*, Oxford University Press, 30 October 2018.

activities with our initiatives for the development of farmers and other households in rural areas.

A Paradigm Shift

A question may arise as to whether there has been any change in the approach to the development of the agriculture sector in the last eight years, beginning with the change in the government at the Centre. The present government has, for the first time, ushered in a paradigm shift in the approach towards the agricultural sector, from the growth of production to an increase in the farmers' income. On 28 February 2016, PM Modi declared that his dream is to see farmers' income double by 2022, to mark 75 years of India's independence.[32] This is a major shift in our approach to agriculture, with a clear focus on farmers and their welfare, rather than simply production and productivity.

For this purpose, a holistic strategy has been visualized for the agricultural sector. Efforts are being made to follow this strategy using an integrated approach to initiate multiple reforms and programmes with an overall objective of increasing farmers' income from agricultural as well as non-agricultural sources. This framework includes the following aspects:

- increase productivity/production and reduce losses;
- increase market access of agricultural produce through marketing reforms, post-harvest infrastructure and value addition;
- reduce input costs of farmers by optimizing resources used as inputs, along with initiatives on 'natural farming';

[32]'My dream is to see farmers double their income by 2022: PM', *The Hindu*, 28 February 2016, https://bit.ly/3s4thO6. Accessed on 2 May 2022.

- undertake governance and structural reforms;
- expand risk mitigation measures to protect farmers against losses due to yield and price risks;
- increase the investment in and for agriculture;
- link development activities in sectors such as water resources, soil health, food processing, rural development, power, IT, environment, fertilizers and other sectors to agricultural development;
- address background risk through initiatives such as ABY, Pradhan Mantri Ujjwala Yojana (PMUY), POSHAN (Prime Minister's Overarching Scheme for Holistic Nourishment) Abhiyaan, the Pradhan Mantri Matru Vandana Yojana, the Sukanya Samriddhi Yojana, the Beti Bachao Beti Padhao Yojana, the PMAY, SBM and Mission Indradhanush.[33]
- promote farmers organizations to overcome the scale disadvantage and impart them with bargaining power;
- higher direct intervention in the marketing of farm produce;
- direct income support to farmers; and
- improved access to institutional credit.

Some of the government programmes and initiatives over the past eight years, particularly those which address price and yield risks, have been briefly discussed below.

In April 2016, the government announced the creation of the National Agriculture Market (eNAM) scheme, which is an innovative marketing platform to revolutionize agricultural markets. It aims to ensure a better price discovery and bring in transparency and competition to enable farmers to get a higher price for their produce. The idea is to move towards

[33]For more details on these initiatives, please see the Annexure.

the vision of 'One Nation, One Market'. The scheme provides an online trading platform for farmers. So far, 1,000 mandis have been integrated with eNAM, and 100 of those are undertaking online trading.[34]

The integration of a mandi with eNAM involves multiple aspects, including:

- identifying private markets;
- direct marketing from farmers to consumers;
- contract farming for aggregation;
- a single-point levy of market fee;
- unified trading license;
- providing electronic trading;
- segregating regulation from operation;
- deregulating fruits and vegetables from the purview of the Agricultural Produce Market Committee (APMC); and
- the presence of quality assaying labs.

In April 2017, the Agricultural Produce and Livestock (Promotion and Facilitation) Act, 2017, which is a model Act, was released for adoption by the state governments. This Act provides for the setting up of private markets, direct marketing, farmer-consumer markets and special commodity markets, and declares warehouses, silos, cold storages and other such structures as market sub-yards. This Act was followed by the circulation of the Model Contract Farming Act in May 2018 to states for adoption. This Act aimed to integrate farmers with bulk purchasers, including exporters, agro-industries, etc. for a better price realization by mitigating market and price risks to the farmers and ensuring a smooth agricultural raw material supply to agro-industries.

[34]eNam: National Agriculture Market, https://bit.ly/3kYGvYB. Accessed on 11 May 2022.

Furthermore, a draft model Agricultural Land Leasing Act was also circulated by the NITI Aayog to the states.

In the 2018 Union Budget, the government introduced a programme for the development and upgradation of 22,000 rural haats as centres of aggregation and direct sale and purchase of agricultural commodities. While the civil infrastructure is to be funded through the Mahatma Gandhi National Rural Employment Guarantee Scheme (MNREGS), the market infrastructure will be funded through the Agri-Market Infrastructure Fund (AMIF) under the National Bank for Agriculture and Rural Development (NABARD), or the Agriculture Marketing Infrastructure (AMI) sub-scheme of the Ministry of Agriculture and Farmers Welfare.

In July 2018, it was announced that the recommendations of the National Commission on Farmers (NCF), also known as Swaminathan Commission, for determination of the Minimum Support Price (MSP), were to be adopted. This was an important step towards providing reasonable returns to farmers. The proposal involved at least a 50 per cent margin over cost, which also includes the imputed value of family labour. In order to help farmers get good returns, a robust procurement mechanism is being put in place.

The Pradhan Mantri Annadata Aay SanraksHan Abhiyan (PM-AASHA) announced by the government is a step in this direction. The scheme comprises three sub-schemes: the Price Support Scheme (PSS), the Price Deficiency Payment Scheme (PDPS) and the Private Procurement and Stockist Scheme (PPSS) on a pilot basis. These are important measures to address the problem of price risks faced by farmers. No doubt, there are economic arguments against the very concept of an MSP that, some contend, distorts the market. However, there are issues of an imperfect market and the risk of survival faced by poor farmers. In the medium-term, and till workable alternatives are put in place, it is difficult to do away with this system.

In 2015–16, there was a tremendous shortage of pulses. With the efforts of the central and state governments and other stakeholders, the production of pulses reached to record levels of 23.13 million tons and 25.23 million tons during 2016–17 and 2017–18, respectively. A comprehensive system for the procurement of pulses and a buffer stock was put in place for the first time. Production of pulses has remained a challenge for many years. The unprecedented increase in production due to the effective measures taken by this government indicates that it is feasible to transform agricultural production.

The Pradhan Mantri Fasal Bima Yojana (PMFBY) introduced from Kharif 2016 (February) is a landmark initiative. As a country, we have been implementing crop insurance schemes for the last three decades. However, there have been issues in their implementation. The PMFBY addresses these earlier shortcomings. It is a bold initiative with affordable premium rates and an ambitious target of covering 50 per cent of the farmers of our large country by 2019–20. One distinguishing feature of this scheme is its use of technology at different stages of its implementation to mitigate problems of misrepresentation, moral hazard and adverse selection. In recent times, however, the coverage has declined, as the scheme has become optional even for those who take crop loans.

The government launched the Pradhan Mantri Kisan Maandhan Yojana (PM-KMY) in September 2019 to provide social security to small and marginal farmers in their old age, when they have no means of livelihood and minimal or no savings to take care of their expenses. Under this scheme, a minimum fixed pension of ₹3,000 per month is provided to small and marginal farmers, subject to certain exclusion criteria, on turning 60. It is a voluntary and contributory pension scheme, with an entry age between 18 to 40 years. The farmers are required to contribute between ₹55 to ₹200 per month to a pension fund depending on the entry age. The central government also contributes an equal amount to the pension fund. This pension fund is being managed by the Life Insurance Corporation (LIC) of India.

The Pradhan Mantri Kisan Samman Nidhi (PM-Kisan) scheme was launched in February 2019 to provide income support of ₹6,000 per year (disbursed in three instalments of ₹2,000) to farmer families to supplement their financial needs in procuring inputs for appropriate crop health and yields. Earlier, only small and marginal landholder farmer families, i.e. families with a total cultivable landholding of up to two hectares, were eligible for the scheme. In May 2019, the Union Cabinet approved an extension of the scheme to all farmer families, irrespective of the size of their landholdings. Initially, the scheme was expected to cover 12.5 crore beneficiaries, but with the increase in its coverage, the revised number of beneficiaries is estimated to be 14.5 crore. As of May 2022, a total of 10.2 crore beneficiaries had been covered under the scheme. However, the number of beneficiaries reached under different instalments varies.

To give further impetus to agricultural reforms, the government introduced the historic new farm laws on agricultural marketing and trade and contract farming in 2020. The laws were enacted through Acts of Parliament by bringing in two new laws and modifying the Essential Commodities Act, 1955 to attract investments in logistics and modern infrastructure. These reforms were debated for a long time and considered essential to address the structural problems of the agricultural sector and transform it by seizing upcoming opportunities. The vision and spirit behind these reforms was enabling farmers to get better prices by enhancing competition, absorbing price shocks and reducing post-harvest losses. This was to be done by creating infrastructure such as cold storage, warehouses, cold chain, processing, etc. The contract farming reforms aimed at price risk sharing between the private sector and farmers. The new Acts gave a range of options to farmers for the sale of produce and diversification towards high-value crops without market risks. However, some sections of farmers opposed these laws. Deferring to the sentiments of farmers, these laws were repealed in December 2021.

A scheme for the formation and promotion of 10,000 farmer producer organizations (FPOs) during a five-year period till 2023–24, with a total budgetary provision of ₹6,865 crore, was launched in February 2020. Under the scheme, each FPO will be adequately handheld for five years from the year of formation—till 2027–28.

An Agriculture Infrastructure Fund (AIF) was launched in August 2020. The fund aims to provide medium- to long-term debt financing for investment in viable projects for the post-harvest management of infrastructure and community farming assets through interest subvention and financial support. The scheme has been planned for 10 years—from FY 2020 to FY 2029. Till January 2021, a total of 3,064 projects of Primary Agricultural Credit Societies (PACS), worth a loan amount of ₹1,565 crore, was sanctioned by NABARD.

The Kisan Rath app, a farmer-friendly mobile application, was launched to facilitate the movement of agricultural and horticultural products for farmers and traders in search of vehicles for primary and secondary transportation. The first Kisan Rail started between Deolali (Maharashtra) and Danapur (Bihar) in July 2020; another Kisan Rail has been operational between Anantpur (Andhra Pradesh) and Adarsh Nagar (Delhi).

Agricultural credit is provided to farmers at a subsidized cost through the Interest Subsidy Scheme, under which an interest subsidy of 2 per cent is provided to farmers on their short-term crop loans of up to ₹3 lakh. An additional interest subsidy at 3 per cent is provided to farmers repaying their loans on time (within a year). There has been a substantial increase in institutional credit, from ₹7 lakh crore in 2013–14 to ₹14 lakh crore in 2019–20.

As part of the AatmaNirbhar Bharat Abhiyan in 2020–21, the Animal Husbandry Infrastructure Development Fund (AHIDF) was set up, with an outlay of ₹15,000 crore. This fund aims to incentivize investments by individual entrepreneurs, private companies, micro, small and medium enterprises (MSMEs), FPOs and Section 8 companies to establish production and processing facilities of animal husbandry products.

The Pradhan Mantri Kisan Sampada Yojana (PMKSY) is an umbrella scheme being implemented since 2015–16 to reduce post-harvest losses and facilitate value chain development. It includes mega food parks, cold chains, food testing laboratories and agro-processing clusters. The Operation Greens scheme was included in this programme in 2018. Different schemes under the PMKSY have benefitted 30 lakh farmers and made it possible to leverage the investment to the extent of ₹9,000 crore. A total of 582 projects have been completed as part of this programme. Some achievements of this programme, based on the data available with the Ministry of Food Processing Industries, are as follows:

- 257 cold chain projects have been created with a capacity of 118 lakh metric ton (MT);
- more than 27 lakh MT of capacities for preservation and processing have been created during the last six years, under the Mega Food Park scheme; and
- over 150 food processing units have been made operational;
- a total of 1.8 crore MT of food processing capacities have been created through different schemes; and
- 118 new food testing laboratories have been set up.

In fact, all the schemes for the value chain development of different departments have contributed to the development of 35 million tons of total cold chain capacities.

In 2020, the Ministry of Food Processing Industries launched the Pradhan Mantri Formalisation of Micro Food Processing Enterprises (PMFME), a new, CSS with a total outlay of ₹10,000 crore for five years. Under the scheme, the 'One District, One Product' (ODOP) status was approved for 137 unique products across 710 districts of 35 states and union territories.

The Operation Greens scheme was announced in the Union Budget for 2018–19 to promote FPOs, agri-logistics, processing facilities and the professional management of tomato, onion and potato (TOP) crops. The scheme was launched in November 2018 on a pilot basis with two components:

- Short-term—Price Stabilization Measures: As part of this measure, a subsidy was announced at the rate of 50 per cent on transportation and storage costs at the time of harvest to take the surplus production of TOP crops from producing areas to consumption centres. The coverage of short-term measures was extended to 41 notified fruits and vegetables as a part of AatmaNirbhar announcement in June 2020.
- Long-term—Value Chain Development Projects: As part of this measure, farmers in the production clusters were organized as FPOs to manage production, post-harvest activities, value addition and marketing of the TOP produce. Assistance was provided for different components of the value chain activities, in the range of 35–70 per cent of the cost.

I have described these initiatives to highlight some distinctive aspects of the Centre's approach to agricultural development during the last eight years. The basic thrust has been addressing the issues raised by various types of risks that adversely affect farmers' income, and having a more comprehensive, integrated and holistic approach to achieve this goal. It is, however, necessary that the programmes are effectively implemented within the given time frame.

The initiatives launched during the last eight years involve continuity with change. Some ideas are not entirely new—they evolve. J.S. Chakravarti, in the book *Agricultural Insurance: A Practical Scheme suited to Indian Conditions,*[35] gives the interesting example of the Diwan Bahadur of Mysore in 1920, who mentioned, in passing, that the distress during a famine is more due to a lack of purchasing power than a shortfall in production. The concept of 'entitlement' put forward by Amartya Sen was based on a similar idea, though not derived from the work of Chakravarti.[36] Similarly, the idea of weather-based crop insurance, advocated by policy analysts and international organizations in the 1990s, was not new. More than half a century earlier, Chakravarti had formulated a scheme of agricultural insurance based on rainfall.

What is relevant is that ideas that are not necessarily new can become useful and fruitful if they are conceptualized, operationalized and implemented with renewed focus and vision. The approach and aspects that I have described earlier should be analysed from this perspective.

The efforts towards agricultural development during the past decades were certainly based on good knowledge, research and technology. Yet, the expected outcomes could not be achieved and farmer distress is apparent. Hence, there

---

[35]Chakravarti, J.S., *Agricultural Insurance: A Practical Scheme Suited to Indian Conditions,* Government Press, Bangalore, 1920.

[36]Mishra, P.K., *Agricultural Risk, Insurance and Income: A Study of the Impact and Design of India's Comprehensive Crop Insurance Scheme,* Avebury, Aldershot, UK, 1996, p. 310.

is a need not only to further refine our efforts in the areas of varietal improvement, transfer of technology and market access but also to analyse why the past initiatives could not accomplish the desired results. It is for this reason that policymakers and practitioners should look at how one can address the problem of farmer's risk in its various dimensions—affecting their income and welfare—and link activities of the non-agricultural sector to those of agriculture. This is also an area that researchers and analysts need to focus on.

I am sure our continued efforts will help us build the desired momentum and design policies and strategies to achieve our collective goal of doubling farmers' income, as visualized by our PM.

This chapter is an updated version of the inaugural address delivered by P.K. Mishra at the 78th Annual Conference of the Indian Society of Agricultural Economics held on 1 November 2018. It has also been published in the Indian Journal of Agricultural Economics, *Vol. 74, No 1, January–March 2019.*

6

THE FUTURE VISTAS

Role of technology in shaping education

The Indian education ecosystem is a large and diverse network spread across multiple geographies and contexts. Its diversity is apparent in the wide array of schools, boards of education and higher education institutions, along with solutions (non-digital and digital) across government, private sector and civil society, languages, mediums and learner needs. The Constitution of India gives 'education' a special position, as both a national and state subject, making the education system both federated and autonomous. The needs of this large and nuanced ecosystem are, therefore, equally diverse.

I was invited to speak about the 'Role of Technology in the Future' at the Foundation Day programme of the Indian Institute of Technology (IIT), Jodhpur. Since it took place on 2 August 2020, when the first phase of Covid-19 was nearing its peak, the programme was hosted online, via a technology platform, without all of us travelling to Jodhpur, which would have meant more time, travelling and other logistical aspects. However, it also deprived us of face-to-face interaction, seeing the ambience of the institute and experiencing the warmth and hospitality of the students and faculty. This brings out the dilemmas, limitations, relevance, use and efficacy of technology, which could pose new challenges in the coming years, particularly in the post-Covid-19 world.

Over the past five years, I have had several opportunities to address students on the occasion of their convocations. On such occasions, I often used to touch upon how technology has been changing the way we live and work, and how game-changing ideas, such as smartphones, AI, augmented reality (AR), robotics, blockchain technologies and the IoT, are likely to usher in changes at an unprecedented pace. However, I had never expected that the situation would transform so dramatically and quickly. Particularly in the last two years, the role of technology has become predominant. Every aspect of our lives has been touched by the improvements in technology, with a wide array of innovations. Undoubtedly, in the coming days, the transformation will be more widespread and comprehensive. This impact will be felt strongly in the field of education.

The way our children are learning things now is very different from how we learnt things even just a few years ago. As is evidenced of late, technology-enabled learning can bring in not only transformational changes in the delivery of online education experience but it can also enhance and supplement regular classroom-based pedagogy. It offers more flexibility and learning support than the traditional formats. Technology offers teachers the opportunity to become more collaborative and extend learning beyond the classrooms. Educators could create learning communities comprising students, fellow educators and global experts from various disciplines. This environment of enhanced collaboration can offer access to instructional materials as well as resources and tools to create, manage and assess the quality and usefulness of such materials.

The PM has repeatedly spoken of the need to give wings to the aspirations of our children and youth through a rich, robust and resilient education system. The use of technology in education is the pillar on which the system can reliably rest and flourish. In schooling, the government has come out with a number of initiatives to realize this objective under the National Education Policy (NEP) 2020. Some of these initiatives include the PM eVIDYA programme, the National Initiative for Proficiency in Reading with Understanding and Numeracy (NIPUN Bharat), the Plan Review Arrange Guide Yak (Talk) Assign Track Appreciate (PRAGYATA) Guidelines on how to use technology for classroom transactions, the National Educational Technology Forum (NETF), the National Digital Education Architecture (NDEAR) and a host of related initiatives that are coming in just in time to meet the aspirations of the youth.

Recent technology initiatives in the school ecosystem that caught the imagination of the country, as reflected in their usage, include DIKSHA, 'one class, one TV channel', podcasts and radio, including community radio. All these initiatives have been a part of the PM eVIDYA programme, under the AatmaNirbhar Bharat initiative.

DIKSHA is a national, AI-based platform for school education in the public domain—an initiative of the National Council of Educational Research and Training (NCERT). It was developed based on the core principles of open architecture, open access, open licensing, diversity, choice and autonomy. DIKSHA has been adopted by 35 states and union territories across the country as well as the Central Board of Secondary Education (CBSE), NCERT and crores of learners and teachers. During the pandemic, DIKSHA brought relief and support to learners by providing free e-content anytime, anywhere, along with supplementary material through QR-coded textbooks. More than 70 per cent of the prescribed textbooks of the country have been energized with e-content tagged to QR codes. Currently, over 215,500 pieces of e-content are live on DIKSHA in 33 languages, including Indian Sign Language (ISL). Talking books for visually impaired children and grade-wise e-content in ISL are also readily available on this platform.

DIKSHA receives close to five crore page hits per day and over 370 crore learning sessions have taken place on it since April 2020. All the courses hosted on the platform are interactive, prepared by the best teachers in the country and are available free of cost to any learner. The student community is free to develop its own solutions, leveraging the DIKSHA infrastructure and assets by taking advantage of its rich set of application programming interfaces (APIs). In fact, the courses on DIKSHA can be utilized in various ways, including online teacher training (through the National Initiative for School Heads' and Teachers' Holistic Advancement [NISHTHA]), item banks, chatbots, quiz competitions, energized textbooks, audios, videos, etc. Similarly, the 'one class, one TV channel' programme was initiated during the pandemic to provide structured and grade-wise lessons to crores of children in remote areas studying in grades 1–12 through the Swayam Prabha satellite-based TV channel.

In recent years, the use of digital technologies in higher education has also received much attention throughout the world. Across the country, the Government of India is encouraging several e-learning projects under the National Mission on Education through Information and Communication Technology (NMEICT) initiatives, such as Study Webs of Active Learning for Young Aspiring Minds (SWAYAM), Swayam Prabha, the National Digital Library of India (NDLI), e-Yantra, Virtual Labs, etc., which help students as well as teachers upskill while providing them quality resources.

SWAYAM is a government programme designed to

achieve the three cardinal principles of education policy: access, equity and quality. This is done through a platform that hosts all the courses taught in classrooms from class 9 till post-graduation. These courses can also be accessed by anyone, anywhere, anytime. These diverse efforts are creating knowledge tools that impart not only quality education accessibly but also encourage creativity and innovation, particularly among younger students.

Towards an India-Centric Education System

The NEP, announced on 29 July 2020, replaced the older policy that had been introduced 34 years ago. It envisages major reforms in the education system, and recognizes and affirms the fourth SDG of 'inclusive and equitable quality education and promote lifelong learning opportunities for all' by 2030. It accords the highest priority to achieving FLN, which stands for foundational literacy (i.e. the ability to read with meaning) and numeracy (i.e. having a clear sense of numbers), among all children by 2025. It advocates the launch of an urgent mission on FLN at the national level. The launch of NIPUN Bharat in July 2021, targeting the learning needs of children in the age group of 3–11 years is a step in this direction. The NEP calls for universalization of early childhood care and education, and aspires to achieve that with the move towards the 5+3+3+4 curricular and pedagogical structure. It also highlights the importance of bringing vocational education and twenty-first-century skill training—e.g. AI, hybrid learning systems online and offline, etc.—into mainstream education, with the intention of giving children flexibility of choice and greater opportunities to obtain gainful employment.

The NEP strongly emphasizes the inclusion of Socially and Economically Disadvantaged Groups (SEDGs), along with marginalized groups and children with atypical needs at every level to ensure that all students thrive in the education system. The education system must aim to benefit India's students so that no child loses any opportunity to learn and excel because of circumstances of their birth or background.

Some of the policy imperatives that the NEP sets for both school and higher education have been listed below:

- flexibility in the choice of subjects and multidisciplinarity;
- Academic Bank of Credits (ABC);
- multiple entry and exit points;
- curricular reforms—including assessment reforms;
- teacher/faculty professional development;
- mentoring of teachers/faculty; and
- professional standards for teachers and institutions.

Technology Use and Integration

The NEP recognizes that:

> India is a global leader in information and communication technology and in other cutting-edge domains, such as space. The Digital India Campaign is helping to transform the entire nation into a digitally empowered society and knowledge economy. While education will play a critical role in this transformation, technology itself will play an important role in the improvement of educational processes and outcomes; thus, the relationship between technology and education at all levels is bi-directional.[37]

It goes on to say:

[37]'National Education Policy 2020', Ministry of Education: Government of India, p. 56, https://bit.ly/3vygF3R. Accessed on 2 May 2022.

> New technologies involving artificial intelligence, machine learning, block chains, smart boards, handheld computing devices, adaptive computer testing for student development, and other forms of educational software and hardware will not just change what students learn in the classroom but how they learn and thus these areas and beyond will require extensive research both on the technological as well as educational fronts.[38]

Clearly, the policy ubiquitously focuses on the use of technology for enhancing and empowering the school and higher education ecosystems. Some of the key areas in education where technology can play a role have been listed below:

- improving teaching and learning opportunities;
- supporting teacher preparation and professional development;
- enhancing educational access by tracking enrolled students and their achievements;
- removing language and other access barriers, improving access and quality of education for students with atypical needs; and
- improving efficiencies and data-backed decision-making in educational planning and management.

In the post-Covid-19 world, as technologies evolve, they will impact social, economic and human activities more comprehensively. The journey ahead may seem uncertain and challenging at times and yet, if used wisely, technology is full of promise and opportunity.

The NEP requires an autonomous body—the NETF—to be set up to provide a platform for the free exchange of

[38]Ibid.

ideas and use of technology to enhance learning, assessment, planning, administration and so on, both for school and higher education. The process has been initiated and it is expected that the NETF will maintain a regular inflow of authentic data from various sources, including educational technology innovators and practitioners. It will engage with a diverse set of researchers to analyse data and facilitate decision-making on the induction, deployment and use of technology, by providing the latest knowledge and research, as well as the opportunity to consult and share best practices.

The NEP provides solutions for future-readiness of the educational sector by requiring the creation of an 'open, interoperable, evolvable, public digital infrastructure in the education sector that can be used by multiple platforms and point solutions, to solve for [*sic*] India's scale, diversity, complexity and device penetration.'[39] In this context, the blueprint for NDEAR was recently launched for the school education sector. It lays down a set of principles and approaches for developing digital platforms and diverse solutions to serve the needs of learners, teachers and administrators of education, through the educational and digital ecosystem in India.

To quote PM Modi, 'N-DEAR will act as a "super connect" between various academic activities in the same way as UPI interface revolutionized the banking sector.'[40] NDEAR will provide a unifying structure and framework for existing infrastructures, platforms and systems, for those that need to be created as per the NEP 2020 and for solutions that the education ecosystem will develop. This architecture will give the education ecosystem the opportunity to innovate, amplify good innovations and solutions and address the needs of all learners

[39]Ibid. 59.

[40]'National Digital Architecture Will Eradicate Inequality in Education: PM Modi', *NDTV*, 7 September 2021, https://bit.ly/37UREqs. Accessed on 2 May 2022.

and teachers, including special, atypical and marginalized learners and teachers, while enhancing the capability of existing applications. NDEAR is now being expanded for the requirements of higher education and skilling too.

A Fillip to Research

A nation that promotes research in all its sectors shall stay ahead in the future. The NEP gives a fillip to research in the higher education sector by defining the need for establishing a National Research Foundation (NRF), which the government is in the process of setting up. It will initiate and expand research efforts in technology. The NRF will play an important role in advancing core AI research, developing and deploying application-based research and advancing international research efforts to address global challenges.

In recent years, as technology has developed and evolved, there have been disruptions everywhere. These disruptions will have even more far-reaching effects in the post-pandemic world. For instance, I am happy to note that, with the support of the Department of Science and Technology (DST), IIT Jodhpur has set up a Technology Innovation Hub on Computer Vision, Augmented Reality and Virtual Reality, under the National Mission on Interdisciplinary Cyber-Physical Systems (NM-ICPS). In the present context, the role of educational and research institutions is extremely critical. It is their work, research and innovation that will enable us to cope with the emerging challenges.

Challenges of the New Normal

The Covid-19 crisis has caused a tectonic shift in our education system. Major universities and higher education institutions have partially or fully shifted to online teaching and learning, and are reporting considerable success in their endeavours. Furthermore, the availability of world-class technology platforms has enabled educational institutions to smoothly transition to online teaching.

Our understanding of the Covid-19 situation continues to evolve. The need for social distancing will continue to affect traditional teaching and learning processes. Evidently, with the improvements in technology and the implementation of automation and other efficiencies, the employment landscape is also evolving rapidly, resulting in greater degrees of specializations as well as glaring redundancies in the job market.

Thus, a new normal might emerge in education that will have a lasting influence on pedagogy, assessment and evaluation modalities. While online education has many merits, it also has challenges, some of which have been listed below.

- Effectiveness: A major limitation is lack, or absence of, face-to-face interaction. This has a different value in education since it enhances the learning abilities of schoolgoing children by positively impacting their cognitive, psychomotor and affective domains, and builds up the culture of all educational institutions. Blended learning, using a mix of online and on-campus resources, could be an option.
- Content-related issues: Curricular changes need to keep pace with the requirements of the twenty-first century, and the pedagogies adopted for transacting this curriculum using technology are still evolving. Another challenge is that of conducting laboratory classes and hands-on exercises for remote students. There may be a need to design and deploy a toolbox of online, virtual and remote labs that can be used

in different courses to bridge this gap. It can be an alternative to a brick-and-mortar lab.

- Quality and cost issues: Conducting remotely proctored examinations is perhaps the most important challenge. It requires pedagogical innovations from the faculty. Change in evaluation modalities, such as replacing examinations with projects or take-home challenges, can provide some viable and cost-effective alternatives. However, it must also be considered that the fast pace of change in technology can make it a huge capital guzzler.
- Equity: In a multilingual country like ours, language barriers create complexities. Cutting-edge research in text translation and machine learning aims to create deep-learning systems that can translate English lectures into a student's native language. Similar advancements in voice recognition and text summarization can be used to transcribe an entire lecture and reduce paragraphs of text into relevant bullet points.
- Capacity issues: Teachers require suitable training and development to be effective online educators. One cannot assume that a good teacher in a traditional classroom is automatically a good teacher in an online classroom. Capacity building of teachers is crucial to the success of use of technology in education.
- Security: Use of technology exposes young students to a variety of cyber security issues. Teachers, students and institutions have a limited capacity to deal with these issues. In the coming days, capacity building for ensuring cyber security shall have to be undertaken for students, teachers, parents and the educational community at large.

It is true that technology will create new opportunities and its adoption will be fast. Simultaneously, technology that could have been subjected to greater regulatory security checks—such as use of AI in healthcare—will likely be fast-tracked and deployed. A possible risk is that some people may be permanently left behind as the process of digitalization is accelerated rapidly. Inequalities could perhaps get aggravated and would need to be addressed.

Learn, Unlearn, Relearn

Today, we are at an unimaginable and unique time in our lives. People have been confined to their homes with their families and loved ones for long periods of time, living with the uncertainty of how this pandemic is likely to unfold. In an unprecedented way, the entire world is fighting an invisible enemy. It has posed a great challenge to science and technology. The following quote from *Chanakya Neeti* (6.7, translated by the author), highlighting the relevance of the wheel of time, is interesting to note,

> कालः पचति भूतानि, कालः संहरते प्रजाः ।
> कालः सुप्तेषु जागर्ति, कालो हि दुरतिक्रमः ।।
>
> Time ripens all beings, Time destroys all creatures.
> Time is awake while all else sleeps, Time is insurmountable!

Time has presented several challenges for us all. It is technology that can help us overcome the challenges. At the same time, new challenges arising due to the use of technology can be addressed by individuals and institutions through learning, teaching and education.

The digital divide presents a major challenge. As the NEP recognizes, the benefit of online and digital education cannot be leveraged unless the digital divide is reduced or even eliminated through considerable efforts and initiatives, such as the Digital India campaign and the availability of affordable computer devices. It is important that the use of technology for online and digital education addresses concerns of equity, such that people who are disadvantaged do not become more deprived with the increasing digitalization of education. Given the actual and expected impact of technology on education, it is essential that we leverage technology to favour equitable access to education, particularly in the case of SEDGs.

I recently read, in an Insight Report by the WEF, that over a century ago, at the time of the Spanish Flu, when people were isolating themselves, many (mostly Americans) turned to the telephone to get in touch with friends and family. At that time, it was a nascent technology. Services quickly broke down due to the increased use. However, the Spanish Flu underscored how essential telecom technology was to modern society. In the subsequent years of the twentieth century, we all know how instrumental the telephone became in shaping the world as a global village. We may be at a similar inflection point today. Years later, historians may look back and assess how the contemporary decision-making around digitalization shaped us as individuals, societies and nations.

PM Modi has given us a clarion call for AatmaNirbhar Bharat, which goes much beyond being a self-reliant nation. It envisages India's leading role in the global arena as a leader in technology and the global supply chain of goods and services. At the same time, it is also a social change paradigm, where every individual is encouraged to strive for excellence in what she does. In this context, the role of education and educational institutions is extremely important. They pave the way for achieving excellence and realizing our national potential.

Moving forward, as trends suggest, the future of learning will always be 'micro'. We will shift from learning for 12 years in schools to a very micro approach of 'I need this just in time'. The future will belong to the adult who has the ability to not only learn but also unlearn and relearn—learning the process of unlearning and then relearning is a lifelong skill. The possibilities are endless, but they will remain possibilities unless we unleash their potential to transform the educational sector. Given the pace at which new technological solutions are being developed, along with capabilities and efficiencies in the education sector, I am convinced that, stepping into the 75th year of our Independence, in the lead up to completing 100 years of Independence in 2047, we will develop our capabilities to use AI, robotics, AR/VR, gamification and more individualized opportunities for learning, and emerge as world leaders in innovation for joyful, engaging, futuristic and resilient education systems based on the effective and efficient use of technology.

This chapter is an updated version of P.K. Mishra's Foundation Day Lecture delivered at the IIT, Jodhpur, on 2 August 2020.[41]

[41]Foundation Day Lecture at the Indian Institute of Technology (IIT), Jodhpur, YouTube, https://bit.ly/3kWSw0E. Accessed on 6 April 2022.

7

PUBLIC HEALTH

Towards a future-ready system

Health outlays and outcomes are never easy to balance, much less, perfectly. Nonetheless, it is necessary to seek some optimal levels of symmetry in them. For instance, it would be a no brainer that even within limited resources, there should be concerted efforts to reduce the sharp incidents of regional inequalities, ensuring minimum access across all levels of health systems and to re-examine our expenditure priorities.

India has made some obvious and notable gains in healthcare. Life expectancy has gone up to 69.96 years (with an average 0.77 per cent increase per annum over the last 50 years); infant mortality and crude death rates have been greatly reduced; diseases such as smallpox, polio and guinea worm have been eradicated; and leprosy is on its way out. However, despite this progress, the health sector in the country has been repeatedly identified as one of the critical areas eluding governance reforms. Literature is replete with analyses by eminent economists commenting that notwithstanding wide-ranging economic progress, our record in the health sector has been extraordinarily limited, unlike some other emerging economies in the region.

Our healthcare infrastructure faces multiple challenges, including insufficient funding, shortcomings in quality of care, neglect of urban health, inadequate number of health personnel and other facilities and the inability to meaningfully integrate the rural healthcare system into the mainstream. This is worrisome considering that 70 per cent of our expenditure on health is out-of-pocket, which is perhaps among the highest in the world. We know that high out-of-pocket expenditure poses serious risks and uncertainties in pushing people back into poverty, particularly those who are living at the critical margins of the poverty line.

India's Public Health Landscape

The first medical institution in India was the Government General Hospital, Madras, established in 1664 as a small hospital to treat soldiers of the British East India Company. In its early years, it was housed at Fort St George, the first English fortress located in Madras. The hospital trained Europeans, Eurasians and Indians alike in western medicine, who were then posted to dispensaries across the then Madras Presidency. By 1820, the institution was recognized as the model hospital of the East India Company.[42]

During the colonial period, healthcare was focused mainly on British citizens living in India. With the establishment of research institutions, public health legislation and sanitation departments, annual health reports were published, stressing the prevention of contagious diseases.

Healthcare reform was prioritized in 1946, at the cusp of

[42]'Institution History', Madras Medical College, https://bit.ly/3KPOxNU. Accessed on 11 May 2022.

Independence. The Bhore Committee, under the chairmanship of Sir Joseph William Bhore, suggested in its report, the implementation of a healthcare system that was financed, in part, by the Indian government. Some of the Committee's objectives in formulating a plan for a National Health Service have been paraphrased below:

- the health services should adequately provide for the medical care of an individual in the preventative and curative fields;
- the services should be as close to people as possible to ensure that they are of maximum use to the community;
- provisions should be made for medical and auxiliary professions, such as dentists, pharmacists and nurses;
- special provisions should be made for certain groups of the population, such as mothers and children; and
- no individual should fail to secure adequate healthcare because they are unable to pay.[43]

Some objectives of the Bhore Committee have been retained in our healthcare provisions even to this day.

Even post-1947, India's public health system has evolved under the colonial influence. So far, health funding in India is directed to helping middle- and upper-income groups, with particular regard to the creation of employment in the health sector, expanding research institutions and improved training. This results in issues of equity for the lower classes, who do not receive the benefits of this funding. A report by the World Bank in 2002 found that states pay for 75 per cent of the public healthcare system but insufficient spending by

[43] 'Report of the Health Survey and Development Committee: Volume II', National Health Portal, 1946, https://bit.ly/3L1q0X5. Accessed on 19 April 2022.

the State neglects the public health system in India.[44] The National Health Accounts' report of the National Health Systems Resource Centre in 2015–16 found that out-of-pocket expenditures on health by households comprised 60.6 per cent of the total health expenditure of India.[45]

Global Developments

Public health is embedded in the history of all ancient civilizations. In Asia, Ayurvedic, Buddhist and traditional Chinese medicine fostered better overall health and regimes to balance bodies, lives and communities. In the early American civilizations, the Mayans and Aztecs used to hold medicinal herbal markets. In Aboriginal Australia, methods of protecting water and food sources were common practice to prevent infections and diseases.

In his book *The Argumentative Indian*, Amartya Sen mentions accounts of several Chinese scholars such as Faxian, who arrived in India in 401 BCE. About healthcare in fifth-century Pataliputra, near modern-day Patna, Faxian writes, 'All the poor and destitute in the country...and all who are diseased, go to these houses, and are provided with every kind of help, and doctors examine their disease.'[46] Similarly, another scholar, Yi Jing, who visited India in 671 BCE, mentions that, 'In the healing art of acupuncture and cautery and the skill of feeling the pulse,

---

[44]Peters, David H., et al., *Better Health Systems for India's Poor: Findings, Analysis, and Options,* World Bank Publications, Washington DC, 1 January 2002, https://bit.ly/3McPPnh. Accessed on 19 April 2022.

[45]'National Health Accounts Estimates for India: Financial Year 2015-16', Ministry of Health and Family Welfare, Government of India, November 2018, https://bit.ly/3L1tzwr. Accessed on 19 April 2022.

[46]Sen, Amartya, *The Argumentative Indian: Writings on Indian History, Culture and Identity,* Penguin UK, 29 August 2006, p.183.

China has never been surpassed [by India]...'[47] The infamous seventh-century Chinese scholar, Xuanzang, visited India in 629–645 CE, during which time he spread awareness about Chinese medicine on his excursions to monasteries, such as the ancient University of Nalanda. In turn, he carried with him the medicinal knowledge from the Buddhist monasteries he visited, including techniques like Ayurveda.

In fact, Ayurveda, which technically means the science of longevity, has deep roots in Hindu mythology. It is often attributed to Dhanvantari, the physician to the gods. It is a form of both preventative and curative medicine—preventative in terms of a strict code of personal and social hygiene as well as bodily exercises like yoga, and curative in terms of herbal medicines, physiotherapy and dietary practices. Early evidence of Ayurveda first appears in a portion of the Vedas dating as far back as the second millennium BCE known as the *Atharvaveda*. The Vedas are replete with instances of treatments for endemic diseases such as fever, cough, tuberculosis, tumours and leprosy. One of the key contributors to Ayurveda was Charaka, known for his foundational texts on Indian medicine and Ayurveda, through his medical treatise called *Charaka Samhita*. It is, therefore, no surprise that Ayurveda was a notable part of the establishment of the Indian Medical Council, set up by the government in 1971.

The development of health systems all over the world has both contrasts and symmetries. For instance, in the UK, with the onset of the Industrial Revolution, living standards in cities among the working population began to worsen. The rapid urbanization of cities, like London, doubled their population, simultaneously exacerbating the spread of diseases. Dr Romola Davenport, a British historical demographer, writes, 'High population densities favoured the transmission of infectious

[47]Ibid.

diseases, and trade and migration promoted the importation of animal and human diseases.'[48] Scholars, such as Thomas Malthus[49] and Jeremy Bentham,[50] became influential for their warnings about overpopulation in the early nineteenth century. Towards the latter part of the century, basic patterns of public health improvement were introduced by private philanthropists, which eventually led to government action and the rapid growth of voluntary hospitals in England. Consequently, the practice of vaccination began in the 1800s, pioneered by Edward Jenner's work in treating smallpox. In 1752, British physician Sir John Pringle introduced the importance of adequate ventilation in military barracks, and in 1754, James Lind discovered the cause of scurvy in sailors, subsequently introducing fruit into the diets of the Royal Navy.

The first attempts at developing public health legislation in England were pioneered by the physician Thomas Southwood Smith, resulting in the Poor Law Commission, set up in the 1830s. In 1838, the Commission reported, 'The expenditures necessary to the adoption and maintenance of measures of prevention would ultimately amount to less than the cost of the disease now constantly engendered.'[51] The Commission, thus, recommended large-scale government implementation of infrastructure projects to alleviate the conditions that lead to the spread of diseases like cholera and

---

[48]Davenport, Romola J., 'Urbanization and mortality in Britain, c. 1800-50', *The Economic History Review*, Vol. 73, pp. 455–85, 2020, https://bit.ly/37EZwMM. Accessed on 11 May 2022.

[49]Malthus, Thomas Robert, *An Essay on the Principle of Population: And, A Summary View of the Principle of Population*. Edited with an Intro. by Antony Flew, Penguin Books, 1970.

[50]'Jeremy Bentham', Stanford Encyclopedia of Philosophy, https://stanford.io/3ybfzwB. Accessed on 11 May 2022.

[51]Poor Law Commissioners, *Fifth Annual Report of the Poor Law Commissioners for England and Wales*, Poor Law Commission Office, London, 1839.

yellow fever. In addition, the Health of Towns Association was formed in 1844 to campaign for the development of public health in the UK. All of these national and local movements led to the Public Health Act, 1848.

With the advent of rapid urbanization and industrialization, the events in the US almost paralleled those in the UK. In the 1700s, the healthcare of sailors and ports was viewed as essential to the development of the country. In 1798, Congress passed the Act for the Relief of Sick and Disabled Seamen, authorizing the formation of the US Marine Hospital Service, which predated the Public Health Service. Eventually, in 1799, the city of Boston established the first board of health and the first health department in the US.

The 1800s further solidified the notion and development of health planning. In 1842, the first US system for recording births, deaths and marriages was established by Lemuel Shattuck, which became a model adopted by other states. Shattuck also made proposals for keeping records of disease, mortality data by age, gender, occupation, socio-economic level and location. The Secretary of the Board of Health of Massachusetts based his plans for public health on Shattuck's recommendations 20 years later.

The Marine Hospital Service was renamed the Public Health and Marine Hospital Services (PHMHS) in 1902. Then, in 1912, this was renamed the United States Public Health Service and was authorized to investigate diseases, such as tuberculosis, malaria and leprosy, as well as issues of sanitation, water supply and waste management.

During the late 1800s, tuberculosis was one of the most fatal diseases in France, especially affecting young people in their twenties. Compared to the Germans, who set up measures for public hygiene and sanitation, France let their private physicians handle the issue, which caused their much higher death rate than Germany. Public health activism was not as prominent in France as it was in the UK, US or even Germany. In France, around the 1880s, issues of public health, including the registration of infectious diseases, mandated quarantines and improving the housing legislation of 1850, were debated at length. Two decades later, in 1902, the first Law on Public Health was passed. This law was finally passed when the government realized that contagious diseases had a national security impact on the military and in keeping the population growth well below Germany's.

The modern Japanese healthcare system developed after the Meiji Restoration in 1866, with the introduction of western medicine. The first form of health insurance was established prior to the 1920s, known as private mutual aid associations for private-sector workers and public mutual aid associations for public-sector workers. This system evolved into the current government-regulated, employment-based health insurance established in 1927. Progressively, in 1938, the National Health Insurance Law (NHIL) was passed along with the establishment of the Ministry of Health and Welfare. However, with the onset of World War I, the National Health Insurance (NHI) only covered two-thirds of the Japanese population. Amendments to the NHIL in 1958 mandated municipalities to have residence-based NHI programmes, leading to full coverage of the Japanese population by 1961.

Traditional Chinese medicine has been an integral part of its culture since the ancient times, even serving as the backdrop and basis of much of China's healthcare history. It was not until the nineteenth century that western medicine was introduced to China. With the rise of communism in 1949, healthcare was nationalized with national attempts to spread awareness on basic healthcare, hygiene and sanitation to rural areas through barefoot doctors and other state-sponsored programmes. However, with the onset of economic reforms in 1978, health standards began to diverge asymmetrically along the urban–rural divide due to the privatization of the health sector. This resulted in a collapse of social security and health benefits, leaving much of the expenses of urban residents to be paid out-of-pocket, while most rural residents could not afford to even pay for healthcare in urban hospitals. Thus, reforms began in 2005 with the launch of the New Rural Cooperative Medical Scheme (NCMS), which aimed to provide affordable healthcare to the rural poor. During this time, medical insurance for the urban areas was increased and made more easily accessible. By 2011, more than 95 per cent of the Chinese population had access to basic healthcare.

International experience on healthcare has shown an increasing awareness to improve health sector outcomes. Nonetheless, if I ask myself, have regional, cross-country and inter-regional heterogeneity and disparities in public health spending increased? Regretfully, the answer may turn out to be positive. The cross-country average of health spending per capita was $1,099 in 2018. While the average was only $40 per person in low-income countries that year, in high-income countries, it was $3,313—over 80 times more.[52]

Besides, even among the low- and middle-income countries, the inter-regional disparities on health expenditure only exacerbate the increasing inequality that many emerging economies are currently facing. This has only worsened as out-of-pocket expenses during Covid-19 have increased. This is notwithstanding the extraordinary support given by the governments, both central and state, which has been widely appreciated.

History often plays a large role in the development of healthcare systems in developing countries. This is true

---

[52]Osewe, Patrick L., 'Universal Health Coverage and the Way Forward', National Health Authority, Government of India, https://bit.ly/3MISOzg. Accessed on 11 May 2022; 'Global spending on health: Weathering the storm', World Health Organization, https://bit.ly/3yjAYDN. Accessed on 11 May 2022.

of countries in Africa and Asia, which were once British colonies, where educational and health programmes had been largely influenced by the colonizers. This is also true of countries colonized by France, the Netherlands and the US. Consequently, the gaps in between the health resources and administrations of developed and developing countries are more pronounced. Within developing countries, complex factors, such as political and societal instability, complicate, and sometimes disrupt, healthcare administration.

There is significant disparity between public health initiatives of developed countries and developing countries, as well as among developing countries. In developing countries, substantive public health infrastructure is still grappling, with issues of inadequate health workers, limited financial resources and insufficient knowledge and education in medical care. The shortcomings of adequate healthcare in developing countries are inextricably linked to poverty. Many African countries, for instance, spend \$8 to \$129 per capita on health,[53] while, in the US, the government spent approximately \$12,530 per capita in 2000.[54]

Public health in Latin American countries substantially differs from Africa and Asia due to their different historical backgrounds. Latin America is generally more affluent than Africa and Asia. On the one hand, in Latin American countries, private practice is more widespread and private agencies are more prominent. On the other hand, auxiliaries—a group of volunteers who offer supplementary support to health centres and institutions, providing comprehensive healthcare for a

---

[53]Gatome-Munyua, Agnes and Nkechi Olalere, 'Public financing for health in Africa: 15% of an elephant is not 15% of a chicken', *Africa Renewal*, 13 October 2020, https://bit.ly/3vIJD0O. Accessed on 11 May 2022.

[54]'Historical', Centers for Medicare and Medicaid Services, https://go.cms.gov/3kDEMYF. Accessed on 11 May 2022.

large number of the population—are less common in Latin American countries than in African and Asian countries. Latin America has been a pioneer in the development of health planning methods, with Chile having one of the most advanced approaches to health planning in the world.

However, Thailand is a country that favours a unique system, even though it was never colonized nor does it have any historical influence. The Thai Ministry of Public Health adopted a universal healthcare plan in 2001 called the Universal Coverage Scheme that was largely supported through government financing and supplemented by private funds. Thailand, thus, has a well-developed system of health centres and hospitals serving both the rural and urban population.

Among the developing countries, Mexico has prioritized issues of health. It has been said that health and development are intrinsically linked. It is not surprising that Nobel Prize winner Robert Fogel commented on the importance of health as a determinant of economic growth.[55] The December 2001 report of the Commission on Macroeconomics and Health (CMH), appointed by the World Health Organization (WHO), in its remarks about Mexico stated:

> In most middle-income countries, average health spending per person is already adequate to ensure universal coverage for essential interventions. Yet such coverage does not reach many of the poor. In view of the adverse consequences of ill health on overall economic development and poverty reduction, we strongly urge

---

[55]Fogel, Robert William, 'New findings on secular trends in nutrition and mortality: Some implications for population theory', *Handbook of Population and Family Economics*, Vol. 1, 1997, pp. 433–81, https://bit.ly/3P8oKEd. Accessed on 11 May 2022.

the middle-income countries to undertake fiscal and organization reforms to ensure universal coverage for priority health interventions.[56]

Investing in Health

Health and economic development are intrinsically linked. A 2001 study conducted by David Mayer-Foulkes[57] showed the direct relationship between health and growth in Mexico using the life expectancy and mortality rates for different age groups. The results showed that health is responsible for one-third of long-term economic growth. In this sense, childhood health is not only an important determinant of school achievement but also an indicator of the income children will receive in their adulthood. Therefore, it can be said that health directly and indirectly impacts economic growth and incidences of poverty over time; this is also called a poverty trap.

Investing in health is warranted from the perspectives of growth and equity. Given the important role that health plays in the economy of a country, protecting health assets from the impact of systemic shocks—such as economic crises and reforms, epidemics, natural disasters, illness and unemployment—is important. However, in spite of this enormous impact, there are no systematic policies and institutions that address the impact of aggregate shocks on health.

Published in 2001, the CMH made several key

---

[56]WHO Commission on Macroeconomics and Health & World Health Organization, *Macroeconomics and health: Investing in health for economic development*, World Health Organization, 2001, https://bit.ly/3rKcQGr. Accessed on 25 April 2022.

[57]Mayer, David, 'The long-term impact of health on economic growth in Mexico, 1950–1995', *Journal of International Development*, Vol. 13, 2001, pp. 123–26. https://doi.org/10.1002/jid.764. Accessed on 25 April 2022.

recommendations for health investment goals to achieve the ultimate goal of economic development. A decade down the line, in 2011, Pamela Das and Udani Samarasekara reviewed some outcomes of the original goals covered in the CMH.[58] This review indicated that the universal health coverage of essential health services had failed to become a core priority in many countries, despite the fact that around 20 national commissions on health had been established. The impact of the recommendations of these commissions had not gained fruitful outcomes. The goal of increasing financing of public health goods through multilateral agencies, such as the World Bank and the IMF, had not been achieved. Adding to this, no mechanisms of accountability had been put in place by these multilateral agencies to support the increase of health expenditure in recipient countries.

Increased international awareness about health spending, with the recommendation of increasing health spending by $23 billion by 2007, is one of the more substantial achievements of the CMH.[59] In the Institute for Health Metrics and Evaluation's (IHME) 2010 report, health spending by developing countries had increased from $128.18 billion in 1995 to $241.33 billion in 2006—an increase of $113.15 billion.[60] Can this increase be attributed to the CMH's recommendations of establishing national commissions? According to Amanda Glassman,

---

[58]Das, Pamela and Udani Samaresekera, 'The Commission on Macroeconomics and Health: 10 years on', *The Lancet*, World Report, Vol. 378, No. 9807, p. 1907–08, 3 December 2011, https://bit.ly/3JCZ5QN. Accessed on 24 March 2022.

[59]Sachs, Jeffrey D., *Macroeconomics and Health: Investing in Health for Economic Development: Report of the Commission on Macroeconomics and Health,* World Health Organization, 2001, p. 18, https://bit.ly/3KLpDPz. Accessed on 11 May 2022.

[60]Institute for Health Metrics and Evaluation, 'The Global Burden of Disease: Generating Evidence, Guiding Policy', IHME, https://bit.ly/3sfA737. Accessed on 11 May 2022.

executive vice president and senior fellow at the Centre for Global Development, these national commissions were 'extremely useful to leverage increased investment in the health sector',[61] especially in Mexico. However, in a 2006 report by the WHO, only 20 countries established national commissions following the recommendations of the CMH, including India.

Experience at Home

The National Commission on Macroeconomics and Health (NCMH) was established in India in March 2004. The report of the NCMH, published in August 2005, discussed the economic basis of investing in health, how public financing could be effectively utilized and the impacts of economic liberalization since the 1990s, which has increased employment opportunities, thereby reducing poverty levels.[62] These economic developments led to lifestyle changes, urbanization and enhanced access to information. Thus, they profoundly impacted the epidemiologic and health-related behaviour of people.

Some of the findings of the report include the following points.

- India's life expectancy has doubled from 32 years in 1947 to 66 years in 2004; the infant mortality rate has fallen by over 70 per cent between 1947 and 1990; malaria has been contained to 20 lakh cases

---

[61]Das, Pamela and Udani Samaresekera, 'The Commission on Macroeconomics and Health: 10 years on', *The Lancet*, World Report, Vol. 378, No. 9807, p. 1907–08, 3 December 2011, https://bit.ly/3JCZ5QN. Accessed on 24 March 2022.

[62]'Report of the National Commission on Macroeconomics and Health', National Commission on Macroeconomics and Health, Ministry of Health and Family Welfare, Government of India, 2005, https://bit.ly/3yuLJDp. Accessed on 11 May 2022.

annually; smallpox and guinea-worm disease have been eradicated; and leprosy and polio are nearing elimination.

- The decreasing public investment, liberalization and privatization that had been happening since the 1990s, the emergence of non-communicable diseases and an effective demand have steadily corporatized medical care. Non-resident Indians (NRIs) and industrial/pharmaceutical companies have set up super-speciality hospitals in India to provide world-class care at a fraction of the cost in the West. This makes India a potential hub for medical tourism. However, this will raise the overall cost of healthcare in the country and create pressure for increased budgetary allocation for government hospitals.
- A survey of eight districts—namely, Khammam (formerly in Andhra Pradesh, now in Telangana), Nadia (West Bengal), Jalna (Maharashtra), Kozhikode (Kerala), Ujjain (Madhya Pradesh), Udaipur (Rajasthan), Vaishali (Bihar) and Varanasi (Uttar Pradesh)—shows a highly skewed distribution of health resources: 88 per cent of towns have a health facility compared to 24 per cent of villages; the private sector has 75 per cent of all specialists and 85 per cent of all the technology in their facilities; 75 per cent of services for non-communicable diseases and about 40 per cent of services for communicable diseases are provided by the private sector.

Nonetheless, the public spending on health has gradually increased from 0.22 per cent in 1950–51 to 1.05 per cent during the mid-1980s, and then it stagnated at around 0.9 per cent of the GDP. Per capita expenditure on health increased from less than ₹1 in 1950–51 to about ₹215 in

2003–04. The Commission recommended increasing public spending from 1.3 per cent to 3 per cent of the GDP in the following years.

From 1990 to 2001, the Centre reduced the funds for health released to the states from 60 per cent to 40 per cent. It spent less than 0.5 per cent of the total public health budget on preventive and promotive health, and underfunded the National Health Programmes, which led to their suboptimal functioning and huge out-of-pocket expenses for services guaranteed under these programmes.

The NCMH recommended a gradual shift towards a mandatory and affordable Universal Health Insurance System for secondary and tertiary care.

MDGs and SDGs: India's Progress

Following the Millennium Summit of the United Nations in 2000, 189 countries made a pledge towards eight international Millennium Development Goals (MDGs) to be achieved by 2015. Briefly, the eight goals are: (1) to eradicate extreme poverty and hunger; (2) to achieve universal primary education; (3) to promote gender equality and empower women; (4) to reduce child mortality; (5) to improve maternal health; (6) to combat HIV/AIDS, malaria and other diseases; (7) to ensure environmental sustainability; and (8) to develop a global partnership for development.

India, as a signatory of the MDGs, witnessed significant progress towards the goals with some targets having been met ahead of the 2015 deadline. On the eradication of extreme poverty, in 1990, the all-India Poverty Head Count Ratio (PHCR) was estimated to be 47.8 per cent. In 2011–12, the PHCR was 21.9 per cent. This indicates that India has achieved the poverty reduction target; however, estimates from 2012 revealed that over 270 million Indians continue to live in extreme poverty. India also made significant progress in combatting HIV/AIDS, malaria and other diseases. For instance, tuberculosis incidences per 100,000 population have reduced from 216 in 1990 to 171 in 2013.[63]

The SDGs were accepted in 2015 as a successor to the MDGs. These 17 goals were established by the United Nations General Assembly (UNGA) to be achieved by 2030. They include: (1) no poverty; (2) zero hunger; (3) good health and well-being; (4) quality education; (5) gender equality; (6) clean water and sanitation; (7) affordable and clean energy; (8) decent work and economic growth; (9) industry, innovation and infrastructure; (10) reduced inequality; (11) sustainable cities and communities; (12) responsible consumption and production; (13) climate action; (14) life below water; (15) life on land; (16) peace, justice and strong institutions; and (17) partnerships for the goals.

India's overall scores across the SDGs improved from 60 in 2019 to 66 in 2020–21 with nationwide improvement in clean water and sanitation, and affordable and clean energy. India has significantly progressed towards good health and well-being. For instance, the mortality rate of infants under five declined from 125 per 1,000 live births in 1990–91 to 50 per 1,000 live births in 2015–16. Maternal mortality rates have also declined from 212 per 100,000 live births in 2007–09 to 167 in 2013.[64]

Planning for Health

The FYPs are integrated national economic programmes to foster development. However, notwithstanding multiple efforts, the health sector, over a prolonged period of overall

---

[63]'Eight Goals for 2015', UNDP India, https://bit.ly/3FhhEZf. Accessed on 11 May 2022.

[64]Ibid.

economic planning through FYPs, did not receive the priority it deserved.

When it comes to healthcare planning, the central government has shaped its health policy through the Central Council of Health and Family Welfare and various committee recommendations via the FYPs, based on which it executes its decisions. During the first two FYPs (1951–61), the basic structural framework of public health remained unchanged. Urban areas received only three-fourths of the resources accorded to them while rural areas received 'special attention' under the CD Programme. This programme, which was launched in 1952, was said to have preluded the health sector even before the second FYP began in 1956 due to its scant attention on social sectors and increased prioritization of agricultural development. Furthermore, the health sector organization, under the CD Programme, was mainly focused on preventative care, such as hygiene, sanitation and the control of and awareness about epidemic diseases. However, medical care was not prioritized. By the time of the third FYP, there was only one primary health unit per 140,000 rural population (14 times lower than the recommendations of the Bhore Committee), one hospital per 320,000 rural population and one hospital bed per 7,000 rural population. In urban areas, there was one hospital per 36,000 urban population and one hospital bed per 440 urban residents.[65]

The Health Survey and the Planning Committee were set up in 1959 to review the progress made in the health sector in the first two FYPs. The Committee's report found that while substantial progress had been made in the control of epidemic diseases, such as malaria, basic health facilities had not reached at least half the country. It was found that primary healthcare

---

[65]Duggal, Ravi, 'Health Planning in India,' *India Health – A Reference Document*, Rashtra Deepika Ltd, p. 43–56, 2002.

centre (PHC) programmes were not given the importance they deserved with issues like understaffing, which led to most of them being run by nurses. The Committee also found that not much was being done to ameliorate the urban–rural divide with priority being given to the expansion of urban PHCs rather than the consolidation of rural PHCs. A large part of the debate rested on the shortage of health personnel, with recommendations to improve PHC infrastructure in rural areas.

Therefore, in the third FYP (1961–66), the issue of inadequacy of doctors, healthcare institutions and other personnel in rural areas was highlighted. This led to increased recruitment of doctors but no other health personnel. While the third FYP seriously considered the expansion of auxiliary personnel, there were no specific steps outlined to reach this goal, with the training and establishment of these auxiliary institutions being underfunded. Meanwhile, proposed outlays for new medical colleges, the completion of the All India Institute of Medical Sciences (AIIMS) and upgradation of departments in medical colleges for postgraduate training continued to be high. Further, following the issues of PHCs in the second FYP, these centres increased in number, but had not improved in quality.

The fourth FYP (1969–74) continued to emphasize the importance of PHCs and, for the first time, PHCs were given a separate allocation. This was so because epidemic diseases, such as malaria, were, once again, on the rise, with cases increasing from 100,000 in 1963–65 to 149,102 in 1966.[66] Family planning was also accorded special emphasis, with India becoming the first country in the world to adopt a population control policy through a government-sponsored family planning programme

[66]*Pocket Book of Health Statistics of India 1981*, Central Bureau of Health Intelligence, Directorate General of Health Services, Ministry of Health and Family Welfare, Government of India, Delhi, 1982.

that had commenced earlier.

During the fifth FYP (1974–78), the government acknowledged the ever-growing divide between rural and urban healthcare. The urban health structure had expanded at the cost of the rural areas. This was evident in the objectives of the plan, including increasing accessibility of health services in rural areas through the Minimum Needs Programme (MNP) and improvements in referral services through district and subdivision hospitals with special attention to diseases in rural areas. However, in the middle of the fifth FYP, a state of national Emergency was proclaimed (1975–77), during which population control was emphasized more than ever before. Family planning took the single largest share in the health sector outlay. Water supply and sanitation were also prioritized, which became especially important during the drought of 1979–80 with the acute scarcity of drinking water. Subsequent FYPs accorded higher priority to the issue of water.

The sixth FYP (1980–85) was greatly influenced by the WHO's 1978 declaration of Health for All by 2000 AD. The plan states that, 'In spite of several significant achievements, the health care system obtaining in the country suffers from some weaknesses and deficiencies.'[67] It recognized that the health infrastructure, both urban and rural, still had a long way to go, with the urban health centres only catering to certain sections of society and the rural areas only catering to a fraction of their population.

This plan, along with the seventh FYP (1985–90), made a lot of radical statements and recommended progressive measures but, ultimately, it fell far short due to inadequate action. Despite the introduction of new schemes, the core of the existing framework remained untouched. This resulted

[67]'Chapter 22: Health, Family Planning and Nutrition', 6th Five Year Plan: NITI Aayog, https://bit.ly/3KlgXiL. Accessed on 27 April 2022.

in the inadequacy of healthcare in rural areas remaining unchanged while urban areas prospered.

In 1983, the first NHP was created, prioritizing the establishment of PHC facilities. This was the first time since the Bhore Committee that the government had prioritized universal comprehensive healthcare. Some of its salient features included a decentralized system of healthcare with low cost, use of auxiliary personnel and community participation, expansion of private practice and the establishment of a national network of epidemiological stations.

The eighth FYP (1992–97) coincided with the economic crisis of 1991. During this plan, the emphasis was no longer on Health for All by 2000 AD, but 'Health for the Underprivileged.'[68] During this period, privatization of healthcare was also encouraged.

The ninth FYP (1997–2002) made a great effort to strategize the achievements and lessons of the past. It contextualized its time and setting against the Bhore Committee report, with the consolidation of PHCs as an important goal. Another unique recommendation was the integration of state-specific strategies to accommodate the different levels of development and healthcare needs of the states. The ninth FYP also reviewed the 1983 NHP in the context of its objectives and goals, concluding that a reformulation was necessary. Thus, the updated NHP in 2002 focused on improving the practicality and reach of the healthcare system as well as incorporating private and public clinics.

The 10th FYP (2002–07) introduced the integration of IT tools into healthcare, with improvements in communication, consultation and referral from primary to tertiary care. The main focus was improving the existing healthcare system with

---

[68]'Objectives and Orientation', 8th Five Year Plan: NITI Aayog, https://bit.ly/3EYiIRJ. Accessed on 27 April 2022.

three new major initiatives: redesigning the Universal Health Insurance Scheme to help alleviate lower classes; introduction of the Group Health Insurance Scheme; and the exemption of income tax for hospitals in rural states.[69]

The 11th FYP. (2007–12) sought to restructure policies to achieve a new vision based on faster, broad-based and inclusive growth. The main objectives were to achieve good health for people, especially the poor and underprivileged and to facilitate convergence and development of public health systems and services to give special attention to marginalized groups, such as adolescent girls, women, children, elderly, disabled and tribal groups.

The 12th FYP (2012–17) developed a system of universal health coverage based on the formulations of a high-level expert group, and other stakeholder consultations. Among its major recommendations (alas, not actions) was the increase of health sector expenditure to 2.5 per cent of the GDP, whereas it was 0.94 per cent during the 10th FYP and 1.04 per cent during the 11th FYP. However, this target was far lower than the global median of 5 per cent, which eventually settled to 2.1 per cent of the GDP by the end of the plan's term.[70] While rural healthcare services were still lacking compared to urban areas, the issue of out-of-pocket expenses arose, even in public-sector hospitals. Although this FYP expressed concern over this issue of out-of-pocket expenditure, it did not lay down any specific target or time frame to address these concerns.

Giant Leaps

---

[69]Suthanthiraveeran, Sathia, 'The Five Year Plans in India: Overview of Public Health Policies', ResearchGate, https://bit.ly/3FfMWzU. Accessed on 11 May 2022.

[70]'Twelfth Five Year Plan (2012–2017): Social Sectors—Volume III', NITI Aayog, https://bit.ly/3KiGSHO. Accessed on 27 April 2022.

There is no doubt that over time, the government has initiated many important health sector priorities, some of which have been discussed below.

The Budget 2022–23 demonstrated a somewhat unprecedented prioritization of the health sector. More importantly, it recognized the interlinkages between health, nutrition, water and sanitation facilities, which reinforce each other. The allocation for the health and wellness sector increased mainly on account of the increased allocation on water and sanitation, from ₹21,500 crore to ₹60,000 crore, and ₹35,000 crore for Covid-19 vaccination. These allocations were over and above the FC grants that are being examined and are to be subsumed in the further rationalization of the CSS.

The launch of the PM AatmaNirbhar Swasth Bharat Yojana (PMASBY) is a decisive step to strengthen the healthcare system in the country. It has an outlay of ₹64,180 crore over six years, which aims to develop capacities at various levels of the health system, create new institutions and strengthen existing ones. However, the budget allocation for the NRHM—which is the core of the National Health Mission (NHM)—in the 2021–22 budget estimate recoded a growth of 11 per cent compared to the 2020–21 BE and remains unchanged compared to the 2019–20 actuals.

The Ayushman Bharat Pradhan Mantri Jan Arogya Yojana (AB-PMJAY), launched in 2018, is the biggest healthcare scheme in the world, providing up to ₹5 lakh per family per year for secondary and tertiary care hospitalization. As a part of the NHP, this scheme is largely aimed at health insurance coverage for low-income earners. Some of its features include no restriction on family size, age or gender, and all previous medical conditions covered along with three days of pre-hospitalization and 15 days of post-hospitalization. It also provides access to free Covid-19 testing. By May 2020, it was announced that more than one crore treatments had been availed through the scheme. Additionally, more than 17 crore beneficiaries have been verified through the Beneficiary Identification System (BIS) of the Ayushman cards. Many economic commentators have highlighted the reversal of the progress on poverty numbers. One of the factors to which this is attributed, apart from other forms of distress, is the number of people who would have been pushed back into poverty due to the out-of-pocket expenses on health. In this context, it would be useful to objectively analyse whether the basic purpose of ABY, which is to prevent the burden of out-of-pocket expenses, has ameliorated their sufferings.

The Ayushman Bharat Health and Wellness Centres (AB-HWCs) is another component that integrates the promotion of health and wellness activities. As of 19 January 2022, the Economic Survey 2021–22 found that a total of 221.99 lakh tele-consultations have been provided under eSanjeevani through 3,017 HWC hubs and 33,819 spokes. It was also found that 96.27 lakh wellness sessions have been conducted at AB-HWCs.[71]

There are two other initiatives worth mentioning: the PM Ayushman Bharat Health Infrastructure Mission (PM-ABHIM) and the Ayushman Bharat Digital Mission (ABDM). PM-ABHIM is the largest pan-India scheme for public health infrastructure since 2005. The ABDM, announced on 27 September 2021, aims to build the digital health infrastructure in India through services like health ID, healthcare professional's registry (HPR), health facility registry (HFR) and personal health records (PHR).

eSanjeevani is an application launched by the Ministry of Health and Family Welfare in the wake of the pandemic. It enables patient-to-doctor tele-consultations in 36 states.

[71]'Economic Survey 2021–22', Union Budget: Government of India, https://bit.ly/3ErOaHJ. Accessed on 27 April 2022.

The application has been integrated with 3.74 lakh Common Service Centres (CSCs) as a driving technological force in equitable healthcare even in rural areas.[72]

The POSHAN Abhiyaan 2022 is a flagship programme aimed at building a people's movement for holistic nutrition to improve outcomes for children, adolescents, pregnant women and lactating mothers. It was launched on 8 March 2018, with an overall budget of ₹9,046 crore for three years. So far, the scheme, which was extended up to 31 March 2021, has had over 10 crore beneficiaries.

The National Digital Health Mission (NDHM), launched in 2020, has sought to improve access and reach, and enhance the doctor–patient consultation experience.

The FC's Holistic Approach

The 15th FC also recommended ₹1.06 lakh crore as health grants for a period of five years (2021–26), out of which ₹70,000 crore will focus on primary healthcare through the third tier of the government. These have been accepted by the government.

In its report, the 15th FC also contained a special chapter on health. This chapter highlights the importance of health funding, especially in the context of the pandemic. Members of the 15th FC felt it was important to renew our engagement with various health sector experts like the Ministry of Health and Family Welfare, the World Bank and the High Level Group on Health under the chairmanship of Dr Randeep Guleria. The group's other members comprised domain experts in the medical sector, namely, Dr V.K. Paul, Dr Devi Shetty, Dr Deelip

[72]'Health Ministry ropes in CSC to provide free medical consultation in rural areas on eSanjeevani app', *ET Government*, 23 June 2022, https://bit.ly/38StNYs. Accessed on 11 May 2022.

Govind Mhaisekar, Dr Naresh Trehan, Dr Bhabatosh Biswas and Professor K. Srinath Reddy. Based on these discussions, we highlighted very short-term, short-term and medium-term measures specific to the pandemic.

Very Short-Term Measures

- The very short-term management of the pandemic may include measures like rapid testing, wide surveillance with the help of chief medical officers and district magistrates for early identification and isolation of cases and containment of infections to avoid clustering.
- Provide rural mobile health units and supply of equipment like ventilators, personal protective equipment (PPEs), masks, continuous oxygen supply, etc.
- Award final-year MD students in various specialties certificates of being 'Board Eligible' and allow them to undertake practice to meet the immediate need of manpower.
- Provide 'flexible money' for the pandemic to help both Union and state governments.

Short-Term Measures

- Put an 'outbreak management plan' in place along with creating more infectious disease/critical care and outbreak management centres.
- Develop a mechanism to shift health resources like manpower and equipment from one state to another. Additionally, start crash courses with the help of IT to train health workers to deal with Covid-19.
- Allow willing medical colleges to run one additional course within their campus with an intake of 100

medical students. Additionally, consider training nurses and, subsequently, allow them to practise as 'nurse practitioners' to prescribe 47 basic drugs. A one-year diploma course after MBBS for lab medicine and ultrasound can also be started. Design incentives for doctors and paramedics to work in rural areas.
- Frame national policy and laws on waste disposal.

Medium-Term Measures

- Increase investment on health to 2.5 per cent of the GDP by 2025, including more investment in PHCs, district hospitals, wellness centres, the national ambulance infrastructure and IT infrastructure.
- Address the shortfall in the health workforce. Include more MBBS/AYUSH (Ayurveda, yoga and naturopathy, Unani, Siddha and homeopathy) doctors in primary and wellness health centres.
- Explore the possibilities of covering the remaining 60 per cent of the population under AB-PMJAY.
- Prioritize the creation of an All India Medical Services, similar to the Indian Civil Services. The All-India Services Act, 1951 has a provision for setting up an Indian Medical and Health Service.
- Explore the possibility of implementing a scheme like the National Health Service of the UK.

The 15th FC recognized that public health forms part of the 11th and 12th schedules of the Constitution, which necessitates the engagement of the third tier of the government. The NRHM provides for the implementation of healthcare programmes through a decentralized system with the involvement of local governments and communities. In fact, rural local governments play a critical role in the planning, implementation and monitoring of the NRHM.

The 11th FYP emphasized the need for greater involvement of local government institutions, right from the village to the district levels, in the public health delivery systems of their respective jurisdictions. The 12th FYP focused on strengthening the initiatives taken in the 11th FYP to expand the reach of healthcare and set up a system of universal health coverage in India. These were, in the past, substantially underfunded.

The pandemic also highlighted the inadequate attention towards urban health systems and the role of municipalities, which play a key role in public health, including air and water pollution, road traffic injuries and pandemic-related vulnerabilities.

So, by assigning ₹70,000 crore to the third tier exclusively for the health sector, the 15th FC sought to address this issue. These funds were assigned to address five critical areas:

- support for diagnostic infrastructure to the primary healthcare facilities;
- block-level public health units;
- urban HWCs;
- building-less sub-centres, PHCs, community health centres (CHCs); and
- conversion of rural PHCs and sub-centres into HWCs.

A New Strategy for Rejuvenation

Going forward, several issues are central to our health strategy. First and foremost, as the Budget 2022–23 has reiterated, we need to clearly recognize that public outlays in areas of health need to be substantially enhanced to 2.5 per cent of the GDP by 2025. According to the Budget of 2022–23, the health expenditure as a percentage of GDP was 2.1 per cent, as compared to 1.3 per cent in the previous fiscal year (FY).

Out of this, 70 per cent of the expenditure was incurred by the states and only 30 per cent by the Centre. This is notwithstanding the NHP, 2017, which aims to increase the states' health spending to more than 8 per cent of their budget by 2020 (currently, 5.18 per cent of the total expenditure of the states) and primary health expenditure to be two-thirds of the total health expenditure (currently, 53 per cent).

Second, we need to address the issue of large interstate variations in terms of health funding as well as health outcomes. States, except Meghalaya, are spending less than 8 per cent of their budget on the health sector, with the average being at 5.18 per cent in 2018–19. Furthermore, the per capita health spending of Bihar, Uttar Pradesh and Jharkhand is about half that of Kerala and Tamil Nadu.

Interstate variations are also evident in the following areas.

- The ratio of doctors and nurses to the total population is very low as compared to WHO standards. In India, the nurse to doctor ratio is estimated at 1.7:1 on the basis of the NSSO, whereas the ratio, according to a report by WHO and the Public Health Foundation of India, is 1:1.[73]
- Life expectancy ranges from 65 years in Uttar Pradesh to 75.2 years in Kerala.
- In states like Tamil Nadu and Kerala, the total fertility rate (TFR) is 1.59 and 1.79, respectively, similar to the TFR in developed countries. However, in states like Bihar and Uttar Pradesh, the TFR is 2.93 and 2.61, respectively.

[73]'Nurse to doctor ratio in India estimated to be 1.7:1 on basis of NSSO data', *Business Standard*, 21 September 2022, https://bit.ly/3vGIAhX. Accessed on 11 May 2022.

- The infant mortality rate ranges from only 4 in Nagaland to 48 in Madhya Pradesh. This disparity is also present in nutritional outcomes, with Bihar, Chhattisgarh, Gujarat, Jharkhand, Madhya Pradesh, Rajasthan and Uttar Pradesh having a very high proportion of children who are underweight and stunted.

Third, we must look into the ongoing regulatory reforms. It is crucial to regulate the health sector to ensure quality, standard of care and the assessment of service providers and hospitals to hold them accountable. Some of the key areas to improve public health spending include:

- Health spending by states should be increased to more than 8 per cent of their budget by 2022.
- Primary healthcare should be the number one fundamental commitment of every state and primary health expenditure should be increased to two-thirds of the total health expenditure by 2022.
- Public health expenditure of the Union and states together should be increased in a progressive manner to reach 2.5 per cent of the GDP by 2025.

Fourth, health is not part of the Concurrent List. In light of the pandemic, it is high time we move health to the Concurrent List. I am still not suggesting that, in the first step, we need to go as far as making this a fundamental right, but the least we can do is make this a concurrent subject.

Fifth, the CSS, co-financed by the government, should be flexible enough to allow states to adapt them and innovate. Top-down mandates and strictures on programme implementation are the antithesis of an open-source model. The CSS should grant states significant latitude to tailor their implementation modalities to local realities.

Sixth, the health sector is in dire need of a health developmental financial institution (DFI). The Budget 2022–23 mentioned setting up a DFI to stimulate investments with an initial corpus of ₹20,000 crore. A health-sector-specific DFI is much needed along the same lines as that of DFIs for other sectors like NABARD for agriculture, the National Housing Bank (NHB) for housing and the Tourism Finance Corporation of India (TFCI) for tourism. Such a health sector DFI would increase healthcare access in tier 2 and tier 3 cities while providing technical assistance that ensures the proper usage of funds.

Seventh, there are several other medical services, such as dentistry and pharmacology, which come under the purview of different laws, rules and regulations. There is a multiplicity of acts, rules and regulations and a mushrooming of institutions, yet the regulation of the sector is far from adequate. There needs to be rationalization and streamlining of these rules, regulations and institutions.

This multiplicity of Acts covers both the central government and the state governments. We need to standardize healthcare codes for both the Centre and states. There is a need for a complete healthcare code for the health ecosystem on similar lines as announced in the Budget 2022–23 for the securities markets (under the Securities Market Code).

Eighth, the 'missing middle' in terms of increasing insurance penetration has become prominent. While the AB-PMJAY covers the bottom two income quintiles, commercial insurance largely covers the top income quintile, thereby creating a 'missing middle' class in between. This refers to people in the middle two income quintiles, where the population is not rich enough to afford commercial insurance and not poor enough to be covered under government-sponsored health insurance schemes. Universalization of healthcare insurance and the development of financial institutions that has no exclusion in terms of disease or category of persons is the ultimate goal to address this issue.

Ninth, given the interstate disparity in the availability of medical doctors, it is essential to constitute an All India Medical and Health Service, as envisaged under Section 2A of the All-India Services Act, 1951.

Furthermore, there are the multiple challenges in the realm of medical training, which have been elaborated on below.

- The MBBS curriculum needs to be restructured to make it competency based. A certain degree of specialization should be included in the curriculum and the Medical Council of India/National Medical Council (MCI/NMC) should develop short courses on wellness, basic surgical procedures, anaesthesia, obstetrics and gynaecology, ophthalmology, otorhinolaryngology, etc. for MBBS doctors. It should also encourage AYUSH as an elective subject for medical undergraduates.
- The asymmetric distribution of medical colleges needs to be addressed, as most of them are situated in the western and southern parts of India. All public health facilities, including district hospitals, private-sector facilities and corporate hospitals, should be utilized for starting specialist DNB courses that will not only enhance the provision of services but will also ensure the availability of trained human resources.
- There is a need to utilize the foreign medical degree holders in the health system of the country to supplement the existing human resources for health. This may be done by designing a skill-based training programme to improve their knowledge and skills so that they meet the professional competencies required

in the screening tests that they have to clear before commencing their practice in the country.

- Nursing professionals need to be assigned larger roles, and the roles of nurse practitioners, physician assistants and nurse anaesthetists ought to be introduced to better utilize nursing professionals. The Budget 2022–23 mentions the Allied Health Services Bill that was introduced in 2020 in the Rajya Sabha and the National Nursing and Midwifery Bill, which will be introduced soon.
- Most recently, on 16 March, the Rajya Sabha passed the National Commission for Allied and Healthcare Professions Act, 2021, which seeks to set up a commission to regulate the allied healthcare sector and standardize training and qualifications across the country. I had dealt with this in the recent report of the 15th FC. We found that there is no higher proportionality between expenditure outlays and the allied healthcare sector. Nurses and allied workers in districts or sometimes even well-run health centres can be trained at a nominal cost.

Our success in overcoming these issues of health planning will depend on us addressing these issues and the key challenges in the health sector that confront us.

A holistic approach to our healthcare strategy must include both financial and non-financial measures. One cannot work without synchronizing with the other. Debilitating rules, procedures and measures could mitigate and reverse the improved outcomes of higher health outlays. They will take time; there is no quick fix. We have, for long, neglected health. The current pandemic gives us a historic opportunity to undo the endemic neglect of the past and seek a better future.

India, as a responsible member of the international community, needs to address its own systemic neglect. Our crucial vaccine initiatives have been widely applauded. We also need to build on and sustain the goodwill developed through India's compassionate and non-political move to address the global need for vaccines.

Moving forward, India can harness a vast reservoir of latent talent through skilful management. A number of regulatory changes have already been introduced. They need expeditious implementation. Strengthening grassroots infrastructure and taking advantage of the new regulation on allied health services can make an enormous difference at the cutting edge. Equally, ensuring that the substantial resources provided to the third tier by the 15th FC are harnessed holistically can make a qualitative difference. Blending these initiatives by channelling the potential of telemedicine with the IoT, 4G—moving towards 5G and beyond—fundamentally alters the health landscape. We have not even begun to seriously study, much less apply, the multiple gains of telemedicine through the potential of technology. Inculcation and application of human skills through regulatory and other changes can position India as a major health destination. This will not only improve the quality of human resources in this country but can also be a force for global good. Healthcare diplomacy and changing patterns of global interdependence have unbounded potential.

India needs to face the challenges in its healthcare planning and spending not only to address its own endemic neglect but also to do so as a responsible member of the international community. We need to build on the various aforementioned initiatives and extract the benefits of the goodwill that these have demonstrated.

This chapter has been extracted from N.K. Singh's keynote address at the NATHEALTH Annual Summit on 26 March 2021.[74]

[74]'Summit Valedictory Session - Session 5 – Skilling', YouTube, https://bit.ly/39SQ8G1. Accessed on 11 May 2022.

8

THE REAL WEALTH OF OUR NATION

Building a post-Covid-19 road map for healthcare systems

The landscape of healthcare systems in India is diverse, given the differences in geography, demography and socio-economic structures of various parts of the country. Efforts have been made in the past decades to improve and reinforce the health delivery mechanism. We have tried to stay abreast of the best practices adopted by other countries while making immense contributions to evidence-based practices that have been indigenously designed.

Several important initiatives have been launched in the last eight years. PM Modi has given a clarion call for the country to strive hard during the coming 25 years—the Amrit Kaal—so that India becomes a developed country by 2047. In this endeavour, the role of the health sector is of critical importance. Economic growth and development depend not only on physical capital but substantially on human capital as well. There is a close correlation between the improvements in the population's state of health and economic development.

The Covid-19 pandemic has posed several challenges to the health system of India, as of other countries, including developed ones. However, our system has responded with alacrity, competence and empathy. Further, we have learnt several lessons that are of immense relevance to our future road map for improving accessibility, equality, affordability and effective delivery of health services. As the post-Covid-19 world emerges, many issues and complexities need to be considered to cope with the new scenario. The role of the health sector will become more predominant, complex and challenging. In the context of the renewed focus on the health sector, it is necessary to look at our recent experiences, recalibrate our systems and approaches and prepare a road map for the future.

Preparedness and Response

India, as a signatory member of International Health Regulations (2005), had adopted measures to strengthen and maintain capacities to respond promptly and effectively to public health risks and emergencies of global concern. Yet, the Covid-19 pandemic, which engulfed the entire world, and its unprecedented scale and spread, posed major challenges to our health system, policy and economy. It brought the health ecosystem across the world to the centre stage of policy priority. How people at the frontlines of the health sector grappled with the rising tide of the virus, learnt to tackle it, made countless sacrifices and saved lives, with overwhelmed health systems all over the world, will be analysed in the years to come.

India wasted no time in acting upon the advice and guidance of experts to control the transmission, spread and ferocity of the pandemic. India's health system is not a homogenous entity. Instead, it is marked with differing levels of adequacy across the states. The nation's substantive approach during Covid-19 has been characterized by five key elements:

- repurposing capacities from multiple disciplines, including their research capacities;
- a context-specific, calibrated approach to scaling diagnostics and clinical management at the facilities;
- an all-of-government approach;
- an all-of-society approach, galvanizing the capacities and cooperation of each and every citizen; and
- a judicious use of technology.

Upon identifying the pathogenic mode of transmission of the disease, a nationwide advocacy about protective and preventive practices, such as respiratory hygiene, hand hygiene and social distancing, was undertaken. The reach and uptake of the advocacy measures were made possible with the joint efforts of frontline workers at the community level, healthcare providers at the facility level, media, law enforcement bodies and the manufacturers of these protective supplies, who met the huge demand. Although, early on, essential supplies were imported to meet the demand, within a short span of time, the nation was not only domestically equipped with an adequate supply of protective items, such as masks, PPEs, ventilators and other medical resources, but was also able to export some of these. Additionally, India was one of the countries at the forefront of both developing vaccines indigenously and manufacturing the ones that had been developed elsewhere.

The requirement of medical oxygen increased manifold during Covid-19, particularly in the second wave. It increased from about 700 MT per day in pre-Covid-19 times to 3,000 MT in the first wave and 9,000 MT in the second wave, putting enormous pressure on the system. We had to divert oxygen used in industries to medical facilities as an emergency measure. Our strong international relationships and diplomacy were reciprocated through goodwill gestures from countries across the globe for supplementing the immediate requirements. Nonetheless, the government developed solutions to increase the domestic capacity with foresight for similar contingencies. In May 2022, the nation had over 4,713 PSA plants for oxygen production at hospitals,[75] along with a strengthened logistic network to augment oxygen availability. As of October 2021, the country had the capacity to produce 14,727 MT of medical oxygen per day.[76]

We rolled out one of the largest vaccination drives as a preventive measure to mitigate the impact of the ongoing pandemic. On 5 April 2022, less than a year since the commencement of the drive, India achieved over 185 crore vaccinations, with the first dose being administered to around 96 per cent of the eligible population and the second dose to around 78 per cent—an achievement truly laudable by global standards.[77] The feat was achieved by leveraging technology platforms, like CoWIN and Aarogya Setu, for extensive and effective nationwide coordination. Looking at the course of the pandemic till now, the nation cannot resign to complacency. Rather, it must implement measures to monitor trends and enhance preparedness and prevention through disease-appropriate behaviour.

The post-Covid-19 world will witness path-breaking changes in India's national policies, priorities and use of technology. It is an opportune time to ensure that the health sector continues

[75]Ministry of Health and Family Welfare, OxyCare – Management Information System, https://bit.ly/3PfUA1K. Accessed on 12 May 2022.

[76]'Preparedness to meet oxygen requirements for possible future surge of Covid-19 cases: Review of progress and the way forward', OxyCare, 5 October 2021, https://bit.ly/3FD7O42. Accessed on 11 May 2022.

[77]'COVID - 19 Vaccination Update - Day 445 India's cumulative vaccination coverage crosses 185 Crore', Press Information Bureau, Government of India, 5 April 2022, https://bit.ly/3yv6b70. Accessed on 11 May 2022.

to receive the renewed focus and attention than what it has received so far. Furthermore, increased investment and an inclusive approach to provide affordable, equitable and quality healthcare to all are also being prioritized.

Strengthening Systems

During the last eight years, the Government of India has taken several steps, including the milestone NHP, 2017, to transform the health sector. The core vision of all the initiatives has been achieving Universal Health Coverage.

As articulated in the NHP 2017, the AB-HWC scheme was launched in 2018. It aimed to transform the primary healthcare landscape in India to ensure availability of free, comprehensive primary healthcare closer to the community through an expanded range of services. The scheme was rolled out to undertake a phased and timed upgradation of 150,000 HWCs by December 2022. As of now, over 100,000 centres have already been operationalized.[78] The scheme aims to create infrastructure to act as the first point of care to bring healthcare closer to the community, and also aims to extend the prevention of diseases and use of telemedicine, and promote wellness activities as parts of a healthy lifestyle. A mid-level health provider leads the team to provide care, dispense medicines and conduct essential tests across 12 packages.

As is evident from the consumption expenditure till date, most of the out-of-pocket-expenditure is incurred on drugs and diagnostics, as well as on availing a higher level of care. To enhance the availability and affordability of healthcare services

[78]'Government of India, Ministry of Health and Family Welfare, Lok Sabha: Starred Question No: 333', Parliament of India, https://bit.ly/3N7MVRk. Accessed on 12 May 2022.

and to mitigate the economic consequences of out-of-pocket expenses, schemes targeting healthcare expenditure have been introduced in the last five years.

The AB-PMJAY, which is another component of ABY, was launched to provide free access to secondary and tertiary care to over half a billion poor and deprived citizens for a cover of ₹5 lakh per family per annum. Through this scheme, the available options for the lower two quintiles of the population to access health services were substantially expanded through an empanelment mechanism. The introduction of the scheme filled the much-needed gap in financial risk protection for secondary and tertiary care services, especially in states that had no such schemes in place.

The 15th FC earmarked funds to the extent of ₹70,051 crore for local governments to strengthen their health systems and redress critical gaps at the primary healthcare level.[79] It also identified interventions that can strengthen primary healthcare services in rural areas. The idea is to support diagnostic infrastructure, block-level public health units, building-less sub-centres, PHCs, CHCs and the upgradation of primary-level facilities into HWCs. In urban areas, local bodies are to work towards strengthening their diagnostic infrastructure and HWCs. Channelling grants through the local bodies not only empowers them to act as supervising agencies but also highlights the health system's accountability to the people.

Considering the system's infrastructural capacity and shortages, the government recently launched PM-ABHIM, which focuses on enhancing the capacity of health institutions across all levels of care to strengthen infrastructure, surveillance,

[79]'Technical and Operational Guidelines: Implementation of 15th Finance Commission (FC-XV) – Health Grants through Local Governments', National Health Systems Resource Centre, p. 3, https://bit.ly/39VTnfU. Accessed on 11 May 2022.

diagnosis, management and research to make the nation self-reliant and enable states to respond effectively to the current and future public health challenges.

In addition to the NHM and grants of the 15th FC, PM-ABHIM, with its CSS, that include some central sector (CS) components, will work towards ensuring universal and comprehensive primary care by strengthening public health institutions and governance capacities for wide-ranging diagnostics and treatment, including critical care services. The scheme envisions the creation of a network of 29,000 HWCs. Additionally, the existing provisions of free drugs and diagnostic services and teleconsultation services would be further expanded under this ambitious scheme so that healthcare services are available and accessible, even in the remotest parts of the country.

This scheme will strengthen secondary and tertiary levels of care by creating specialized critical care hospital blocks in various districts. It aims to provide 37,000 beds with ICUs, ventilators and oxygen support, institute 4,000 block- and district-level primary health units and labs and make a full range of diagnostic services available in the districts.[80]

In the context of the pandemic, measures were taken to upgrade the eSanjeevaniOPD application to enable patient–doctor teleconsultations to provide free-of-cost health services to people at home. Telemedicine services were rolled out in 36 states and union territories to expand the outreach of health services; the eSanjeevaniOPD application has been integrated with 3.75 lakh CSCs to provide healthcare in remote areas of the country.[81]

---

[80]'Pradhan Mantri Ayushman Bharat Health Infrastructure Mission', Press Information Bureau, Government of India, 30 November 2021, https://bit.ly/3NccvnZ. Accessed on 11 May 2022.

[81]'Government of India, Ministry of Health and Family Welfare, Lok Sabha:

CoWIN 2.0 is a unique digital platform that displays activities, such as registering for vaccines, tracking the Covid-19 vaccination status of every beneficiary, stocking and storing vaccines, the number of people who have been vaccinated and generating digital certificates in real time. It can also be utilized for the delivery of many other health-related services.

In addition, PM-ABHIM envisages the development of an institutional approach to holistic healthcare by developing the National Institution of One Health (NIOH), achieving bio-security preparedness and strengthening pandemic research through four new National Institutes of Virology (NIVs) and 15 Biosafety Level-3 (BSL-3) labs. The existing surveillance system will also get reinforced with 20 metropolitan surveillance units, five new regional branches of the National Centres for Disease Control (NCDC), Integrated Health Information Platform (IHIP) in all states and the strengthening of 50 international entry points aimed at preventing future disease outbreaks.

To integrate all the efforts and information sharing, the ABDM has been launched to create a seamless, interoperable digital health ecosystem. It will revolutionize healthcare, the way the Universal Payments Interface (UPI) revolutionized payments. The mission envisions leveraging digital technology to strengthen accessibility, quality and equity of health services as well as a continuum of care by creating unique health IDs for every citizen, HPR, HFR and facilitating telemedicine. The programme will benefit citizens by also providing a choice to access both private and public health facilities.

Unstarred Question No – 575', Parliament of India, https://bit.ly/3yv84R8. Accessed on 12 May 2022.

Healthcare Financing

As envisaged by the NHP 2017, overall systemic efficiency can be ensured through appropriate resource allocation, strengthening institutional mechanisms for consultative decision-making and coordinated implementation by the Centre, states and local bodies as a way forward. As we move towards the goals of the NHP, the National Health Accounts (NHA) estimates show progressively increasing government health expenditure since 2013–14, alongside gradually declining out-of-pocket-expenditure.

Capacity Building, Infrastructure, Training and Practice

There has been a substantive improvement in the area of medical practice, education and training during the last five years. The transformative enactment of the National Medical Commission (NMC) Act, 2019, has paved the way for much-needed professionalism and credibility to the medical education regulator. The NMC also mandated the setting up of emergency medicine departments in all medical colleges by 2022 to enhance the reach of the much-needed emergency services for citizens. As part of this endeavour, the quality of human resources is more important than the physical infrastructure, equipment and medicines. After over two decades, the medical curriculum was revised to focus more on competency-based training, to enable the providers to become patient-centric, gender sensitive and outcome- and context-oriented. In addition, to augment human resources, postgraduate medical seats have been increased by 80 per cent and undergraduate MBBS seats have been increased by 50 per cent. Other initiatives to improve the quality of human resources in health include sanctioning 157 new medical colleges, with the objective of having a medical college or institution in every district and widening the scope for telemedicine-supported outreach, where voluntary efforts can supplement formal initiatives.

The Pharmaceutical Industry

The private sector—including healthcare providers, the pharmaceutical industry, the medical devices and technology industry, insurance and others—constitute a significant part of our healthcare system. The Indian pharmaceutical industry is the third largest by volume globally, with India being the largest supplier of low-cost generics and vaccines in the world. It is well known that India contributes over 60 per cent of the world's vaccines. The industry responded to the pandemic outbreak by developing (Covaxin, ZYCoV-D) and manufacturing (Covishield, Sputnik, Covavax and Johnson & Johnson) vaccines for emergency use. The government undertook initiatives, such as introducing Production Linked Incentive (PLI) schemes for pharmaceuticals and a scheme promoting bulk drug parks, to further expand the country's supply of drugs and reduce imports, improve the domestic manufacturing of critical key starting materials (KSMs)/drug intermediates and active pharmaceutical ingredients (APIs) and promote the domestic manufacturing of medical devices.

The introduction of Janaushadhi Kendras made quality generic drugs available at an affordable price. Now, we have over 8,500 Janaushadhi Kendras supplying generic medicines.[82] Simultaneously, the nation needs to focus on research and discovery of new molecules, promotion of different therapy areas, biosimilars and adult vaccines and emerging technologies

[82] 'Government of India, Ministry of Chemicals & Fertilizers, Department of Pharmaceuticals: Annual Report 2021–2022', Pharmaceuticals & Medical Devices Bureau of India, p. 41, https://bit.ly/3l3zWUH. Accessed on 12 May 2022.

using AI and machine learning for process optimization.

Several path-breaking initiatives have been introduced during the last eight years to realize the objective of the NHP 2017 and the SDGs. More importantly, we—the people of the country, health workers, health system, government and other agencies—spared no efforts in meeting the challenges of the pandemic. Even before the pandemic, we were striving to achieve the many objectives of the NHP 2017, including increased government health expenditure, which have become much more urgent in the current scenario.

We need more research, equipment, infrastructure, facilities for the delivery of health services and universal health coverage. All these will require adequate financial resources. However, the key element is the knowledge, skills and availability of human resources at all levels of the health workforce and health systems. Management of human resources for health necessitates developing a health workforce and sustaining them through prioritized actions for their recruitment, placement, retention, productivity and motivation. Thus, effective delivery of health services will require not only core health activities but also appropriate skill development and training management across disciplines and sectors.

The attainment of health outcomes depends on concerted endeavours in the field of public health, drinking water, sanitation, education, food security, nutrition, social empowerment and effective management. Our health sector programmes should account for the complex interplay of the determinants of peoples' health, capability and productivity.

This chapter is an updated version of the keynote address delivered by P.K. Mishra during the Platinum Jubilee Global Conclave of SCB Medical College, Cuttack on 26 November 2021.

9

A NEW EPOCH BEGINS

Covid-19 and the future of disaster risk management

The Covid-19 pandemic has sparked a debate on how the world should deal with the risk of low-frequency, high-impact events. This includes not only pandemics but also other extreme events of natural or man-made origin that may have a cascading impact across the global system. We need to learn from the pandemic and create a bridge between the traditional practice of disaster risk management and how disaster risk management ought to be practised in the twenty-first century—particularly to deal with uncertain scenarios in the context of climate change and due to some of the underlying drivers of risk inherent in the current global system.

Over the last four decades, the practice of disaster risk management has evolved significantly. It has come from the margins to the centre stage of our development discourse. It is no longer seen as a narrow, specialized field but as something that requires the engagement of multiple disciplines—not just science, technology, engineering and mathematics (STEM) disciplines but also the social sciences. For example, we now understand that a building being built poorly in an earthquake-prone area is, of course, an engineering problem. However, it is also a governance-related, social and economic problem. As significant as these changes of the last four decades have been, it appears certain that Covid-19 will mark the beginning of a new epoch.

Innovative Solutions and Blind Spots

In the four decades prior to Covid-19, the practice of disaster risk management in India went through multiple transitions. Discussion and debate stirred by large disaster events, such as the 1999 Odisha super cyclone, 2001 Gujarat earthquake, and 2004 Indian Ocean tsunami, combined with global policy processes, such as the International Decade for Natural Disaster Reduction (IDNDR 1990–99) and the Hyogo Framework for Action (HFA) propelled these transitions. I have had the opportunity to shape some of these transitions in my present assignment as well as in my early years as the agriculture secretary, the secretary to the National Disaster Management Authority (NDMA), the CEO of the GSDMA, and before that in several other departments of the state government.

Looking back, one can discern three main transitions in the disaster risk management system of the country:

- transition towards a multi-tiered disaster risk management system backed by dedicated disaster management legislation;
- much greater focus on linking science to society, characterized by a people-centric approach to early warning; and
- transition towards an all-of-government and all-of-society approach.

These transitions are still works in progress and probably will remain so for some time. However, it is clear that these evolutions have borne results. We have seen a consistent decline in the mortality from some disasters, most notably from cyclones and heatwaves. Our success in reducing cyclone-related mortality has been lauded globally. Public awareness about disasters is at an all-time high at all levels in the country. There are efforts from all strata of society to foster innovative solutions to address specific disaster-related problems.

Going beyond our own needs, after the Indian Ocean tsunami, we played a pivotal role in establishing the end-to-end Indian National Tsunami Early Warning System for the Indian Ocean. In recent years, India has been playing an increasingly important role in disaster risk management globally through a range of bilateral and multilateral initiatives. This includes the PM's initiative to establish the Coalition for Disaster Resilient Infrastructure (CDRI), the bilateral support for response and recovery after major disasters in neighbouring countries and regional disaster preparedness exercises within the framework of the Bay of Bengal Initiative for Multi-Sectoral Technical and Economic Cooperation (BIMSTEC), the South Asian Association for Regional Cooperation (SAARC) and the Shanghai Cooperation Organisation (SCO). Consequently, the world has come to expect India to play a leadership role in the area of disaster risk management beyond its borders.

While we need to celebrate and consolidate our accomplishments, we must acknowledge that we have a long way to go in building a resilient future. The pandemic is a sobering reminder that there are vulnerabilities lurking across the global system. These vulnerabilities can come in contact with a rare event—in this case, an unknown virus—and have a cascading impact of unimaginable proportions. So, it is important that the international community gives greater attention to managing the risk of such low-frequency, high-impact events.

In 2015, when 187 countries, including India, adopted the Sendai Framework for Disaster Risk Reduction (SFDRR) 2015–2030, the discourse centred around two types of disaster risks:

- extensive disaster risk or the risk of low-severity, high-frequency hazardous events and disasters, such as localized floods and landslides; and
- intensive disaster risk or the risk of high-severity, mid- to low-frequency disasters, such as a strong urban earthquake, a tsunami or a major storm.[83]

Both these types of risks can be identified, quantified and evaluated. The deliberations recognized the need for addressing both these types of risks in a comprehensive manner. This would require a multi-tiered disaster risk governance system in each country as well as regional and international collaboration.

Looking back, in the context of Covid-19, it appears that there was a blind spot in our thinking in 2014–15. We did not consider ways to manage the risk from rare events. During the preparatory discussions for the Sendai Framework, there was little discussion on 'Black Swan' events—the kind of rare events that have outsized impacts, are hard to fully anticipate and it is harder still to model their impacts.[84] Yet, in this century we have seen Black Swan events with global implications.

---

[83]'Report of the open-ended intergovernmental expert working group on indicators and terminology relating to disaster risk reduction', UNDRR: PreventionWeb, https://bit.ly/3LJ00QR. Accessed on 29 April 2022.

[84]Nassim Nicholas Taleb, a Lebanese-American scholar, made the concept famous in his 2007 book *The Black Swan: The Impact of the Highly Improbable* (Random House). Unlikely events seem impossible when they lie low in the unknown or in the future. But after they happen, people try to rationalize them into their conception of the world. Experts debate whether someone had predicted such an event or why someone could not have predicted it.

- First, the Indian Ocean tsunami of 2004 that simultaneously affected a large number of countries, and caused over 200,000 deaths of not only nationals from the Indian Ocean Rim (IOR) countries but also tourists from many parts of the world.[85]
- Second, the crash of the US housing market during the 2007–08 financial crisis is a well-known Black Swan event. The effect of the crash was catastrophic and global, and only a few outliers were able to predict it happening.
- Third, in 2011, we saw the triple disaster in Japan, where an earthquake led to a tsunami, which then affected the Fukushima nuclear plant. While a strong earthquake in Japan is entirely expected and its impacts can be modelled, it would be very difficult to model the concatenation of an earthquake, a tsunami and a nuclear disaster. How do we prepare for that?
- And finally, the ongoing Covid-19 pandemic, which some would classify as a Black Swan event. While the notion of pandemic preparedness has been on the radar of the global public health community, the way the current pandemic has panned out shows the limits of our ability to anticipate and prepare for Black Swan events. In India, floods, cyclones and chemical disasters have also coincided with the pandemic. While we know how to assign probabilities to each one of these events separately, how do we calculate the likelihood of all of these events coming together, leading to larger impacts? This is a question we must ponder over not only for the Indian context but for an increasingly interconnected world.

---

[85] Shaw, Rajib (ed.), *Recovery from the Indian Ocean Tsunami: A Ten-Year Journey*, Springer, 2015, p. 4.

Lessons from the Pandemic

In India, we recognized the threat posed by Covid-19 early in its trajectory. We correctly gauged the enormity of the problem and committed ourselves to a scientific, evidence-based approach. Even after the first wave subsided, we were monitoring the number of infections. As the cases began to rise in late February and early March of 2021, there was constant dialogue with, and review of, the states where we saw an early trend of a rising number of infections. We expected an increase but we did not anticipate such a steep rise during the second wave. We prioritized the vaccination of health workers and frontline workers in early 2021, as a part of our preparedness for the second wave.

Under PM Modi's leadership, the country put up a united fight against the pandemic. All strata of society—across social and economic groups, different regions of the country, the civil society and the industry—came together to take on this common challenge. It has been clearly recognized that everyone is susceptible to the virus—rich or poor, from the east or the west—and this has to be a united, collective fight.

While our public health workers, the corona warriors, have been at the frontline, risking their own safety for the sake of their fellow citizens, the non-pharmacological response has also been unprecedented. Constant communication between different parts of the society—between central and state governments, among state governments, between the government and civil society—has been the hallmark of our response. While the fight against Covid-19 continues, we can take pride in the fact that, as a country, we have come together in a remarkable way. Our substantive approach to the pandemic has been characterized by five key elements: repurposing capacities, scaling diagnostics and clinical management facilities, an all-of-government approach, people's participation and the use of technology.

From a disaster risk management perspective, we can identify the following key lessons from the experience of managing Covid-19 thus far.

Need for More Dynamic Risk Assessment Tools

In line with our commitment to a scientific evidence-based approach to mitigating and managing the impacts of Covid-19, the government has been open to receiving scientific inputs from all possible sources—from epidemiological modelling of the disease to anticipating its geographical spread or conducting a gap analysis of our health infrastructure. Some conventional disaster risk assessment tools were used to map various hazards, vulnerability and exposure parameters—such as the current incidence of the spread of the virus, the infection doubling rate, population density, age structure of the population and the state of health facilities—and estimate the risk of the spread of the disease in different locations. By early 2021, the government was taking into account epidemiological modelling outputs from at least five different sources. A big challenge in assessing the risk has been the wide variance, sometimes by an order of magnitude, in the projections provided by these models.

Such analyses, while useful in visualizing the scope of the problem, also had major limitations, which have been listed below.

- The information was not granular enough. In the Indian context, even a district is too large a unit of analysis. A district may be 'red', and consequently, close down all its economic activity but, in reality, the risk may be confined to a small part of the district.
- The information was not dynamic enough. In a rapidly spreading epidemic, we needed updates to be provided at shorter time intervals.

- The analyses were not adequately informed by the local drivers of risk.

The disaster risk management community should take stock of these lessons and refine these tools to meet future needs.

No Substitute for Community Action

Covid-19 is caused by an invisible agent. The virus has insidious ways of jumping from one host to another. While an efficient test-isolate-treat regime is essential for its containment, in a populous country like India, there is no substitute for community action. In states where communities are active drivers of surveillance rather than subjects of the system, efficiency in containing the spread of Covid-19 is higher. Greater community involvement and leadership enables the government to keep an ear to the ground, anticipate unintended consequences of government action and take corrective steps.

Risk Is Global, Resilience Is Local

Covid-19 is affecting the entire world. In some sense, everyone lives downstream. The emergence of the virus and the actions taken (or not taken) elsewhere increase its spread. Global interconnectedness is a major driver of the spread of this disease. However, in the current scenario, how this disease impacts different locations seems to be determined by the resilience of communities and robustness of the local-level public health systems. For the scale of the Covid-19 disaster, there needs to be more global cooperation to proactively share good practices on efficient surveillance systems, treatment protocols and methods for repurposing existing resources to fight Covid-19. For the future, this has two implications: one, greater investment in local-level resilience and self-reliance, as reflected in the PM's call for AatmaNirbhar Bharat; and two, even greater international cooperation towards fighting global disasters.

From Managing Risk to Managing Uncertainty

Covid-19 is riddled with several uncertainties. While the characteristics of the strain of coronavirus that causes Covid-19 have been studied, there are many uncertainties about how it progresses. There are contradictory reports about its effects on different age groups, the effectiveness of different treatment protocols and the likelihood of a population achieving herd immunity. The emergence of new variants of coronavirus and the level of their virulence and infectiousness adds another dimension to this uncertainty. This was one of the major drivers behind the second wave in India. Similarly, globally, although the vaccines were developed in record time, the advice in terms of the ideal gap between doses was modified as more information became available. At the same time, there were greater uncertainties about the local drivers of risk. All through the pandemic, policymakers have had to make decisions under great uncertainty. The traditional disaster risk management paradigm is attuned to using the analyses of past events—their frequency, intensity and impact—to quantify risk and devise risk management strategies for the future. We need to bridge the gap between traditional disaster risk management and risk management in an uncertain environment.

From Risk Reduction to Resilience

This lesson is a corollary of the previous one. In our country, for the last two decades, we have been talking about a paradigm shift from 'relief and response' to 'preparedness and mitigation' or 'risk reduction'. It is apparent that we are poised for the next leap: from 'risk reduction' to 'resilience'. During the pandemic, we witnessed the limits of a traditional 'risk reduction' approach, which assumes that risks can be precisely identified, mapped, quantified and reduced. But how do we manage risks that are not yet fully understood, let alone quantified? Should we allow for more redundancies in our economic system? Or should we continue to focus on extreme efficiencies in our economic system? I do not want to imply that we should abandon traditional disaster risk reduction. That would be erroneous. We must do a much better job of reducing the known risks too, but in the twenty-first century, that will not be enough. We must focus on systemic resilience by building redundancies, developing strong feedback mechanisms and investing in stronger modular systems at the local level.

Towards More Antifragility

Many public policymakers and analysts have referred to Covid-19 as a Black Swan event. For most of us, this event came from nowhere. Everything was normal and suddenly the virus started affecting all parts of the world.

A pandemic is not something unknown. However, in the context of the Covid-19 pandemic, this would have been a moot point if the magnitude, spread and impact of the virus had been predicted. The way it has overwhelmed most countries of the world, the pressure it has exerted on the medical infrastructure and the ferocity of its economic impact have perhaps been unthinkable. One can only imagine whether the memories of the Spanish Flu of the last century could have, or should have, guided us to anticipate the nature of the current pandemic. Interestingly, a few months after the pandemic started, Nassim Nicholas Taleb said that the Covid-19 pandemic was not a Black Swan event; it was a White Swan event, if ever there was one, because it could have been predicted.[86]

[86]'Covid was not "Black Swan" event, says Nassim Nicholas Taleb', *ET Now News*, 22 March 2021, https://bit.ly/3LKqPUa. Accessed on 7 April 2022.

Regardless of whether we call it a Black Swan event, the pandemic has pointed to the need for engaging in a forward-looking conversation on how we can be better prepared and build robustness to face negative events—not only a pandemic but also any event that has a similar disproportionate impact. As the early nineteenth-century Danish philosopher Søren Kierkegaard said, 'Life can only be understood backwards; but it must be lived forwards.'

Even as we retrospectively analyse Covid-19, it is more important to work towards minimizing the negative outcomes of a future extreme event that is not as yet on our horizon. Taleb, in his 2012 book *Antifragile: Things that Gain from Disorder*, introduced the concept of 'antifragile' as a solution to Black Swan problems. According to him,

> Antifragility is beyond resilience or robustness. The resilient resists shocks and stays the same; the anti-fragile gets better. This property is behind everything that has changed with time: evolution, culture, ideas, revolutions, political systems, technological innovation...[87]

Proliferating global networks, both physical and virtual, lead to more interdependent and fragile systems. Not only risks such as pathogens but computer viruses, hacking of information networks, reckless actions of financial institutions or spectacular acts of terror can also make the system fragile. Any adverse event can cause a rolling and widening collapse—a Black Swan event—in the same way the failure of a single transformer can collapse an electricity grid. For Taleb, an antifragile country would encourage the distribution of smaller, more local, experimental and self-sufficient entities. The government should be an insurer of healthcare, although

[87]Taleb, Nicholas Nassim, *Antifragile: Things That Gain from Disorder*, Random House, 2012, 544.

Taleb prefers to not have a centrally run medical care system but a decentralized system with smaller jurisdictions. In the Indian context, I propose that our efforts to become more antifragile or more resilient to rare events should rest on the following five pillars.

Community-Level Initiatives

In the course of fighting Covid-19, almost all the states encouraged local-level innovations to seek people's active cooperation in bringing about behavioural changes and alleviating collective distress. This included setting up community surveillance mechanisms, enlisting the support of volunteers, disbursing cash assistance to the people who were stuck, organizing community kitchens and providing essential supplies to the people in containment zones. We also saw the local-level mobilization through Accredited Social Health Activists (ASHAs), Anganwadis (rural child care centres) and multipurpose health workers across the country, which helped us reach out to the masses for testing, isolating and treating people. These community-level initiatives have played an important role in our efforts to manage the pandemic. However, these initiatives need to be supported and reinforced through the efforts of the central and state governments. We cannot realize their potential without adequate capacities and resources for risk management at the local level. We need to strengthen institutions like the District Disaster Management Authority (DDMA), Indian Red Cross Society and similar institutions at the local level

Resilient Infrastructure

One of our success stories has been the maintenance of supply lines across the length and breadth of the country in the midst of nationwide lockdowns. There was no major disruption to essential supplies, as our trucks moved incessantly on roads.

Not just that, the private sector joined our extraordinary efforts to augment essential health supplies, such as testing kits, masks, PPEs and sanitizers across the country. We organized the Vande Bharat Mission (VBM) and Shramik Special (SS) trains (special trains for migrant labourers) to bring millions of stranded people back to their homes. It speaks of the resilience of our infrastructure, which also helped us deal with several other crises during this period, including floods, cyclones, desert locusts and the crisis at our northern borders.

During the second wave of the pandemic, the requirement for oxygen, particularly in North India shot up exponentially. There was a mismatch in the geographical areas where oxygen was produced and where it was needed. Particularly in the first two weeks of the second wave, the distress caused by the scarcity of oxygen was of grave concern to all the levels of the government. However, at the same time, the various arms of the government and the private sector rose to the occasion. The production capacity for liquid medical oxygen (LMO) was expanded more than 10 times, from a pre-pandemic 700 MT per day to over 9,000 MT per day in May 2021, accompanied by a similar increase in cryogenic tanks in hospitals, along with oxygen cylinders, oxygen concentrators and pressure swing adsorption (PSA) oxygen plants. Special 'Oxygen Express' trains were organized to transport large quantities of oxygen. Over time, this not only served our own needs but we were also able to transport oxygen to Bangladesh. Many of these life-saving emergency measures were implemented by repurposing capacities from other sectors, such as industry, railways and defence.

Our infrastructure systems need to be strengthened further by building multiple redundancies. The government has initiated a specific multilateral initiative—the CDRI—to work with key infrastructure sectors on improving resilience in this sector. One of the areas that need special attention is improving the resilience of our digital communication. Since digital access has emerged as the most empowering tool, it has become an area that we need to develop with a sense of urgency.

A Robust Financial System

Cash transfers through the Direct Benefit Transfer (DBT) mechanism have been an important form of support for the people who have suffered the most from these disasters. Under the Pradhan Mantri Garib Kalyan Yojana, the government transferred ₹69,000 crore (approximately $9.25 billion) to 420 million people. Further, 750 million people got free food grains. These provided the much-needed support to the people reeling under the impact of Covid-19. It clearly points to the need for improving access to financial services for the people. Be it the Pradhan Mantri Jan-Dhan Yojana (PMJDY), through which people are getting linked to banks, or the Pradhan Mantri MUDRA Yojana (PMMY), through which people are getting cheaper loans, people have benefitted from their integration into an expanding national financial system. Needless to say that agricultural insurance will play a significant role in addressing the risks faced by farmers, particularly small ones. This integration needs to be reinforced further in several ways, by encouraging enterprise, bringing more economic activities into the formal sector and increasing people's awareness of diversity of financial services. The stronger the outreach and depth of our financial system, the greater the resilience at the household and community levels.

Social Protection

The spread of the pandemic not just in India but across all countries has clearly shown that social protection will always be an important strand of our intervention. Even the most developed nations needed to extend social protection to their people, as people lost their jobs and income. We have a functional social protection system in the country, which is implemented through cash transfers via the DBT, food supplies through the Public Distribution System (PDS) and cash for work through the MNREGS. In addition, all state governments took several steps to help people with the provisions for quarantines, cooked food and cash assistance. Both the important initiatives—Pradhan Mantri Garib Kalyan Package and AatmaNirbhar Bharat—have included strong elements of social protection. Despite these efforts, social protection can always be improved further with the support of civil society. With all the enabling mechanisms available through the digital infrastructure, we can improve our social protection and ensure a more efficient transfer of benefits, particularly for weaker social groups, women and informal workers.

Sustainable Natural Resource Management

Finally, we need to pursue a strong sustainability angle. In many ways, the pandemic has come across as a backlash against the excesses of our consumption. We need to take a step back and assess how we can find a better balance with nature. This clearly implies that we must value our natural resources, like rivers, wetlands, mountains, forests, coastlines and biodiversity. As we accelerate our economic recovery and push the country towards becoming a global manufacturing hub, we also need to improve the management of natural resources, ensure clear water and air, maintain our rivers and coastlines and enhance peoples' access to these environmental resources. These resources enrich our inner and outer lives, and build our defences against different risks, including natural hazards and the risks arising from the industrial and information economy.

It's Everybody's Business

India's achievements in the area of disaster risk management over the last two decades have been more than satisfactory. However, this is not enough. On one hand, we have a lot more to do to reduce the risk of losses from common disasters, and on the other hand, we must be prepared for the less understood or expected disaster risks. In the coming years, the compartmentalization of different risks will be increasingly difficult and even impractical. At the same time, the past is no longer a good guide for the future. Climate variability and change, combined with continued population increase and economic growth, are driving a rapid overall rise in global disaster risk. Although India is at the forefront of climate change mitigation efforts, we are also at a high risk of losses from extreme events related to weather and climate. Covid-19 has shown us the power of the exponential. It has shown us how impacts can escalate quickly. Is it analogous to what might happen when we suddenly reach the climate change tipping points and a very large number of people are affected? While investing in our resilience, there are two specific opportunities that we can and should pursue.

Here, it is important to highlight the recommendations of the 15th FC for the 2021–26 period. For the first time, we have a predictable way of financing all aspects of disaster risk management. We now have dedicated resources for the entire complement of disaster mitigation, disaster preparedness, disaster relief and rescue, and disaster recovery and reconstruction. This is an unparalleled opportunity to holistically pursue disaster risk management in the country. It is important to ensure that these funding windows are meaningfully utilized. The preparatory work for instituting the right kind of implementation mechanisms will require us to collectively draw upon all our past experience, while exercising our imagination to pursue a broader resilience agenda. Otherwise, there is a danger of disaster risk management being reduced to a mechanical process of only applying some administrative norms without adequate focus on the outcomes.

We have to pursue disaster risk management, and more broadly, resilience, as a strategic area of national interest. Over the past eight years, we have increasingly worked with other countries on various aspects of disaster risk management. We now lead a global initiative on disaster-resilient infrastructure. On various aspects of disaster response, we have engaged with the world within the framework of various international groupings like SAARC, BIMSTEC, SCO, the Indian Ocean Rim Association (IORA) and the Forum for India-Pacific Islands Cooperation (FIPIC), as well as our bilateral relations. We have to embrace knowledge and experience sharing as an essential element of building resilience. We have to pursue resilience at home as well as in the global system.

The country has a policy environment that is conducive to innovation and we are already making efforts in the direction of antifragility. In fact, several elements of the PM's AatmaNirbhar Bharat initiative, as well as reform measures in various sectors, with a medium- and long-term perspective, will bring about far-reaching changes in our economy and polity, making us more resilient and antifragile. Further, the NEP 2020 takes a comprehensive approach to enabling young people to innovate and be better equipped to face the uncertainties of the future.

Over the past decades, India and the world have seen unprecedented progress in economic and human development. However, Covid-19 and other events of the last two decades have demonstrated that all of this progress is at risk, and there are consequences of failing to reduce these risks. A large part of this risk is well understood, and collectively, the world has the wherewithal—experience, expertise and resources—to manage them. However, we also must build our robustness and resilience to risks that may not be known or may not be fully understood yet. Going forward, we need to continuously innovate to develop systems that are antifragile. Just as the Covid-19 cases are gradually coming down in India, we have to not only continue to be vigilant and try to get the pandemic under control but we also have to renew our resolve to build a bright future for all our people. The dream of becoming a $5 trillion economy is critical to ensuring the well-being of each and every citizen, especially the poorest and the most vulnerable. The key lesson from the pandemic is that the principles of resilience and antifragility must be integral to India's growth story. This would mean that risk management has to become everybody's business and not just remain in the domain of agencies like the NDMA. Risk management must become our second nature in all spheres of our national life.

This chapter has been extracted from the Professor Jai Krishna Memorial Lecture by P.K. Mishra at the IIT, Roorkee, in November 2020,[88] *which was later published in the journal* Progress in Disaster Science.[89] *The author would like to thank the journal for the permission to use the material presented in the original paper. He would also like to acknowledge the inputs and feedback provided by Kamal Kishore and Krishna S. Vatsa, members of the NDMA, and Vishal Sharma towards the development of the ideas presented in this paper.*

[88]Prof. Jai Krishna Memorial Lecture, YouTube, https://bit.ly/39tSafu. Accessed on 6 April 2022

[89]Mishra, P.K., 'Covid-19, Black Swan events and the future of disaster risk management in India', *Progress in Disaster Science*, Vol. 8, 2020, https://bit.ly/3s1ADlb. Accessed on 29 April 2022.

10

OUR HOME ON FIRE

From climate despair to action

We are in what may be called an existential crisis: a crisis that involves the survival of our blue planet. This is inextricably linked to water—an important factor determining overall climate conditions. Water availability, scarcity and contamination are all key elements on which human life survives. Even though we have made spectacular progress in exploring other planetary constellations, in the foreseeable future, the earth is the only home we have. However, we are living on this planet as if we have another one to go to. Solar energy and the hospitable atmosphere of our planet offset the fluctuations in weather patterns, preserve our sources of water, enable gainful agriculture and permit us, as a species, to evolve and adapt. There have been debilitating changes to this delicate equilibrium between many variables that enable life to prosper. Experts have expressed the need to limit global warming to 1.5–2 °C above pre-industrial levels to maintain this equilibrium. It has been established that a rise in temperatures beyond 1.8 °C would have debilitating and far-reaching consequences. Congruent efforts at the national and international levels aim to limit climate change preferably below 1.5 °C.

This existential crisis also raises moral issues of multiple kinds. The basic moral issue is that the countries that have come to cause the most damage to the ozone layer due to emissions of carbon dioxide are unwilling to reduce their carbon consumption to enable other parts of the world to have a fair and equitable share of the carbon footprint. Equitable carbon consumption involves not only countries with higher carbon footprints reducing their carbon consumption but also acumen, innovation, technology and finance for less energy-intensive activity patterns.

The other broad moral issue is that of common but differentiated responsibility towards mitigating the climate crisis. All nations have a common responsibility towards addressing this issue because it pertains to humanity as a whole, affecting all nations by influencing their right to development through harnessing their natural resources. Simultaneously, this is a differentiated responsibility because those who have achieved higher levels of economic development are technologically and financially better placed to bear the burden of an orderly transition to mitigate the climate crisis, unlike those who are economically underdeveloped or developing. The differentiated obligation must be distinguished based on each country's typology of development and the thresholds of economic progress reached by each of them.

The issue of intergenerational equity is connected to the common but differentiated responsibility. Is it morally irresponsible of the present generation to utilize their carbon credit so inefficiently that it prevents successive generations from exercising their right to achieve the levels of development and quality of life to which they are entitled? It is said that we do not inherit the earth from our ancestors but borrow it from our children. The intergenerational issues of equity further highlight these moral hazards.

No other issue that we confront today will need a compact among all stakeholders. Such a compact entails issues of geopolitics, the inherent competition between nations to maximize the use of natural resources and altering the pattern of economic activities, like agriculture, livelihood and services, all of which are interconnected. Equally important is the issue of harnessing technology, which offers boundless opportunities for enabling a non-disruptive energy transition from fossil fuels to renewables for regions and countries. Since technology is not bound by geographical or other restrictions, it is full of both potential and danger. Misuse of the new technological frontiers can have a debilitating impact on all that we have pursued so far in our climate and sustainability goals.

I have been connected with the debate on global warming and climate change ever since I was appointed the first chairman of the Global Environment Facility (GEF) created by the World Bank in the aftermath of the Rio Earth Summit on global warming in 1992.

The issues pertaining to global warming and climate change fall into two broad categories—first, issues of international action, and second, challenges of national endeavours. Of course, regional and international actions also have national consequences.

The challenges for India include:

- developing a climate action plan with the Centre and states acting in concert;
- the energy- and water-intensive patterns in agriculture;
- changing practices in animal husbandry;
- industry moving away from excessive fossil-fuel-generated inputs, like cement or steel; and
- reducing fossil-fuel-based energy by enhancing renewable energy through public and private initiatives.

It must be ensured that these measures do not disrupt employment and livelihood, and provide access to both affordable technology and affordable finance. This entails multiple issues of interregional and intra-regional equity.

International Action

So far, the Conference of the Parties (COP), which is the supreme decision-making body of the United Nations Framework Convention on Climate Change (UNFCCC), has met 26 times between 1995 and 2021. All the nations that are parties to the UNFCCC are represented at the COP, where they review the implementation of the UNFCCC and take necessary decisions to promote the consensus reached in it. Invariably, the deliberations of the COP are informed by the IPCC. The most recent Sixth Assessment Report (AR6) of the IPCC addressed concerns relating to climate change under three working groups: The Physical Science Basis; Impacts, Adaptation and Vulnerability; and Mitigation of Climate Change. According to this report, it is only possible to avoid warming of 1.5 °C or 2 °C if massive and immediate cuts in greenhouse gas emissions are made. *The Guardian* described the findings of this report as 'IPCC's starkest warning yet' of 'major climate changes [being] inevitable and irreversible.'[90]

The COP26 met at the Glasgow Climate Change Conference from October–November 2021. In an outstanding article in the *Financial Times*, well-known economic commentator and my friend, Martin Wolf, describes the outcome of COP26 with the headline 'Dancing on the edge of climate disaster'. In this

[90]Harvey, Fiona, 'Major climate changes inevitable and irreversible – IPCC's starkest warning yet', *The Guardian*, 9 August 2021, https://bit.ly/3KRSfr3. Accessed on 18 April 2022.

piece, he argued, 'It would be reasonable to conclude that it [COP26] was both [a] triumph and [a] disaster – triumph, in that some notable steps forward have been taken, and disaster, in that they fall far short of what is needed.'[91] Analysts have argued that a 1.5 per cent ceiling remains elusive. It has been pointed out based on the Climate Action Tracker that under the current scenario,

> [...] the world is set for a median increase in temperature of 2.7C above pre-industrial levels; with the targets for 2030 alone, this would fall to 2.4C; Full implementation of all submitted and binding targets would deliver 2.1C; and, finally, implementation of all announced targets would deliver 1.8C. Thus, if the world delivered everything it now indicates we would be close to the recommended ceiling of a rise of 1.5C.[92]

India played a significant role in COP26. So, what has been its outcome? What were the gains? What were the hits and misses, so to say? And what are the continuing challenges that need to be addressed?

First, the question of whether climate change has been caused by anthropogenic reasons has firmly been answered. In a book review of Bjørn Lomborg's *False Alarm: How Climate Change Panic Costs Us Trillions, Hurts the Poor, and Fails to Fix the Planet*, economist Joseph E. Stiglitz wrote about some key issues in the book regarding the relationship between the environment, sustainability and the economy.[93] Stiglitz and Lord Nicholas Stern, of the London School of Economics

---

[91]Wolf, Martin, 'Dancing on the edge of climate disaster', *Financial Times*, 23 November 2021, https://on.ft.com/3JkuM13. Accessed on 20 March 2022.

[92]Ibid.

[93]Stiglitz, Joseph E., 'Are we overreacting on climate change?' *The New York Times*, 27 July 2020, https://nyti.ms/3inQ7uw. Accessed on 20 March 2022.

and Political Science, are part of an international panel called the High-Level Commission on Carbon Prices, supported by the World Bank. Stiglitz and Stern have concluded that the economic cost of limiting climate change to 1.5–2 °C above pre-industrial levels is affordable. Fortunately, this time, no one raised the issue of the consistency and credibility of scientific evidence about global warming and climate change.

The second important achievement of COP26 is India's announcement of achieving net zero emissions by 2070—the net zero commitments now cover 80 per cent of the total emissions. The issue of methane gas, which impacts agricultural practices, also came into sharp focus. Of course, implicit in such a pronouncement is the complex issue of carbon pricing, elimination of the subsidy on fossil fuels, explicit regulations on internal combustion engines and transparency of data.

Third, for the first time, there was an implicit need to accept obligations without the mechanical correlation between accelerating efforts towards a phase-down of unabated coal power and an inefficient fossil fuel subsidy. It is important that COP26 recognized the importance of the role and contribution of private-sector initiatives towards climate financing and climate change goals. The Glasgow Financial Alliance for Net Zero (GFANZ) is based on private-sector contributions.

However, the biggest disappointment was the issue of climate finance. The failure of developed countries to prepare a credible plan to deliver on the commitment of $100 billion, undertaken in 2009 at the United Nations Climate Change Conference in Copenhagen (Denmark), is tantamount to a breach of trust. It is another matter that subsequent developments have rendered this number increasingly irrelevant since Lord Stern, who has played a pioneering role in issues of climate change and finance, along with other domain experts, like Amar Bhattacharya of the Grantham Research Institute on Climate Change and the Environment, have called this a small change. According to them, emerging markets and developing countries, other than China, including India, will need to invest an additional $0.8 trillion by 2025 and close to the $2 trillion per annum gap on climate mitigation and adaptation as well as restoration of natural capital by 2030. Clearly, this will require massive efforts from multiple stakeholders.

I had worked on the issue of climate and sustainable finance in a working group with Professor Nick Robins of the Grantham Research Institute and others in the run-up to COP26. Clearly, several actions need to be taken. Some of them have been listed below.

First and foremost, enhanced public outlay and bilateral financial commitments from the Group of Seven (G7) countries. This, of course, will raise the next issue of modalities for sustaining higher public outlays. In addition to this, catalysing private investment will be key to reaching anywhere near the necessary finances. The option of public–private blended finance needs to be imaginatively explored. De-risking and flattening the risk curves of private capital will be the centrepiece of these efforts. De-risking and risk insurance mechanisms are innovative ways of crowding-in private capital, either based on guarantees from public entities or through other modalities.

Second, in this context, reforms to the perspective of multilateral development banks (MDBs) play a crucial role. Here are a few suggestions for climate finance.

- The World Bank and other regional development banks need to reform the ethos of their lending operations. A mechanical correlation between quotas of lending and climate finance is impractical. The quotas were designed for a different set of developmental challenges. The emission intensity of individual developing countries, particularly those where the per capita emission entity is exceedingly low, needs to be managed by the World Bank to act with greater imagination.

- Much higher levels of lending, and exempting the application of debilitating rules, like the single country borrower limit, need the urgent attention of the governing board of the MDBs. A substantial part of higher lending to low-emission countries, like India, can go towards deleveraging the risk of private capital.
- MDBs must also recognize the need to invest in higher lending to low-emission countries to deleverage the risk of private capital and shift their focus to such de-risking activities rather than plain vanilla project financing that tends to crowd-out, rather than crowd-in private investment. This de-risking and pooling of risks across projects and geographies must be obligations recognized by the MDBs.

Connected with this is the third issue of the lending window of the IMF. The basic ethos of the lending programmes of the IMF aims for stable, orderly economic growth. It has, traditionally, been used for BoP support. The special drawing rights (SDR) of $650 billion should not be parcelled out in accordance with the current policy. A substantial part of these SDRs should be earmarked for climate finance, particularly risk mitigation. Countries who meet the criteria of being included in the SDR basket[94] need not meet the quotas again but the per capita

[94]Currencies included in the SDR basket have to meet two criteria: the export criterion and the freely usable criterion. A currency meets the export criterion if its issuer is an IMF member or a monetary union that includes IMF members, and is also one of the top five world exporters. For a currency to be determined 'freely usable' by the IMF, it has to be widely used to make payments for international transactions and widely traded in the principal exchange markets. Freely usable currencies can be used in Fund financial transactions.

'Special Drawing Rights (SDR)', International Monetary Fund,

energy emission for the proposed utilization of the SDR. The reforms and altered role of all multilateral development entities, which includes the World Bank, the ADB, other regional development banks, the International Finance Corporation (IFC) and other specialized entities, would be critical in the ability to garner adequate climate finance.

An important dimension in the decision-making process of private investment is the regulatory entities in emerging markets. This includes, no doubt, the role of the central banks of all countries with emerging markets or other sectoral regulatory institutions. The rules of these regulatory entities must prioritize and encourage lending for climate finance. An altered regulatory regime within the parameters of the working of the central bank and in line with the norms of the Bank for International Settlements would be an important signal to domestic lending institutions for climate finance.

National Reach

Apart from international action, the achievement of climate goals is predicated on the nationally determined contribution. As an off-shoot of this contribution, during the Paris Summit in 2015, PM Modi launched the International Solar Alliance (ISA). India is perhaps the only country that has fully implemented the commitments of the Paris Summit as part of its nationally determined contribution. During COP26, the US continued the endeavours of the Paris Summit by joining the ISA, which now has 101 participating nations. A subsequent bilateral initiative between India and the UK called the One Sun One World One Grid (OSOWOG) initiative makes the alliance globally operational because it envisions an interconnected solar grid.

---

https://bit.ly/3w5Axuf. Accessed on 11 May 2022.

The Economic Survey 2021–22 mentions two more initiatives: the Lifestyle for Environment (LIFE) and the CDRI. LIFE was introduced by PM Modi at the COP26 as a mass movement to endorse an environmentally friendly lifestyle with the aim of revolutionizing various sectors, such as agriculture, wellness, water management, fashion, tourism and energy. Since its launch in 2019, the CDRI's membership has expanded to 28 countries and seven multilateral institutions, with the commitment of providing financial and technical assistance to its member countries. India has, so far, provided $70 million, with the UK, US and the Netherlands pledging £1 million, $9.2 million and €100,000, respectively, to the CDRI's programmes and projects. Some projects of the CDRI include the third International Conference on Disaster Resilient Infrastructure (ICDRI) and Infrastructure for Resilient Island States (IRIS). India plays an active part in both these projects.

PM Modi's five-point visionary statement, called the 'panchamrit', was a bold step that received international applause. These five steps involved fundamental changes. The first will be raising India's non-fossil fuel energy capacity to 500 gigawatts by 2030. Second, by 2030, 50 per cent of India's power requirements will be met by using renewable energy. Third, for the first time, a few nations have committed to reducing carbon emissions by one billion tons between now and 2030, and fourth, they will aim to reduce carbon intensity by 45 per cent by the same date. Finally, fifth, India is committed to achieve net zero emissions by 2070. India has taken these actions unilaterally, even though it has used only 1.3 per cent of the total carbon space, whereas, on the basis of its per capita income, it is entitled to over 17 per cent of the total space. Each of these commitments made by India is a daunting challenge and entails multiple actions, including greater investments in renewable technologies, transition to electric vehicles, production of solar photovoltaic cells, storage capacity and the pursuit of the green hydrogen mission.

From a conceptual point of view, there are four broad areas that the 15th FC identified from a national perspective in its deliberations: mitigation and adaptation; strengthening regulations; reducing risks and vulnerabilities; and building greater resilience at the level of the state and civil society.

Mitigation of disasters is closely related to climate change adaptation. Many interventions—such as water resource management, deforestation and livelihood diversification—are understood to be helping disaster mitigation as well as climate change adaptation. In linking mitigation and climate change adaptation, the 15th FC has recommended the need for mitigation funds at both national and state levels under the provisions of the National Disaster Management Act, 2005.

Further, in combating climate change, India has launched eight missions under the National Action Plan on Climate Change (NAPCC) in the areas of solar energy, energy efficiency, water, agriculture, Himalayan ecosystem, sustainable habitat, green India and strategic knowledge on climate change. At the state level, climate actions are based on the State Level Action Plan on Climate Change (SAPCC). These actions outline sector-specific and cross-sectoral priorities in climate change actions. In addition, the Union Government is also implementing the National Adaptation Fund for Climate Change (NAFCC) to support the adaptation measures for the states and union territories in areas that are particularly vulnerable to the adverse impacts of climate change. The NAFCC is currently implementing 30 projects that have been sanctioned in 27 states to tackle climate-related issues, some of which include a climate resilient livestock production system in Punjab, water conservation in Odisha, sustainable livelihoods of agriculture-dependent rural communities in Himachal Pradesh and scaling climate smart agriculture in Bihar. India's success in achieving its SDGs and its commitments to the Paris Agreement will be greatly influenced by the success of the missions launched under the NAPCC.

Furthermore, in accordance with India's commitments under the UNFCCC and the Paris Agreement, India submitted its Nationally Determined Contribution. The commitments therein include:

> (i) reduce the emission intensity of GDP by 33 to 35 per cent by 2030 as compared to 2005 level; (ii) create an additional carbon sink of 2.5 to 3 billion tonnes of CO2 equivalent through additional forest and tree cover by 2030; and (iii) achieve about 40 per cent cumulative electric power installed capacity from non-fossil fuel energy resources by 2030.[95]

Subsequently, India submitted its third Biennial Update Reports (BUR) findings to the UNFCCC in 2021, which stated that India reduced its emission intensity by 24 per cent of the GDP during 2005–16. Additionally, the *India State of Forest Report 2021*[96] in January 2022 noted that the total carbon stock in all Indian forests is 7,204 million tons, with an increase of 79.4 million tons since 2019. Finally, according to the Central Electricity Authority, on 31 December 2021, the share of non-fossil fuel energy comprised 40.20 per cent.

In the Budget 2022–23, it was declared that energy transition and climate action will be an important developmental goal for the Amrit Kaal agenda. In her Budget speech, FM Nirmala Sitharaman announced several environmental initiatives, in accordance with sustainability goals, including, 'Four pilot

---

[95]'Economic Survey 2021–22', Union Budget, January 2022, p. 228, https://bit.ly/3ErOaHJ. Accessed on 18 April 2022.

[96]'ISFR 2021', Forest Survey of India, Ministry of Environment, Forest & Climate Change, https://bit.ly/3lwbQ4Y. Accessed on 19 May 2022.

projects for coal gasification and conversion of coal into chemicals required for the industry will be set up for technical and financial viability.'[97] Another important area mentioned in the Budget is the issuance of sovereign green bonds for mobilizing resources for green infrastructure. The proceeds of these green bonds will be deployed in public-sector projects to reduce the carbon intensity of the economy.

Challenges on the Horizon

India still faces several daunting challenges to achieving sustainable development. Some of these have been detailed below.

First, transitioning to non-fossil fuel-based renewable sources of energy has unique country-specific challenges. In India, coal has traditionally been the single largest source of electricity. Renewable energy, by way of hydro or nuclear energy, has played an insignificant role. Recently, solar and wind energy have begun occupying an understandably larger role. Nonetheless, India's coal transition plan is an important challenge to enabling a non-disruptive transition to renewable energy.

Second, ironically, the poorest parts of India have the maximum concentration of inefficient coal plants. Massive external finances will be necessary to address the human and social consequences of coal transition. The paucity of external finances will inhibit an orderly transition to an era of renewable energy. Equally, we need to minimize the human and social costs of such an orderly transition. We now await a national coal plan that brings together actions on coal and the human front.

Third, on the issue of transitioning to an era of renewable

[97]'Budget 2022–2023: Speech of Nirmala Sitharaman, Minister of Finance', Union Budget, 1 February, 2022, https://bit.ly/39TVYXJ. Accessed on 18 April 2022.

energy, the decision to make the railways—India's largest public-sector undertaking—net zero by 2030 is a signal. Other public-sector undertakings at both national and regional levels must now start working towards net zero emissions as well.

Fourth, on the issue of promoting renewable energy, the multiplicity of actions entails enhanced direct public outlay, congruence with the infrastructure pipeline project, based on PM Gati Shakti—a ₹100 lakh crore national infrastructure master plan that will provide an integrated path for the Indian economy—and the prioritization of climate-related actions. In addition to a higher public outlay, the modalities of private capital in the area of renewable energy create enormous opportunities and entail an assured availability of capital. Regulatory changes and de-risking private investments—past and proposed—require coherent action. Retrospective changes in the PPAs between states and private entities on renewable energy, based on subsequent technological changes, which alter the pricing matrix, are a complex and challenging issue. Many companies that have signed long-term PPAs expect those agreements to be honoured, even as technology has made it possible to lower the cost of such energy. Governments are driven by public good and argue that it would be against people of the State or users having to pay significantly higher costs of energy than those that technology can offer today. At the same time, those who have made past investments, based on the regime that existed earlier, need to be protected. These are complex subjects that need greater discussion and consensus to arrive at decisions, which balance the conflicting objectives of the need to honour contracts and the need to make energy most efficiently available.

Connected to the issue of private investment, India's target of 500 gigawatt (GW) of non-fossil electricity capacity by 2030 will require unprecedented amounts of capital. The Council on Energy, Environment and Water (CEEW) estimates that achieving 450 GW of renewable energy by 2030 would require $200 billion for the generating capacity alone, with significant amounts of additional capital for accompanying storage and transmission costs. Renewable energy infrastructure investments will require large-scale mobilization of the debt capital. But domestic banks and non-banking financial companies (NBFCs) do not have the resources to keep lending at the pace required to meet the targets.

A limited-period subsidized credit enhancement facility of ₹4,543 crore ($649 million), spread over a defined period of five years, can open up the domestic bond market to renewable energy developers by mobilizing the domestic bond market capital to the tune of ₹75,984 crore ($10.85 billion). This amount of capital is sufficient to debt finance approximately an additional 30 GW of solar capacity. This amounts to over a 60 per cent increment above the current 48 GW of installed solar capacity in the country.

We also need a Climate Credit Enhancement Fund of ₹10,000 crore, spread over five years, which could be housed within the Ministry of Finance. This fund should be designed to help renewable energy developers get greater access to the domestic bond market, reduce risk for bond issuers and increase the flow of capital for India's ambitious renewable energy targets.

We need to constitute a Committee on Climate Risk Insurance to assess the exposure of the insurance industry to climate risks, as well as the extent of uninsured infrastructure, and consider solutions to increase the insurance coverage for key built infrastructure, including roads and bridges, telecom and power grids, ports and airports, housing, etc. A Climate Risk Insurance Facility of ₹4,000 crore could be introduced as a blended finance special purpose vehicle to leverage public funds and crowd-in private insurance coverage at lower risk premiums. The budgetary allocations to the facility can increase year-on-year while the risk premiums would reduce as more infrastructure gets insured against far greater losses from extreme weather events.

Finally, regarding the nationally determined contribution, we require institutions to work together coherently. Given the multiplicity of entities and agencies, a National Environment Council, headed by the PM, could align the varying concerns and objectives of several ministries and institutions. We also need to ensure that in a federal entity, the role of the states, subnational governments and, indeed, the third tier remains significant. We must consider and reinforce arrangements that enable partnerships with the states. As far as state governments are concerned, apart from action taken by them, they should find modalities for the fullest participation of the third tier—the ULBs and panchayats—in the pattern and nature of their development projects.

The issues of global warming and climate change are past their hour of action. We have made enormous progress both at the global level and by way of the nationally determined contribution. Our goals and challenges have become more daunting. Allowing more time to pass would exacerbate the problem. It would threaten our lives and the lives of our future generations. While complacency and despondency must be buried, optimism and hope must be grounded in actions at the national and international levels. We cannot afford not to act cohesively and urgently with moral purpose and zest that are driven by reason and our innate instincts to survive.

This chapter has been extracted from N.K. Singh's speech at the 104th Annual Conference of the Indian Economic Association on 25 December 2021.

Section 3

FISCAL MATRIX AND BEYOND

11

REGULATION MEETS INNOVATION

Revisiting competition laws

Covid-19 is not the first time we have encountered a pandemic. The last pandemic, namely the Spanish Flu, only left us around 1920. We have no memory of the earlier pandemics, but there are anecdotal accounts and evidence of them, such as the bubonic plagues and viruses of multiple kinds, for which, at that time, the treatment protocols or vaccines were somewhat unknown. In an interdependent world, the pandemic has unintended, far-reaching consequences. A world critically dependent on the broad philosophy of liberalization and value-added chains was forced to go back to the drawing board. It was forced to revisit many areas hitherto taken for granted, such as social security systems, pedagogy for education skills, the protocols on health systems, employment, migration and the structure of the economy itself. It has forced us to push the reset button on the broader issues of the historically evolved social contract.

In the Indian context, apart from the necessity of balancing and optimizing on the issues of life and livelihood, the Covid-19 pandemic necessitated the fast tracking of many features of economic reforms that had been long overdue. It shook us out of a period of prolonged complacency on key economic parameters that were long overdue for structural reforms. Take, for instance, the need to transition out of an era of a socialist hangover to a newer regime that believes in maximizing the value of embedded assets in the large number of public-sector undertakings to improve logistics and infrastructure. Equally, tinkering with erstwhile sacred cows, like the nationalization of banks and insurance by looking at the privatization of two public-sector banks and an insurance company to begin with. The disinvestment and privatization programme, while unfreezing unproductive assets, would unleash a new momentum in the economic strategy not only for privatization but fostering competition as well. So, how will the present regulatory framework governing competition laws deal with these emerging challenges?

Understanding Competition

Generally, in economics, competition is seen as rivalry among firms for a larger share of the market, which leads to internal efficiency and lower prices for consumers. It can be defined as a process through which cost-efficient production is achieved with easier entry and exit, a reasonable number of players (producers and consumers) and close substitution between products of different players in a given industry. It is necessary and important in any normal pattern of economic activity because it helps promote safety, a quest for innovation and additional gainful employment opportunities.

A competition policy is a critical component of any overall economic policy framework. Not only does it promote efficiency and maximize consumer/social welfare but it also helps promote the creation of a business environment that leads to efficient resource allocation and mitigates the abuse of market power.

All stakeholders (producers and consumers) benefit from competition, as opposed to a monopoly. In a monopolistic market, there is only one firm that dictates the price and supply levels of goods and services and that firm has total market control, with serious entry and exit barriers. Similarly, market duopoly, or even oligopoly, has disabilities in securing wider benefit from enhanced competition. Thus, competition is necessary, especially if the objective of the economy is maximizing societal good.

Thus, both competition and markets have numerous multiplier benefits. At the same time, markets have infirmities. They cannot play God. As the Hungarian-American investor George Soros observed, 'Markets are imperfect. So you do need regulation, knowing that the regulators are also human.' Unbridled competition can become counterproductive without going through the economics of what is sometimes called 'natural monopolies' or 'controlled competition.' Both public and private entities play an important role in maximizing societal good.

A review of cross-country literature suggests that there is a positive association between GDP growth and enhanced competition. Empirical studies of select industries in several OECD countries suggest that competition enhances productivity at industry level, generates more employment and lowers consumer prices. Illustratively, in the Indian context, increased liberalization and competition have, in many cases, brought about enormous multiplier gains. Take, for instance, modes of communication. Telephone density in India has risen from mere 2.32 per cent in 1999 to about 86.37 per cent in 2021. From the consumers' points of view, there has been a dramatic fall in telecom tariffs from ₹16 per minute to ₹1 or less per minute with increased competition in this sector. Free talk time is normal and data is priced at affordable rates. The proliferation of technology platforms has enhanced consumer choice. Consumers have benefited similarly from competition in other sectors of important economic activity, such as civil aviation, automobiles, newspapers and consumer electronics.

Cross-Country Comparisons

Competition law is a body of legislation designed to restrain the market distortion caused by the anticompetitive practices of businesses. Therefore, it is also called antitrust legislation. The purpose of competition law is to guarantee a good marketplace for customers and producers by discouraging unethical practices designed to garner a larger market share than what can be reasonably accomplished through honest competition. The consequences of anticompetitive practices include difficult entry and exit for smaller firms, poorer service quality and a waning innovation drive.

In the 1800s, in the US, large manufacturing conglomerates began to emerge in great numbers and were perceived to have excessive economic power. Thus, various antitrust laws, such as the Interstate Commerce Act of 1887, the Sherman Antitrust Act of 1890 and the Clayton Antitrust Act of 1914, were enacted. The Federal Trade Commission Act (FTCA) was adopted in 1914 to create the Federal Trade Commission (FTC), an independent agency of the US federal government, charged with giving the government a full complement of legal tools to use against anticompetitive, unfair and deceptive practices in the marketplace. The FTCA was designed to achieve two goals: ensuring fair competition between businesses and protecting consumers against fraudulent business practices.

In the UK, competition law is affected by both British and European entities. For cases that are within the national sphere, the Competition Act of 1998 and the Enterprise Act of

2002 are the most important statutes. But for cases that reach across the border, the EU has the competence to deal with all problems and the EU law used to be exclusively applicable. However, after Brexit, this overlap needs to be re-examined. The Competition and Markets Authority (CMA) enforces the competition law in the UK. The CMA merged the Office of Fair Trading with the Competition Commission after the Enterprise and Regulatory Reform Act of 2013. The main objectives of the CMA are to protect consumer welfare and public interest. Competition law in the UK is closely connected with laws on deregulation of access to markets, state aids and subsidies, the privatization of state-owned assets and the establishment of independent sector regulators.

In Japan, competition law consists mainly of the Antimonopoly Act (AMA). Prior to World War II, Japan had no antitrust laws. The AMA was, therefore, introduced during the post-war US occupation of Japan. During this period, President Harry S. Truman issued a presidential directive to dissolve Zaibatsu structures. It generalized prohibitions against three types of anticompetitive conduct: private monopolization, unreasonable restraints of trade and unfair methods of competition. The AMA led to the formation of the Japan Fair Trade Commission (JFTC), which is a commission of the Japanese government responsible for regulating economic competition as well as enforcing the AMA.

Evolution of Competition Law

India adopted its first competition law in 1969 in the form of the Monopolies and Restrictive Trade Practices (MRTP) Act. The MRTP Bill was introduced in Parliament in 1967 and the same was referred to the Joint Select Committee. The MRTP Act, 1969 came into force with effect from 1 June 1970.

The enactment of the MRTP Act was based on the socio-economic philosophy enshrined in the Directive Principles of State Policy contained in the Constitution of India. The Act was amended in 1974, 1980, 1982, 1984, 1985, 1986, 1988 and 1991. The amendments introduced in 1982 and 1984 were based on the recommendations in the Report of the High-Powered Expert Committee on Companies and MRTP Acts, published in 1978. This report was authored by a committee that was constituted by the government under the chairmanship of Justice Rajindar Sachar in 1977.

However, as the times changed, the need was felt for a new framework on competition law. With the introduction of the new economic policy and the opening up of the Indian market to the world, there was a need to shift the focus of public policy from curbing monopolies to regulating a new framework of competition laws. Needless to say, monopolies are the antithesis of competition.

In October 1999, the Government of India constituted a high-level committee under the chairmanship of S.V.S. Raghavan to devise a modern competition law for the country in line with international developments and to suggest a new law or suitable amendments in the MRTP Act, 1969. The Raghavan Committee presented its report to the government in May 2000. With the changing nature of business behaviour, the markets and the economy, both in India and elsewhere, there was a necessity to replace the obsolete law with a new competition law. And so, the MRTP Act was replaced with the Competition Act, 2002.

The Competition Act provides for the establishment of the Competition Commission of India (CCI), a quasi-judicial body bound by principles of rule of law (i.e. predictability in reasoning and uniform and consistent application of the law) in giving decisions and the doctrine of precedents. There are three major elements in the Competition Act: anticompetitive agreements, abuse of dominant positions and combinations.

The Act empowers the CCI to order remedial measures including prohibitory direction to cease and desist, impose penalties, award compensation, directly modify agreements, recommend the division of a dominant enterprise and pass such other orders as it may deem fit. The CCI has all the powers of a civil court for gathering evidence. The range of powers given to the CCI allows it to structure remedies to the facts of each case and the need thereof to be used judiciously.

The State and Competition

The basic tenets of democracy and market competition are ingrained in the same value system—freedom of individual choice, abhorrence of concentration of power, decentralized decision-making and adherence to the rule of law.

The goal of both democracy and market competition is the same—to enhance public welfare. While the nature of the market mechanism is judged by its 'allocative efficiency', democratic institutions are judged by the degree of equity they create. The concepts of working for the benefit of the weaker sections and the greater good of greater numbers are of prime importance in both a democracy and competitive market mechanism. The concepts of 'consumer sovereignty' in economic literature and 'voter rights' in a democracy have the same philosophical groundings. 'Equality of opportunity' and the 'freedom to trade' are sacrosanct in both the systems.

The Constitution of India guarantees certain basic freedoms that include the fundamental right to engage in any occupation, trade or business under Article 19(1)(g). Competition law reinforces this fundamental right by prohibiting unreasonable restraints on the exercise of this right through anticompetitive practices.

Economists such as Amartya Sen have consistently

maintained that a democratic state makes it much harder for the ruling government to be unresponsive to the needs and values of the population at large.[98] Competitive markets and democratic governments are, therefore, considered complementary and need to interact in a manner that maximizes the larger public interest. There are domain experts who also believe in the necessary complementarities of markets and democratic governments to achieve social and economic justice to protect the interests of society. However, he also maintains that there are 'government failures' as there are 'market failures' and as markets need to be made more efficient, governments also need to be made more effective.

Competition law and policy are also tools towards better governance since they advocate for lesser control and discretionary powers in the hands of government functionaries. Compliance with competition law is akin to good corporate governance at the level of the enterprises. Corporate governance, as normally understood, ensures ethical conduct within the internal environment of the company. Similarly, compliance with competition law ensures ethical conduct in the external environment of the company, principally in the marketplace. These cover a wide gamut of subjects like trade, industry, privatization, intellectual property rights (IPR), taxation and environment.

Key Issues and Challenges

India will inevitably enhance its global interdependence. In the process, its harmonious functioning and symmetry will be under scrutiny. Some of these challenges have been discussed below.

---

[98]Drèze, Jean and Amartya Sen, *India: Development and Participation*, OUP; 2nd edition, Oxford, 2002.

Multiplicity of Sectoral Regulators

There have been perceived conflicts between the CCI and sectoral regulators. These could be caused by legislative ambiguity, jurisdictional overlap or both. Interpretational bias could aggravate conflicts. Conflicts between the two may also be generated by the market players and legal arbitrators.

Conflicts and uncertainties magnify investment risks and costly delays with onerous compliance. The allocation of specific areas of work to sectoral regulators does not appear to have been done very carefully. The tangled understanding of the framers of the legislation is evident in multiple legislations.

Some of the examples of overlapping jurisdictions are:

- **Petroleum and Natural Gas Regulatory Board (PNGRB)**: The PNGRB is mandated to be mindful of competition while dealing with access to common carriers or contract carriers as well as distribution networks. Specifically, if the PNGRB is interested in declaring an existing pipeline or distribution network as a common carrier, it still needs to be guided by the principles of competition.
- **Central Electricity Regulatory Commission (CERC)**: The Electricity Act was passed in May 2003, following the enactment of the Competition Act, 2002. One of the objectives of the Act is the promotion of competition, a primary function of the CCI. Indeed, the framers of the legislation also conferred power upon the regulator to deal with anticompetitive agreements, abuse of dominant position and mergers related to impeding competition in electricity. Subsequently, each state government has also set up their own independent electricity regulators.
- **Airports Economic Regulatory Authority of India (AERA)**: The objective of AERA is to regulate tariff

for aeronautical services, determine other airport charges for services rendered at major airports and monitor the performance standards of such airports. The operating environment in the domestic airline industry has become extremely competitive over the last few years, with an increase in the number of players leading to a fragmented market share, growing competition and pricing pressure on players. The scope for competition in the provision of air navigation services is limited, and direct competition between different air navigation service providers within the same airspace is not a practical possibility. Therefore, to protect the user from the abuse of dominant position, greater transparency is inescapable.

- **Telecom Regulatory Authority of India (TRAI):** TRAI is another interesting instance. It was established, inter alia, to ensure orderly development of the telecom sector. Accordingly, one of the critical functions of the telecom regulator is to 'facilitate competition and promote efficiency'. Nevertheless, the appellate authority established to adjudicate telecom disputes excludes competition matters, besides those arising under the old MRTP Act.[99]

[99]In the case of *Consumer Online Foundation vs Tata Sky Ltd. & Other Parties* (2009), Dish TV submitted that the CCI could not claim jurisdiction over this matter, as the TRAI and Telecom Disputes Settlement and Appellate Tribunal (TDSAT) were already vested with the '[...] jurisdiction and responsibility to govern and regulate the telecommunication industry covering telecom, broadcasting and cable TV services [...]'. The CCI held that any matter that raises competition concerns would fall within the purview of the Competition Act, 2002 enabling it to exercise its jurisdiction.

Intersectoral Regulatory Conflicts

Having settled for some sort of framework overseeing business conduct, Indian policymakers will face the dilemma of choosing between sectoral regulation and competition law. In order to foster a symmetrical approach between sectoral regulators and competition authorities, there are three broad options available.

- Clear separation of competition enforcement functions from technical functions: The sectoral regulator may be vested with powers of ex ante control and the competition authority may be given the ex post authority. For instance, fixing electricity tariffs may be left to the electricity authority constituted under the Electricity Act unless the prices are claimed to be excessive or predatory, which, then, may require an ex post review by the competition authority.
- The competition authority substitutes the sectoral regulator: Another option is to make the competition authority responsible for both sector-specific regulation as well as overarching competition enforcement. This approach is advantageous because it reduces the problem of multiplicity of regulators and enhances domain expertise. Indeed, Australia has taken this approach to settle for an economy-wide economic regulator that integrates technical and competition regulation. However, experts have expressed their concern that this may lead to a complex bureaucratic structure. There is also a lingering danger that the regulator may prefer using direct regulatory power over indirect competition enforcement powers.
- Concurrent existence of a competition authority and a sectoral regulator: Institution building is a complex,

time-consuming exercise. At a pragmatic level, sector-specific regulators are here to stay because it would be practically impossible to abolish the authorities that have already come into existence. Further, experiences of other countries are not valuable guidance. There is a wide diversity in the available models. While Australia privileges its competition authority, the UK grants explicit concurrent powers to its sectoral regulators.

The Financial Domain

In the financial domain, we have a multiplicity of regulators as well: the RBI is one of the oldest regulators; there are also the Securities and Exchange Board of India (SEBI) and the Insurance Regulatory and Development Authority of India (IRDAI). There is no overarching super regulator. This has created some ambiguity. For instance, there has been a lack of clarity as to which regulator—the RBI or SEBI—regulates the National Stock Exchange (NSE). Even regulation of the debt market has suffered since banks are getting regulated by the RBI but SEBI has a mandate to regulate financial markets. The current Financial Stability and Development Council (FSDC), chaired by the FM, is a high-level coordinative entity, which includes all other finance regulators, without any legislative reach.

Inter-Corporate Rivalries

We need to address issues of inter-corporate asymmetries to ensure a level playing field. Rivalry among businesses can influence varied aspects of an organization or their products and services. For instance, rivalry can encourage managers to seek externalities of scale, but it can also enhance the possibility of unethical behaviour. Are these inter-corporate rivalries to be resolved by the CCI? What role can the CCI play to enforce ethical behaviour?

Issues of Mergers and Acquisitions

Combinations like mergers and acquisitions are common practices among business entities. The purpose of the combinations is accelerating economic growth and enhancing trade practices that are beneficial to consumers. However, combinations may not always be beneficial and may cause socio-economic disruptions. Nonetheless, they could be designed to bridge competition and lead to dominance in the future.

Under a 2007 Amendment to the Competition Act, issues like mergers, acquisitions and amalgamation were made integral parts of its jurisdiction. This vested immense responsibility in the CCI to mitigate adverse issues that can be detrimental to the interests of consumers. To fulfil this obligation, the CCI has been encouraged to take the assistance of various experts from diverse fields. The CCI needs to invest significantly in broadening and deepening the training and capacity building of its personnel. It needs to be ahead of the curve. The pace of technology is dramatic and identifying detrimental business practices will be a dynamic challenge.

Foreign Investment by Big Companies

Globalization entails and confers multiple advantages. Simultaneously, it poses more difficult choices. e-Commerce is a reality and will increasingly seek greater space in our economy. It has great advantages from the viewpoint of making goods and services available at more efficient, cheaper costs and with less onerous logistics. But, how does one ensure that this does not lead to the displacement of a number of mom-and-pop shops, which were a huge repository of employment and livelihood for the informal sector? How does one balance out the gains to the consumers with the overall gains of the economy in terms of the facility and access that e-commerce provides? What are the best international benchmarks? Will this abuse of market dominance be mitigated by balancing the interest of consumers and all other stakeholders in a fair and equitable manner?

Strategic Disinvestment and Creating Fiscal Space

There has been a tectonic shift in our approach to central public sector undertakings (CPSUs). This shift has been triggered by the policy decision for all CPSUs to be progressively privatized except in strategic sectors. The embedded value in these policy decisions can be utilized for financing infrastructure and improving the overall competitive efficiency of the economy. On the basis of some calculations done by the NITI Aayog, 77 strategic units are to remain public entities. Four hundred and thirty-nine public-sector enterprises, including their subsidiaries, are also being considered for privatization.[100] One hundred and fifty-one non-strategic CPSUs are to be progressively transitioned to the new approach. Among these 151, 83 are holding companies, while 68 are subsidiary entities.[101] These are huge numbers.

In due course, apart from freeing valuable financial resources, creating fiscal space for the government for its priority capital expenditure, both physical and social infrastructure, and improving logistics, this move will also generate enhanced competition. The nature of the disinvestment and ensuring that market dominance and market abuse can be obviated in the process will be a challenge for the years to come. How is the CCI equipping itself to fulfil the broad mandate of fostering competition, while preventing its abuses to multiple forms of

---

[100]Dhoot, Vikas, 'The Hindu Explains | How will the new disinvestment policy oversee future of public sector enterprises?' *The Hindu*, 21 February 2021, https://bit.ly/37ciKsK. Accessed on 4 May 2022.

[101]Dhoot, Vikas, 'Disinvestment will be squeaky clean, says DIPAM Secretary', *The Hindu*, 7 February 2021, https://bit.ly/37gwRgO. Accessed on 4 May 2022.

financial engineering? This will be an ongoing dynamic but an important obligation for an overarching entity like the CCI.

The Road Ahead

Going forward, the first thing we need to do is reconcile issues of market dominance with optimizing externalities of scale. When does dominance become abusive and when do we reach that point? These questions need to be balanced with advantages to the consumer, given externalities of scale in terms of cost, quality and delivery efficiency.

Second, how does one deal with the issue of large foreign investments, either in Indian corporates or other institutions which alter the market equilibrium, within the overall regulatory framework? Often, subtle forms of market engineering alter the pace and flow of such foreign investments. The alacrity with which issues of competition are addressed invariably needs reliable data and judgment calls.

Third, given the inevitable sectoral regulators, what kind of an organizational forum would be appropriate for intersectoral regulatory coordination? Since all the laws enacted by Parliament stand on an even keel, what kind of a role can an overarching non-economic regulator like the CCI play? Will this require legal changes or can consultative mechanisms and forums be created through practice to promote harmonious coordination? The CCI and the sectoral regulators could meet on a regular basis through this forum with a view to promote policy-level coordination and make sectoral regulation as competition driven as possible. Unlike the FSDC, this coordination must be done at the technocratic level.

Formal schemes for coordination can also be considered, as is done in various countries. For example:

- the right to participate in/observe proceedings before the other;
- formal referrals;
- appeal to a common authority;
- non-interference in the other's jurisdiction;
- delineation of jurisdictions; and
- the presence of a competition authority on a sectoral regulator agency.

As a matter of policy, formal and informal exchanges between various sectoral regulators and the CCI should be encouraged. The consultation process could happen at two levels—one, at the policy level and two, with respect to individual cases.

Other mechanisms for coordination should also be explored, such as:

- using experts from each other for facilitating enquiry/investigations;
- exchanging personnel through deputations or internships;
- participating in each other's training programmes, workshops, seminars, etc.; and
- finally, the CCI should be conducting regular training programmes for representatives of the sectoral regulators so that they are in a better position to appreciate various competition issues.

Fourth, given the fact that significant privatization of CPSUs is underway, how will this alter the overall milieu for orderly competition? How does one promote the maximum realization of the embedded values? At the same time, how does one ensure that their sale or divestment does not distort broad principles of fair competition? How does one enhance data quality for exercising judicious functions? Data, its availability and dynamics, in terms of real-time data, must be an important tool for guiding pronouncements.

Fifth, apart from CPSUs, state governments should be encouraged to adopt a similar practice. Many state governments already have independent regulators in some key sectors, like power. How does one ensure uniformity in the application of the working of state-level regulators with not only the central regulator but also under the overarching coordinative role of the CCI?

Finally, we must press the reset button in the post-pandemic era. The interface between emerging technologies and harnessing technological possibilities has altered the way in which not only technology-based companies function but also has radically changed which of their applications will influence multiple spheres of economic activity. The role of technology in this reset button needs careful delineation. The CCI, which deals with technology companies, needs to be mindful of its broader implications to multiple facets of economic activity.

We undoubtedly need greater awareness and education on the role of independent regulators. Therein lies the importance of the CCI in being the overarching regulator. The CCI Act needs to be strengthened in this manner. It may not be appropriate to have an overarching regulator to override all sectoral business but what about new issues of competition that are coming into play? Who would be their final arbitrator?

As the government takes major steps towards disinvestment, giving a new impetus to privatization, the role of the CCI becomes more significant to ensure that these discussions enhance competition, economic efficiency and gains for all. The design of privatization should allow us optimum room for competition. Moreover, the strategic disinvestment programmes should be incentivized by the Centre to extend this reform to the myriad of state-owned public-sector enterprises to create the much-needed fiscal space.

The world is at the cusp of change, so is India and so is the CCI. After all, as former treasury secretary of the US, Henry Paulson said, 'Regulation needs to catch up with innovation.'

This chapter has been extracted from N.K. Singh's speech at the National Conference on Economics of Competition Law on 5 March 2021.

12

THE FISCAL CONUNDRUM

Promoting responsible growth

Common sense tells us that no one can live beyond their means in perpetuity. What is true of individuals is equally true of nations. Since one cannot spend one's way to prosperity, increasing the means for finance and optimizing expenditure responsibly is at the heart of all fiscal policies. There is also the question of intertemporal equity. It would be irresponsible to utilize all available resources in a manner that leaves little for our children. The former President of the US, Herbert Hoover, famously said, 'Blessed are the young for they shall inherit the national debt', which re-emphasizes intergenerational inequity. The need for adopting policies that maximize the virtues of macroeconomic stability, yet secure long-term economic growth to improve quality of life remains our guiding principle. The international debate on fiscal policies has evolved over time, and so has the optimum mix of fiscal approaches. There are, however, some settled issues that are worth reiterating.

Unbridled fiscal deficit leads to unsustainable levels of debt. This raises the question of debt sustainability and determining appropriate levels for it. Generally speaking, we need a prudent debt anchor that steers clear of what may be called a fiscal cliff. The anchor ties down the final role of policy and the expectations of economic agents adjusted accordingly. By acting as the constraint on policy discretion, an anchor disincentivizes inconsistencies. In a more technical sense,

> The standard government solvency constraint suggests using debt as the ultimate objective of fiscal policy. The solvency constraint implies that at some point a solvent government has to run primary surpluses; in technical terms, it is called a 'no-Ponzi condition', i.e. the present discounted value (PDV) of the terminal government debt should be equal to or less than zero.[102]

Of course, debt and fiscal deficits may not be mutually exclusive choices. Cross-country comparisons suggest that a fiscal rule must be comprehensive and a debt ceiling combined with fiscal deficit as the operational target jointly provide a robust fiscal framework.

There could be other approaches to determine sustainable levels of public debt with intertemporal budgetary constraints. All these imply that we must stay far away from a debt cliff or the concept of debt intolerance. Debt intolerance is a term introduced by Carmen Reinhart, Kenneth Rogoff and Miguel Savastano, which refers to levels of debt where emerging markets have difficulty in accessing capital markets. It can be explained by many variables, including the country's default

---

[102]FBRM Review Committee, 'FRBM Review Committee Report: Volume-I', Department of Economic Affairs, Government of India, January 2017, p. 50, https://bit.ly/3jP5qNI. Accessed on 18 April 2022.

and inflation history, and can be subjected to widely varying comparisons.[103]

Based on all the aforementioned approaches, while international debate on fiscal deficit has evolved, suffice it to say that the choice invariably implies a mix of five rules: debt rule, budget balance rule, structural budget balance rule, expenditure rule and revenue rule.[104] The consensus during a pandemic is clearly to seek contracyclical action; namely, to ameliorate the economic downturn, provide a stimulus to the recovery process and act in tandem with monetary policy to revive the growth momentum.

Evolution of Fiscal Policies

In the Indian context, the Constituent Assembly, while passing Articles 292 and 293 (adopted as Articles 268 and 269 during the discussion on the Draft Constitution), discussed the borrowing powers of the Centre and states at length. It is pertinent to note that many of the members were in favour of placing a limit on the borrowing powers of the executive government by Parliament.

Professor K.T. Shah, a Constituent Assembly member, in his speech while debating the issue, said,

---

[103]The issue of debt sustainability has been analytically examined in the FRBM Review Committee Report: Volume-I (pp. 50–51). Connected to this is the concept of growth theory, which assumes the existence and a fully functioning modern capitalist economy with entrepreneurs and investors who, through economic incentives, drive growth. This is expressed through the Harrod–Domar growth equation of $g= s/k$, where g is the total growth output, s is the savings ratio and k is the capital-output ratio.

[104]FBRM Review Committee, 'FRBM Review Committee Report: Volume-I,' Department of Economic Affairs, Government of India, January 2017, p. 36, https://bit.ly/3jP5qNI. Accessed on 18 April 2022.

> As I have said before, while I have always suggested that the supreme power should be vested in Parliament here is an instance in which, by the Constitution, I would limit the power even of Parliament to allow any borrowing within and much more so outside the country.[105]

In response to this, Dr Ambedkar said,

> This article specifically says that the borrowing power of the executive shall be subject to such limitations as Parliament may by law prescribe. If Parliament does not make a law, it is certainly the fault of Parliament and I should have thought it very difficult to imagine any future Parliament which will not pay sufficient or serious attention to this matter and enact a law. Under the article 268, I even concede that there might be an Annual Debt Act made by Parliament prescribing or limiting the power of the executive as to how much they can borrow within that year.[106]

This debate took place on 10 August 1949 and the Constitution was promulgated on 26 January 1950. For almost five decades, there was no law to limit the borrowings by the Centre and states.

Paradigm Shift

During the early years of economic policymaking, there was popular belief that a nascent, emerging market like India could not rely on the private sector. Hence, large public outlays, particularly on infrastructure, had to be financed from

[105]'Constituent Assembly Debates on 10 August, 1949 Part II', Indian Kanoon, https://bit.ly/3L6rMWG. Accessed on 23 March 2022.
[106]Ibid.

government borrowings or fiscal deficit. It was a predominant thought that such investment would create a virtuous cycle of having multiplier effects on growth and development in the long run. It was expected that this would also bring down fiscal deficit. Private capital, especially foreign capital, was highly regulated and, hence, limited. India's foreign exchange requirements were largely met from the capital flows of donor communities or multilateral institutions. This led to some BoP difficulties during this period. Frequent BoP crises and the consequent fiscal profligacy during the 1980s culminated in a paradigm shift in the economic policy in 1991.

In 1985, the Sukhamoy Chakravarty Committee presented a report on the 'Review of the Working of the Monetary System in India'. The report recommended that the fiscal deficit is a better and more accurate representation of the government's draft on credit available in the economy rather than uncovered deficit. Only six years later, fiscal deficit made its first appearance in the Economic Survey of 1990–91 under the shadow of the IMF's structural adjustment programme. Later, fiscal deficit made its way into the Union Budget of 1991–92. Figure 1 maps India's fiscal deficit over the last four decades.

In an increasingly interdependent world, India wanted to attract foreign and private capital for investment. Large foreign investors were looking at rating agencies to get a sense of India's macroeconomic stability. This prompted the observance of fiscal prudence and adherence to fiscal norms. It was realized that fiscal prudence could create space for private investment and deliver better quality of infrastructure for the country. However, this period of fiscal prudence did not last too long and fiscal consolidation started faltering again by 1997–98. At this point, the government acted with some alacrity and introduced the FRBM Bill in Parliament. This was enacted as the FRBM Act in 2003. This Act legally obligated the central government to reduce its fiscal deficit to 3 per cent and maintain it below that level over a period. After the central government enacted the FRBM Act, with incentives and nudges from the FC, such legislation was enacted in most states by 2007, placing a limit on the borrowings of the states.

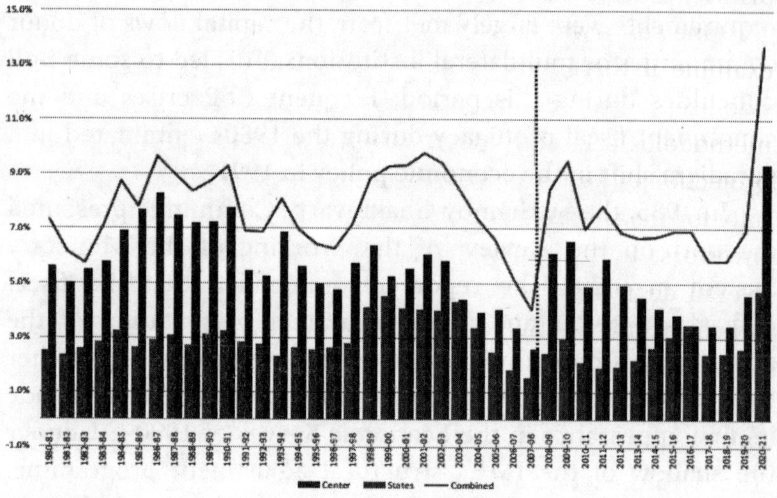

Figure 1: Fiscal deficit (per cent of the GDP) over the last four decades

Source: Reserve Bank of India database

For inexplicable reasons, notwithstanding the 1991 economic crisis, the first FRBM Act was not enacted until PM Vajpayee did so in 2003. The Act had a salutary effect on overall fiscal management. This effect was further reinforced by the acceptance of the 11th FC's recommendations enjoining the state governments to enact similar state-level legislations. Thereafter, as mentioned above, exogenous and other expenditure compulsions led to long periods of pause or inactivity of the FRBM legislations. It was not until the return of the National Democratic Alliance (NDA) government in 2014 that we, once again, refocused on the broader issues of macro stability and reactivated as well as made changes to the original FRBM Act through amendments to the 2018 Union Budget. My own experience with PM Modi suggests that under his leadership, conformity to the amended FRBM and its centrality in macroeconomic management received the priority it deserves.

One can always seek to recalibrate the fiscal regulations to examine if there can be greater flexibility through automatic stabilizers and contracyclical action, notwithstanding the methodological and other complexities in making such projections. These projections, of course, will need to be made not only for the central government but also for state governments. Investors, both domestic and foreign, invariably look to the overall debt and the fiscal picture of the general government, which includes both the central and state governments.

Consolidation in the Post-FRBM Era

The FRBM Act, 2003 provided a legal framework for fiscal consolidation of the central government finances for the first time. It mandated the following targets.

- Reduction of the fiscal deficit to 3 per cent of the GDP by 2008–09, with an annual reduction target of 0.3 per cent of the GDP per year by the central government.
- Revenue deficit reduction by 0.5 per cent of the GDP per year with a complete elimination of revenue deficit by 2008–09.
- Prohibition of borrowing by the government from the RBI, thereby making monetary policy independent of fiscal policy.
- Banning the RBI from purchasing the primary issues of the central government securities after 2006, preventing the monetization of the government deficit.

After the enactment of the FRBM Act, there was a clear improvement in the fiscal position of the government. The general government deficit declined from a peak of 9.6 per cent in the FY 2002 to 4 per cent in FY 2008. In fact, the central government deficit declined to 2.5 per cent of the GDP in FY 2008, a year before the 3 per cent deficit target was to be achieved. The debt to GDP ratio also declined during this period from 83 per cent in FY 2003 to 71 per cent in FY 2008.

Post the global financial crisis in 2008, many of the earlier gains in fiscal consolidation were eroded and fiscal deficit again started soaring high. It also impeded the credibility of the FRBM Act. FM Pranab Mukherjee, in his 2009–10 Budget speech, announced a return to the FRBM target for fiscal deficit at the earliest, as soon as the negative effects of the global crisis on the Indian economy were overcome. Thus, amid considerable uncertainty about returning to the FRBM Act road map, the deficit rules remained in abeyance for a period of five years. In the Budget speech of 2012–13, Mukherjee announced his intention to reoperationalize the FRBM Act and proposed several amendments to the Act in the Finance Bill, 2012. These included pushing the deadlines for numerical targets from 2009 to 2015 and introducing a new fiscal indicator, viz., the 'effective revenue deficit' (revenue deficit excluding grants for creating capital assets). However, he later postponed the deadlines for meeting the numerical targets from 2015 to 2018 to create fiscal space for public expenditure. During this period, while India performed well in terms of growth, inflation and current account management, its fiscal performance remained an outlier among its peers, as can be seen in Table 1 on the next page.

Under such circumstances, and because of changes in the external environment, a review of the FRBM Act became necessary.

Table 1: India's fiscal performance compared to other countries

Country	*Real GDP*			*Consumer price index (CPI)*			*Current account balance*			*Fiscal balance*		
	(per cent year over year)			*(per cent year over year)*			*(per cent of the GDP)*			*(per cent of the GDP)*		
	2012–14	*2015–17*	*2018–20*	*2012–14*	*2015–17*	*2018–20*	*2012–14*	*2015–17*	*2018–20*	*2012–14*	*2015–17*	*2018–20*
India	6.4	7.7	1.1	8.4	4.3	4.8	-2.6	-1.2	-0.7	-7.2	-6.9	-8.9
Brazil	1.8	-1.8	-0.3	6.0	7.1	3.5	-3.6	-1.8	-2.6	-3.8	-9.0	-8.8
China	7.7	6.9	5.0	2.4	1.7	2.5	2.1	2.0	0.9	-0.7	-3.4	-7.4
Indonesia	5.5	5.0	2.7	5.6	4.6	2.7	-3.0	-1.8	-2.0	-2.0	-2.5	-3.3
Russia	2.2	0.0	0.6	6.8	8.8	3.6	2.5	3.0	4.4	-0.6	-2.8	0.3
South Africa	2.1	1.0	-1.6	5.8	5.4	4.0	-4.9	-3.1	-1.3	-4.0	-4.0	-6.4
Turkey	6.1	5.6	1.9	8.4	8.9	14.6	-5.1	-3.7	-2.4	-1.6	-1.9	-4.9

Source: 'World Economic Outlook October 2021', International Monetary Fund, https://bit.ly/36w7hnG. Accessed on 12 April 2022.

Review and Recommendations

Since the FRBM Act was first enacted in 2003, India has seen significant changes both in its internal and external fiscal environment. India is increasingly being financially integrated in the world economy and foreign capital flows have significantly increased. India's trade as a percentage of its GDP has significantly increased during the last decade. Globally, thinking on fiscal rules has also changed. Most countries now have multiple rules and allow for higher fiscal space during exogenous shocks. Such rules are also being complemented by independent fiscal councils, escape clauses and automatic correction mechanisms in many countries.

Domestically, India has had many financial sector reforms like lowering the statutory liquidity ratio (SLR) for banks as well as including some part of the SLR in the liquidity coverage ratio (LCR) for better prudence under Basel-III norms. The Monetary Policy Committee (MPC) and the recent amendments to the RBI Act enjoin the RBI to secure a central target of 4 per cent inflation. Against this public and legislative commitment, a profligate fiscal policy would force the RBI to tighten the monetary policy to perhaps higher-than-optimal levels. This requires a rethink of how fiscal consolidation has been carried out so far as well.

In the Union Budget 2016–17, FM Arun Jaitley proposed to constitute a high-level committee to review the implementation of the FRBM Act and to give recommendations on the way forward. Elaborating on this point, the FM said,

> The FRBM Act has been under implementation for more than a decade. Both Central and State Governments have made significant gains from the implementation of this Act [...] While remaining committed to fiscal prudence and

> consolidation, a time has come to review the working of the FRBM Act, especially in the context of the uncertainty and volatility which have become the new norms of global economy. I, therefore, propose to constitute a committee to review the implementation of the FRBM Act and give its recommendations on the way forward.[107]

The FRBM Act Review Committee was constituted under my chairmanship in May 2016, with the following terms of reference (ToR):

- to review the working of the FRBM Act over the last 12 years (2004–16) and to suggest a way forward, keeping in view the broad objective of fiscal consolidation and prudence, and the changes required in the context of the uncertainty and volatility of the global economy;
- to look into various aspects, factors and considerations that go into determining the FRBM targets;
- to examine the need and feasibility of having a 'fiscal deficit range' as the fiscal deficit target in place of the existing fixed numbers (percentage of the GDP) for this target; and if we are to do so, providing the specific recommendations of the committee thereon; and
- to examine the need and feasibility of aligning the fiscal expansion or contraction with credit contraction or expansion, respectively, in the economy.

The committee, after extensive consultations and deliberations with all stakeholders, submitted its report to the government in January 2017. Following are its key recommendations for a legal framework on fiscal consolidation.

---

[107]'Union Budget 2016–17: Full Text of Arun Jaitley's Speech', *Mint*, 29 February 2016, https://bit.ly/3vccUzo. Accessed on 11 April 2022.

- Enact a new Debt and Fiscal Responsibility Act, and in pursuance of the new Act, enact and adopt the Debt and Fiscal Responsibility Rules, as per drafts suggested by the committee.
- Adopt a prudent medium-term ceiling of 60 per cent of the GDP for general government debt, to be achieved by no later than FY 2023.
- Within the overall ceiling specified above, adopt a ceiling of 40 per cent for the Centre, and the balance 20 per cent for the states.
- Adopt fiscal deficit as the key operational target consistent with achieving the medium-term debt ceiling.
- Adopt the path for debt-to-GDP ratio and fiscal deficit as well to be achieved by FY 2023.

Apart from these, the committee also recommended the inclusion of an escape clause in the law. The following triggers were recommended to activate the escape clause with a stipulated magnitude of deviation in the fiscal deficit target of 0.5 percentage points in a year.

- Overriding considerations of national security, acts of war, calamities of national proportion and collapse of agriculture severely affecting farm output and incomes.
- Far-reaching structural reforms in the economy with unanticipated fiscal implications.
- Sharp decline in real output growth of at least 3 percentage points below the average for the previous four quarters.

To symmetrically apply this response, the committee also recommended that if there is a sharp increase in the real output growth of at least 3 percentage points above the average for the previous four quarters, fiscal deficit must fall by at least 0.5 percentage points below the target.

Further recommendation on institutional reform included a proposal to create an autonomous Fiscal Council. The suggested roles of such a council would include:

- preparing multi-year fiscal forecasts;
- recommending changes to the fiscal strategy;
- improving the quality of fiscal data;
- advising the government if conditions exist to deviate from the fiscal target;
- advising the government to take corrective action for non-compliance with the Bill; and
- issuing detailed policy guidelines on the procedure for the central government's consent to state borrowings under Article 293 of the Constitution of India, as a proactive guidance to the state governments.

Debt as an Anchor

A transparent and predictable policy framework is rule-based. The concept of an anchor is central to a credible framework. As the committee observed in its report,

> An anchor ties down the final goal of policy, and the expectations of economic agents adjust accordingly. By acting as a constraint on policy discretion, an anchor dis-incentivizes time inconsistency, including due to pressures from interest groups. There are four key economic arguments that form the basis for moving to debt. First, the standard government solvency constraint suggests debt to be the ultimate objective of fiscal policy. Second, there was broad consensus that a debt ceiling combined with fiscal deficit as an operational target can jointly provide a robust fiscal framework for India.

> Third, India, with a public debt close to 70 per cent of GDP, currently stands out as among the most indebted countries in the relevant peer group of emerging markets. Finally, public debt exemplifies an important factor in the assessments of rating agencies. In addition to these economic arguments, a non-economic, albeit powerful and convincing rationale for moving to debt as the anchor put forth by several members of the committee and considered to be particularly relevant in the Indian ethos, was that 'debt', and 'debt repayments' are concepts that can be communicated easily to the public and are also embedded in the psyche of the ordinary citizen.[108]

Several approaches can be employed to determine an appropriate or prudent debt ceiling for India. For example, a debt threshold can be calibrated by estimating the level of debt to the GDP at which debt has a negative effect on economic growth. A second approach could be on the concept of 'debt intolerance', which refers to the levels of debt at which emerging markets have difficulty accessing capital markets. Based on this approach, the maximum threshold that will keep India from dropping to a more debt intolerant club was estimated by the committee. Although every approach has limitations, taken together with cross-country evidence and assessment methodology of rating agencies, the committee suggested a ceiling of around 60 per cent of the GDP for the general government debt in India. A 60 per cent of the GDP debt ceiling would still be above the average for emerging markets, but it would provide sufficient space for greater private investment and higher growth, offer a sufficient buffer

---

[108]FBRM Review Committee, 'FRBM Review Committee Report: Volume-I (p. 50)', Department of Economic Affairs, Government of India, January 2017, https://bit.ly/3jP5qNI. Accessed on 18 April 2022.

when the country is subject to macro and fiscal shocks, make available some headroom for future contingent liabilities and would also be a level of debt that is sustainable under plausible assumptions on primary balances and interest-growth differentials. The committee's analysis also suggests a ceiling of around 40 per cent for the central government debt. This was based on multiple rounds of modelling to determine an appropriate level beyond which additional borrowing would crowd-out space for productive investment and social spending, and have an adverse effect on economic growth. The committee considered the balance of 20 per cent of the GDP as a prudent ceiling for the states.

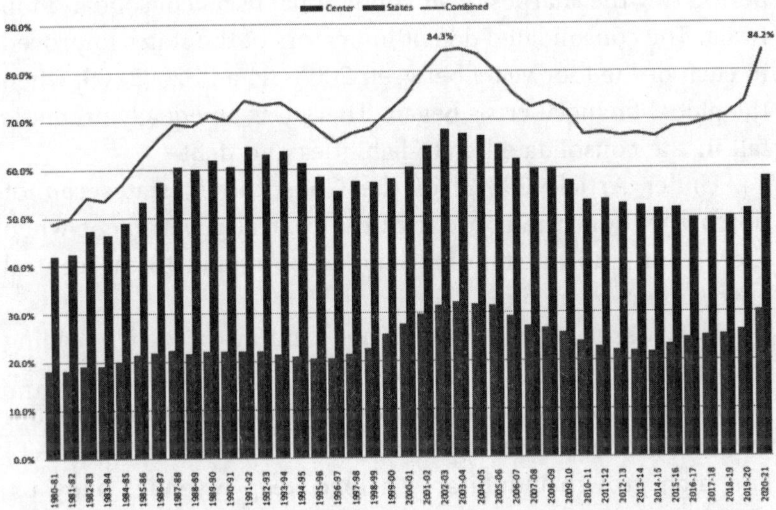

Figure 2: Debt (per cent of the GDP) over the last four decades

Source: Reserve Bank of India database

The report of the committee was accepted by the Union Government in its Budget and the amended FRBM Act came into force from 1 April 2018.

Subnational Finances

Subnational governments, in India as well as in the world, have been entrusted with greater responsibilities towards the delivery of public goods and services and these responsibilities are further increasing. This requires significant higher public investment and financing. Hence, it has become imperative to analyse the borrowing patterns of states vis-à-vis their repayment capacities.

After the enactment of the central FRBM Act in 2003 and with a push from the 12th FC, states also enacted their respective Fiscal Responsibility Legislation (FRL) in the following years. By 2008–09, most states had their FRL in place. The post-FRL period saw the sharpest ever subnational fiscal consolidation in India. The consolidated deficit indicators of the states improved in each of the four years between 2003–04 and 2008–09, when the global financial crisis began. There was an equally dramatic fall in the consolidated state liabilities and debt.

Under Article 293(3) of the Constitution, states cannot borrow without the consent of the central government when there is still an outstanding loan to be repaid to the central government by a state.

It is observed that the 3 per cent fiscal deficit ceiling and the target of zero revenue deficit were complied with an account of buoyant revenues as well as active expenditure control. While the introduction of the value-added tax (VAT) and high growth indubitably helped keep revenues buoyant, the fact that revenue buoyancy was seen across rich and poor states indicates that there was a collective effort to achieve revenue targets to facilitate FRL compliance. It was also observed that the state governments did not fully utilize their higher revenues to increase expenditures in good times, a course of action that is politically very attractive. State-specific characteristics, such as the level of per-capita income, the size of the state government and the level of state's own revenue, do not have a significant impact on debt and deficit control by individual states. In fact, evidence shows that following the execution of the state FRLs, the correlation between fiscal performance and state-specific characteristics has reduced sharply; poor and rich states are equally fiscally prudent.

It has also been pointed out by successive FCs and successive reports of the Comptroller and Auditor General (CAG) of India that while FRLs have been complied with, states have moved to less transparent means of financing their expenditure through off-budget borrowings. Hence, some individual states' finances do remain a concern.

As there is significant heterogeneity in debt levels and fiscal consolidation of the states, and their aggregate public debt depends on actions taken by individual states, it is important to draw a debt consolidation path for all states individually by distributing aggregate targets in inter se manner. This task can be better handled by the FC, as it deals with individual state finances in a detailed manner.

Fiscal Architecture in Contemporary Times

The fiscal architecture of any economy in the twenty-first century inevitably rests on three pillars: fiscal rules, financial management process and fiscal institutions. The first phase covered these rules by stipulating norms relating to fiscal deficit targets, consistent with macroeconomic stability.

In the second phase, we recognized that fiscal management must be guided by principles of equity, efficiency and transparency. These rules must be applied to all levels of government, including the subnational levels and budgetary institutions as well as management practices. The question of raising the quality and efficiency of public spending remains a continuing challenge. Equally, the availability of credible data across levels of government remains elusive. The classic questions of raising the quality and efficiency of public spending is a continuing challenge. The strain on public finances during the Covid-19 crisis especially highlights the importance of reprioritizing expenditure. How quickly expenditures are reprioritized for financing health, skill inculcation and infrastructure accentuates the importance of ensuring public financial management policies. These policies encompass processes and systems.

The second-generation fiscal rules have increasingly recognized the need to adopt more than one fiscal rule to balance competing options and enhance credibility. The need to create a fiscal anchor, the challenge of having multiple rules and the inconsistencies in seeking to monitor, verify and communicate remain problematic. Fiscal data on all the contingent liabilities incurred by the sovereign, subnational and parastatals, and recourse to off-budget borrowing are also problematic. These issues distract from the credibility of debt numbers. The second-generation fiscal rules typically rely on escape clauses or equivalent mechanisms in using structural deficiencies to create flexibility. Countries very often adopt automatic correction mechanisms, which also need to specify in advance how deviations from the general rule must be handled. This inevitably implies the need for medium-term fiscal policies to be adopted with multiple fiscal indicators. Moreover, having public debt as a principal macroeconomic anchor is widely accepted.

However, several questions remain unanswered. What levels of public debt would be acceptable based on conditions that are country-specific and have been worked out in accordance with international benchmarking? The Reinhart–Rogoff suggestion of external debt becoming a problem at around 60 per cent of the GDP and growth turning negative at 90 per cent of the GDP[109] must be interpreted in a broader context. The differentiated nature of various economies will need country-specific models, keeping in view the need to avoid the debt cliff. Countries with significantly higher per capita incomes have significantly higher debt levels without compromising their long-term macroeconomic stability.

Budget 2022–23: Recalibrating the Fiscal Road Map

Budget 2022–23 was presented during the stressful period of an ongoing pandemic. The contours of this somewhat recalibrated fiscal road map have been outlined in Table 2 below.

Table 2: Medium-Term Fiscal Policy cum Strategy Statement

	Revised estimates (in percentages)	*Budget estimates (in percentages)*
	2021–22	*2022–23*
Fiscal deficit	6.9	6.4
Revenue deficit	4.7	3.8
Primary deficit	3.3	2.8
Tax revenue (gross)	10.8	10.7
Non-tax revenue	1.4	1.0
Central government debt	59.9	60.2

Source: Sitharaman, Nirmala, 'Statements of Fiscal Policy as required under the Fiscal Responsibility and Budget Management Act, 2003', Ministry of Finance, Budget Division, February 2022, https://bit.ly/3OQFpf8. Accessed on 11 May 2022.

---

[109] Reinhart, Carmen M. and Kenneth S. Rogoff, 'Growth in a Time of Debt', *American Economic Review: Papers & Proceedings*, Vol. 100, No. 2, May 2010, pp. 573–78, https://bit.ly/37iGADk. Accessed on 11 May 2022.

The fiscal deficit for 2021–22 will likely adhere to the budget estimates with a nominal difference of 0.1 per cent, ending at 6.9 per cent rather than 6.8 per cent. In the following year, the fiscal consolidation of 0.5 per cent of the GDP is inconsequential given other stressors and uncertainties. The fiscal trajectory of achieving 4.5 per cent by 2024–25 has remained unchanged, even though the path and strategy for realizing this target have not been articulated. Apart from fiscal deficit itself, a debt of 90 per cent would prove stubborn and the best-expected outcome can only be a change in the directions by the terminal year 2024–25. A dramatic reduction in debt target, considering its stock, is not feasible.

A positive factor, however, is continued revenue buoyancy. To some extent, apart from the performance in the current year, a further improvement on tax buoyancy, currently at a modest 1 of 1.4 per cent assumed in the Budget, coupled with further tax reforms both on the GST and direct taxes, will make a substantial difference in creating greater fiscal space. A strategy for retiring public debt over the medium-term during periods of continued tax buoyancy would be a worthwhile strategy to pursue. Fortunately, the debt being largely domestic rather than foreign and our comfortable external reserves, mitigate the possibility of reaching anywhere near a debt cliff and tantrums connected with sustainable debt management, notwithstanding the sharp reduction in the imported energy price. Over the medium-term, a more articulate debt strategy would be central to continued investor confidence, both in domestic and foreign macroeconomic policy.

Challenges in a Post-Pandemic World

In the context of the pandemic, we need to focus not on fiscal rectitude but on fiscal forbearance. Fiscal norms designed for normal times are not appropriate in distressed times like these. The last major global pandemic happened 102 years ago, long before the UN and other sister agencies of the Bretton Woods family, namely the World Bank and IMF, were established. The multilateral institutions are, thus, confronting the challenges of a pandemic of this nature for the first time. There are no past precedents for such an event, and we need to address the present complexities. The first challenge for these institutions is how to determine fair, appropriate and consistent norms of fiscal forbearance that address the health emergency, build economic recovery, accept the fiscal shock and address its nature, and reform the international debt architecture.

The uncertain nature of the pandemic is a continuing challenge for finance ministers globally. For instance, a classic question is: what should be the appropriate levels of fiscal stimulus? And in determining fiscal stimulus, should we occupy the fiscal space fully, given the fact that we cannot predict the nature of the pandemic?

The next issue is connected with the balance between actions of the sovereign government and the activities of the central bankers. Seeking synchronization between the policies of the sovereign and the central bankers is critical to address the ongoing pandemic. This is true, not only for the non-banking financial sectors, like the cooperative sector but also for private corporate entities. Such entities that are seeking a restructuring of the debt process would need the advice and guidance of central bankers. There are no hard and fast rules to address these. Evolving norms on some of these issues will remain a continuing challenge.

While it is necessary, and perhaps easier, to argue in favour of fiscal forbearance—and taking recourse to escape clauses or such flexibilities that these norms prescribe—it is equally important to get back on track as soon as the pandemic is under control. Fiscal forbearance must be followed by fiscal rectitude. The path to this shift must be central to these norms. It is easier to exit than to re-enter. At what point will nations determine that the pandemic has started waning and we need to reconfigure the contours of macroeconomic stability?

In the Indian context, the focus is on the optimum mix between monetary and fiscal policies. As inflation rises globally, monetary authorities will inevitably need to review their strategies. A northward direction from the more accommodative interest regime appears inescapable, and yet, there is evidence that, given the uncertainty of the pandemic, the recovery process, particularly in the service sector, remains uncertain. The absence of credible data in relation to the informal sector is a continuing challenge. While this is scarcely a time for deep fiscal consolidation, fiscal policies must inevitably assist the recovery process. A differentiation in the expenditure pattern, namely to incentivize capital expenditure rather than revenue expenditure, has multipliers in terms of employment, output, demand creation and capacity utilization.

Clearly, investment in infrastructure through multiple initiatives, like the National Infrastructure Pipeline project and enhanced outlays for roads, highways, airports and ports, are a no-brainer. However, given the needs and lags, the needs of the micro, small and the informal sector must be addressed. The distress of the informal sector cannot be overstressed. The service sector, or in a more limited sense, the contact-based patterns of activity, including retail outlets, micro, self-employed activity, travel and hospitality, have suffered enormous economic hardship. Putting resources directly in their hands along with continuing support to the PDS or rural employment have to proceed alongside the support of capital expenditure with high growth multipliers. Those who advocate the need for contracyclical fiscal action have to reckon with the difficulties of determining parts of the cycle, measuring output gaps, their geographical and spatial distribution and designing a framework which does not contribute to inflationary trends. The contracyclical action and automatic stabilizers embedded in the escape clause of the fiscal policy have been understandably already resorted to. The issue is whether the magnitude of these interventions is adequate to sustain the recovery process.

In this endeavour, one cannot be unmindful of the rising debt stock. The FRBM Act adopted by the central government in 2003 as well as by the state governments much later stipulated that fiscal deficits should not exceed 3 per cent of the GDP; adding them together resulted in a desirable split of 6 per cent. In a certain sense, if this split of 6 per cent equally between the Centre and the states had been based on the savings of the informal sector and the tolerable current account deficits of 1.5 per cent of the GDP, the debt profile would have looked vastly different than what it is today. This assumes that, at that time, the desirable sustainable debt level of 60 per cent over a medium-term, disaggregated as 40 per cent for the central government and 20 per cent for the state government, seemed like an optimum arrangement. All norms of managing fiscal deficit were calibrated on this assumption. Since then, as the report of the 15th FC recognized, we have developed a more realistic debt and fiscal trajectory, as illustrated in Figure 3.[110]

---

[110]'Finance Commission in COVID times: Report for 2021–2026,' Finance Commission India, October 2020, p. 11, https://bit.ly/3jPhMVZ. Accessed on 19 April 2022.

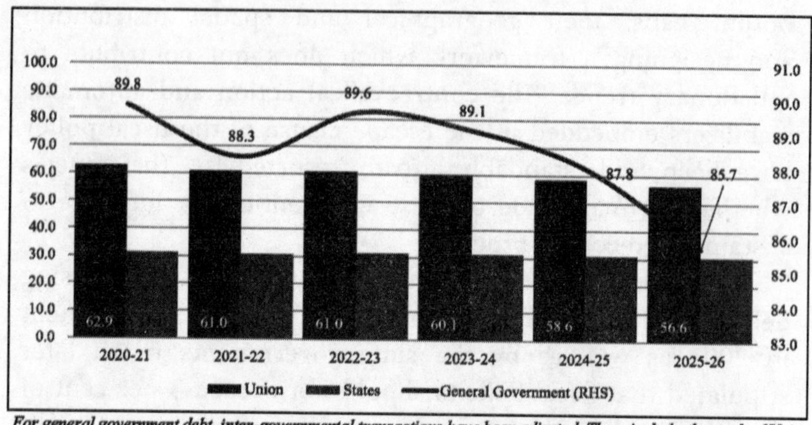

For general government debt, inter-governmental transactions have been adjusted. These include the stock of Union Government loans to the States, the stock of NSSF securities and Treasury Bills held by the State Governments.

Figure 3: Recalibrated debt and fiscal projections

Source: Finance Commission in COVID times: Report for 2021–2026

Even this somewhat more realistic recalibration from the 15th FC report looks misaligned with the current realities. If by a conservative estimate, current debt to GDP ratio is around 85 per cent, getting it back to 60 per cent, from where it all began, will be a daunting challenge, as will recalibrating the break-up of the debt plan between the Centre and the states. No doubt, one must recognize the enormous gains that greater transparency and data credibility have brought in favour of our reputation for responsible growth. Taking and assimilating all contingent liabilities fully into our accounting process has demonstrated that the earlier figures were a total suppression of the actual debt, and credit rating agencies have realized this throughout.

We need a new National Debt Plan that is applicable both to the Centre and the states. Differentiating between national and subnational entities would be generic in this process. Recalibrating fiscal deficit to this revised debt plan needs both partnership and, more importantly, concerted action. Initiating credible action will enhance the confidence of investors. From this point of view, some of the suggestions made in the 15th FC report for an intergovernmental group embracing both the Centre and the states, deserve further consideration. Any concerted plan must also be cognizant of the new challenges in terms of uncertainties of the emerging geopolitical scenario, behaviour of oil prices, policies of monetary authorities globally and trade frictions between large economies. A new legal framework on debt and fiscal consolidation must be designed to address these challenges.

Connected with these challenges are some other issues, which have been detailed below.

First, the need for credible fiscal institutions. The case for an independent fiscal council acting in an advisory capacity has been in the public domain for a long time. Successive FCs have reiterated their recommendations that now over 80 countries, including emerging markets, have adopted fiscal councils in one form or the other. The IMF, in a study on fiscal councils, suggested that these councils may:

- contribute to the use of unbiased macroeconomic and budgetary forecasts in budget preparation (through preparing forecasts or proposing prudent levels for key parameters);
- identify sensible fiscal policy options, and possibly, formulate recommendations;
- facilitate the implementation of fiscal policy rules; and
- cost new policy initiatives.[111]

Second, and connected with the fiscal council, is the issue of compliance and endorsements. Clearly, unlike

[111]'The Functions and Impact of Fiscal Councils: Executive Summary', International Monetary Fund, 16 July 2013, https://bit.ly/3sKI80a. Accessed on 19 May 2022.

many countries, the sovereign cannot be bound down by any legislative requirement, particularly if Parliament endorses these actions. This would be equally true of state governments seeking the approval of the state legislatures. Nonetheless, the issue has arisen whether this latitude and flexibility offers adequate protection against irresponsible populism. The continuing cycle of elections offers enormous opportunities for varied political parties to make promises, which, by any stretch, are financially irresponsible. If elected to power, they are obligated to implement these commitments with far-reaching, irreparable damages to the finances of the state. Mitigating the impact of irresponsible populist action would be integral to any compliance process. In the 15th FC report, three compelling arguments have been outlined in this regard:

- to bridge the gap between the high-level public financial management framework in the Constitution and the detailed guidelines, rules, regulations and manuals and, thereby, codify the principles and processes, while providing them statutory strength;
- to enable a review and rationalization of the existing rules and regulations, some of which date back to the pre-Independence era and make them internally consistent between the Union and the states;
- to build a more resilient public finance framework with the capacity to better manage and mitigate future shocks.[112]

There are a few other issues in India's fiscal policies that have assumed contemporary relevance.

[112]'Finance Commission in COVID times: Report for 2021–2026', Finance Commission India, October 2020, p. 392, https://bit.ly/3jPhMVZ. Accessed on 19 April 2022.

The first issue is the relentless electoral cycle. While the central government is elected for a term of five years, its focus on governance is constantly interrupted by unabated state elections. Each state election entices governments towards populist measures, known as 'freebie promises', in common parlance. This has become particularly endemic in recent times, where more and more freebies are being offered to influence the electoral psyche. There are serious financial consequences of fulfilling these promises in case political parties who made these commitments are voted to power. The tendency to demand large sums of money from the central government are embedded in those promises, which compound the challenges.

There is no mechanism for the central government, except in times of emergency like pandemics, natural disasters and urgent relief, to transfer large resources to the consolidated funds of state governments. The transfer mechanism to states is primarily governed by successive FCs. This system inadequately considers constitutional and legal provisions. Furthermore, FCs invariably make their recommendations on the percentage of devolution to states based on intensive analysis, interactions and what is formulaic and normative. In addition to the direct transfers from the divisible pool, recommendations made under Article 275, by way of revenue deficit grants, are also based on a normative approach but these outgoes are charged to the Consolidated Fund of India. Being grants, they can be performance-based or conditional. At any rate, the revenue deficit grants are outgoes based on norms of acceptable behaviour, which will enable, based on expenditure and revenue buoyancy, the states to not be in deficit at the end of the award period. The politics of freebies trumps the norms of such responsible behaviour.

Unfortunately, there is no recourse mechanism to ensure the availability of these resources to be calibrated during the award period. The logic of this would suggest that there may be some advantages in making annual recommendations rather than making them for a full five-year period. Of course, it is only legitimate that states would expect similar norms to be followed by the central government as well. Annual devolutions create uncertainties and unpredictability. The mechanism for reconciling predictability with responsible behaviour based on electoral promises is an area that deserves greater debate and consensus.

Second, is the issue of financial mismanagement by the states, which raises issues of overall stability and solvency. This leads to the question: should there be constitutional provisions to define the parameters of what is described as subnational bankruptcy among federal entities? The recourse to Article 293(3) by the central government is designed to regulate the borrowings of state governments and is necessary to secure the prior approval of the central government. Notwithstanding this, state governments have often resorted to what was characteristically known as accommodation by way of overdrafts for very limited periods. The issue of subnational bankruptcies and its implications for the rating of the central government or the sovereign rating needs wider debate.

The third issue is with the mechanisms that would allow the voice of the market, so to say, to be permeated and appreciated by subnational and parastatal entities. How can markets recognize and differentiate the cost of borrowings by states between those whose finances are better managed than others with fiscal profligacy? As long as there is an implicit sovereign guarantee, any such mechanism is unlikely to be meaningful. At any rate, the FC recommends that all state governments should have a fiscal or debt management cell. This cell, coupled with the obligation for getting a credit rating to enable market differentiation, would encourage prudent behaviour among state governments.

Last but not the least, parliamentary awareness and

understanding on fiscal issues remain somewhat rudimentary. I had, in my autobiography *Portraits of Power*, lamented the absence of parliamentary scrutiny in the working of our overall strategy. Fiscal issues are an integral part of overall macroeconomic management. Parliament, in taking up the Finance Bill, has rarely debated the issue of compliance with the FRBM targets and their rationale for significant deviations. Creating mechanisms for greater parliamentary engagement in economic issues would improve the quality of parliamentary debates on them. Holding the executive more meaningfully responsible for deviations from the macroeconomic trajectory contained in the legislations would fortify investor confidence.

Mahatma Gandhi said, 'Economics that hurts the moral well-being of an individual or a nation are immoral and therefore sinful.' Rising expenditure financed through unsustainable borrowings and high public indebtedness hurts the moral well-being of a nation. This is why responsible growth must be an obligation and necessity for us.

This chapter has been extracted from N.K. Singh's keynote address to the Commonwealth Finance Ministers Meeting 2020[113] *and N.K. Singh and P.K. Mishra's presentation at the 14th Annual Meeting of the OECD Network on Fiscal Relations Across Levels of Government, 19–20 November 2018.*[114]

---

[113]'Securing Fiscal Sustainability: Options for Navigating Covid-19 Crisis: Norms for Fiscal Forbearance | N.K. Singh's Keynote Address to Commonwealth Finance Ministers', Press Information Bureau, Government of India, https://bit.ly/3vLeeuW. Accessed on 11 May 2022.

[114]'Fiscal Matrix – The Indian Experience', SlideShare, https://bit.ly/3N2iqMw. Accessed on 11 May 2022.

13

THE FINANCE COMMISSION

Continuity and stability over seven decades

The FC is integral to our Constitution. It has often been described as the balancing wheel in the matrix of fiscal federalism. The FC irons out the asymmetries in the amount of resources to be left out of the divisible pool to assign to the Union and the states. It harmonizes the resources between the states and, overall, fosters higher growth rates while seeking convergence in varied growth patterns. It also sets the norms regarding, and seeks symmetry in, the estimates of the states' expenditure outlays during the period of the FC's awards, along with the revenue buoyancy to determine the need for revenue deficit grants. Similarly, for the central government, the FC looks into its own permitted expenditure liabilities on the capital and revenue account, as well as the likely revenue buoyancy. Based on the total divisible resources, the FC determines the percentage of the divisible revenue that should be assigned to the states and, by implication, the amount which would be available to the central government. In a broader sense, the FC has represented continuity and stability for over 75 years. It has often been described as, and earned the title of, a 'Legacy of Trust'. Is there a need to reinvent the FC and make it more purposive to address emerging and contemporary challenges?

Evolution of the Finance Commission

The concept of the FC is embedded in the constitutional history of this country. In a sense, it is even older than our Constitution. Thus, it is important to understand its evolution from the pre-Independence period.

Pre-Independence

Government of India Act, 1919

Fiscal federalism in India is embedded in the Government of India Acts of 1919 and 1935. The Act of 1919 was the result of the Montagu–Chelmsford Report, 1918. As a step towards autonomy, the earlier classifications specifying an ambiguous separation between the revenue of the Centre and the provinces were abolished. This Act made the provincial heads responsible for the fundamental functions of government, the enforcement of law and order and administrative duties. The Act allowed the provinces considerable autonomy in financial matters. They were, for instance, given the power to float loans in India and abroad against the security of their revenues. The Act was seen as a halfway house between control and autonomy, as the provinces were able to withdraw from the same public account and any overdrawn amount was to be reimbursed before the end of a financial year.

Government of India Act, 1935

It is broadly agreed that the FC is rooted in the Government of India Act, 1935. This Act embodied the basic principles of federalism by allowing the Centre's revenues to be shared with the provinces. This was the British Indian government's first attempt at federalism for the Indian subcontinent, which was, till then, divided into British-ruled areas and fiscally independent princely states. For the provinces to share the Centre's revenues and receive grants, the Act mandated that federating states would have to surrender their right to levy certain taxes, such as income tax, excise duties, export duties and duties on salt. Their powers and functions were divided into three lists: the Federal List, the State/Provincial List and the Concurrent List, akin to the current Seventh Schedule of the Constitution. Through the Act, provincial governments obtained their resources as direct grants from the Crown. This Act was the foundation for the provisions of fiscal federalism in the Constitution of 1950.

On vertical and horizontal devolution, the Act of 1935 did not prescribe the exact ratios but had left this up to the His Majesty in Council, who formed the federal government in its absolute discretion. The Act did not provide for an institutional mechanism, such as the FC, for the discretionary aspects of the transfers. However, the British Indian government appointed a one-man committee under Sir Otto Niemeyer to make recommendations on the aforementioned discretionary parts of the fiscal transfers. The Niemeyer Committee made recommendations to the government under Sections 138(1) and (2) (relating to income taxes), 140(2) (relating to the net proceeds of jute export duty) and 142 (relating to the grants-in-aid) in the 1935 Act, subject to the approval of both Houses of Parliament. Finally, the Niemeyer Report, which was officially titled the Indian Financial Enquiry Report, made 69 recommendations regarding horizontal and vertical devolutions, which prevailed from 1936 to the period of Independence in 1947.

The Niemeyer Committee concluded that the net proceeds

of income tax to be shared with the provinces should be 50 per cent. However, Niemeyer put a rider to the effect that after the first five years of the award being operational, the share of the provinces would be reduced by amounts that would make the central government's share in the divisible pool of ₹13 crore. This rider was permissible under Section 138(2) of the 1935 Act. As a result, the actual transfers to the provinces remained far less than 50 per cent, which Niemeyer justified on the ground of 'financial stability and credit of India as a whole being of paramount consideration'[115], for which it was essential to maintain the solvency of the central government.

On the horizontal sharing of the proceeds of income tax among the provinces, Niemeyer used two criteria: the population and the realized source of collection for some reference year. Regarding the weightages, he did not indicate any relative statistical data but rather used his own discretion in the matter.[116]

The ToR of the Niemeyer Report sought to address the issue of the 1935 Act in Section 142,

> Such sums as may be prescribed by His Majesty in Council shall be charged on the revenues of the Federation in each year as grants in aid of revenues of such provinces as His Majesty may determine to be in need of assistance, and different sums may be prescribed for different provinces.[117]

The Constitution of India contains a similar provision. These two sources would eventually become the blueprints for the ToR of the FC post-Independence.

---

[115]Niemeyer, Otto, 'Indian Financial Enquiry Report', DSpace Repository, https://bit.ly/3MAAtJm, Accessed on 27 April 2022.
[116]Ibid.
[117]Ibid.

During the period of Independence, the recommendation of the Niemeyer Award, under which 50 per cent net proceeds of income tax went to the states, remained in vogue. In fact, the 1935 Act continued to be operational until the Constitution of 1950 repealed its provisions under Article 395. Under the 1935 Act, it was permissible to share the proceeds of the Union excise duties. However, the Government of India decided not to extend these shares to the provinces/states. Regarding the inter se share of the divisible pool, the government took an executive decision to the shares attributed to the divided Punjab and Bengal, which had become part of the newly formed Pakistan. Thus, the provincial shares were revised under the Indian States Finances Enquiry Committee 1948–49, set up in October 1948, with V.T. Krishnamachari as the chairman. The Committee's primary focus was on Part B States[118] and Baroda's merger with Bombay.[119]

Constituent Assembly Debates

The financial provisions in the Draft Constitution were referred by the Constituent Assembly to an Expert Committee under the chairmanship of Nalini Ranjan Sarkar, with V.S. Sundaram

---

[118]Part A States were the former Governors' provinces of British India, comprising Assam, Bihar, Bombay, Madhya Pradesh, Madras, Orissa, Punjab, Uttar Pradesh and West Bengal.

Part B States were former princely states or groups of princely states, comprising Hyderabad, Jammu and Kashmir, Madhya Bharat, Mysore, Patiala and East Punjab States Union (PEPSU), Rajasthan, Saurashtra and Travancore–Cochin.

Part C States were the former Chief Commissioners' provinces and some princely states, comprising Ajmer, Bhopal, Bilaspur, Coorg, Delhi, Himachal Pradesh, Cutch, Manipur, Tripura and Vindhya Pradesh.

The sole Part D territory was the Andaman and Nicobar Islands, administered by a Lieutenant Governor.

[119]'Chapter II: Evolution of Financial Relations between the Centre and the States', Report of the First Finance Commission 1952', Finance Commission India, https://bit.ly/3EQxBFL. Accessed on 28 April 2022.

and M.V. Rangachari as members. The N.R. Sarkar Committee recommended a pattern of division of tax sources between the Union and states that was broadly adopted in the Constitution. Customs and excise duties were to be retained by the Union, while income tax was to be shared. The Committee recommended the sharing of corporation tax with the states, whereby 20 per cent, 35 per cent and 5 per cent of the proceeds would be distributed on the basis of population, collections and an adjusting factor, respectively. After detailed discussions in the Constituent Assembly, the provisions currently in the Constitution were accepted.

As the FC could be set up only after the Constitution came into force on 26 January 1950, the states' share of the income tax and its distribution and the payment of grants-in-aid under Articles 273 and 275 of the Constitution had to be regulated by a presidential order for the period between the commencement of the Constitution and the appointment of an FC. Some states were dissatisfied with the way the government arranged for the allocation of income tax and jute export duty immediately after Partition. Further, the debates of the Constituent Assembly were replete with instances of differences and divergence of opinions on the modalities for the sharing of the resources between the Union and the states. Hence, it was decided that these matters should be referred to an impartial authority for reconsideration. It is in this context that, in 1949, an interim FC was appointed under the chairmanship of C.D. Deshmukh to consider the distribution of resources between the Union and the states. The Deshmukh Award came into effect from 1 April 1950 and remained in force for two years, ending on 31 March 1952.

Thereafter, the First FC was constituted by a presidential order dated 22 November 1951 with K.C. Neogy as its chairman. There have been 15 FCs ever since. The constitution of the FC is governed by Article 280 of the Constitution, which spells out, in conjunction with other provisions, the manner and modality for the management of the finances of the Union and the states as well as the principles for governing the divisible resources.

There were some debates in the Constituent Assembly regarding income tax which are relevant today, a few of which I shall mention below.

Article 251 of the Draft Constitution corresponds to Article 270 of the Constitution of India. This was discussed in the Constituent Assembly on 5 August 1949. A number of amendments were proposed, but only some of them were moved. The main speakers who participated in the debate on Article 251 were Upendranath Barman, Shibban Lal Saxena, Biswanath Das and H.N. Kunzru.

Barman, in his amendment, proposed the following:

- Union emoluments should not be excluded from the computation of the tax on income, as the Expert Committee has suggested.
- The share of the provinces should be fixed in the Constitution itself. He proposed a share of 60 per cent.
- As for the distribution of income tax among the provinces, a fixed minimum percentage should be assured for each province and the balance should be left to the Committee.[120]

Saxena's main point was that the phrase 'prescribed by the President by Order' mentioned in the Draft Article should be substituted by 'prescribed by Parliament by Law'. He was not comfortable with the fact that 'such wide powers of distribution of hundreds of crores of rupees between the Provinces and the Centre should be vested in the President.'[121]

---

[120]'Constituent Assembly of India Debates (Proceedings) - Volume IX', Parliament of India: Lok Sabha, 5 August 1949, https://bit.ly/3MzmDHb. Accessed on 28 April 2022.

[121]Ibid.

Das vehemently objected to collection being a major criterion for the distribution of income tax among the provinces, as Niemeyer had recommended in the Niemeyer Award. The Expert Committee had recommended that the share of the provinces be raised to 60 per cent, but Das was of the opinion that the Committee should have given even more. He felt that this did not do justice to the underdeveloped provinces. Subsequently, Das cited the recommendations of the B.N. Adarkar–B.K. Nehru Committee (set up to study the financial relation in Australia and its applicability to India) that population and collection be the criteria for the distribution of income tax among the provinces, with collection having the lowest weight.[122]

Kunzru made a spirited defence of the Draft Article. He argued that Burman's proposal could not be accepted because the financial position of the Union had deteriorated since December 1947, when the Expert Committee had submitted its report recommending the provincial share at 60 per cent. He suggested that the fiscal relations between the Union and the provinces could be reconsidered if the financial position of the provinces improved and that this was one of the purposes of the proposed FC. As for distribution among the provinces, the basis of collection could not, according to him, be accepted as a sound one.[123]

While concluding the debate, Dr Ambedkar said that he could not accept either of the amendments moved by Burman and Saxena,

> This question whether the percentage of revenue collected by way of income tax should be prescribed in the Constitution itself either as 60 per cent of any other

[122]Ibid.

[123]Ibid.

> percentage or should be left to the President to decide is a matter over which considerable thought has been bestowed both by the Central Government as well as the provincial Governments in the Conference which took place the other day to discuss this matter. It was agreed that the best thing would be to leave the matter to be prescribed by the President and our scheme is to allow the President and that no proportion should be fixed in the Constitution itself [...] Our scheme is to allow the President to prescribe the proportion in the first instance by himself and in the second instance after consideration of the recommendations of the Finance Commission. We do not propose to bring the Parliament in [...] to leave the matter to the Parliament practically means leaving it to the voice of those provinces who happen to have a larger representation at the Centre, and that I think, would cut at the root of the justice which you want to be done to the various provinces.[124]

All these suggestions were discussed by the Drafting Committee, which accepted the recommendations of the N.R. Sarkar Committee in most respects. For the long term, it had recommended the setting up of an expert body to make periodic recommendations. This would be known as the FC and it would focus on three broad issues:

- the allocation of centrally administered taxes between the provinces;
- considering the application for the Government of India Act for provinces and recommending thereon; and
- considering and reporting on other matters referred to it by the President.

[124]Ibid.

The Constitution indicates the broad framework for the ToR of the FC but also allows the Commission to determine its own principles for making its recommendations in relation to the ToR. In addition, Parliament enacted the Finance Commission (Miscellaneous Provisions) Act, 1951, which prescribes the qualifications of the chairman and other members of the FC. It also suggests the procedures that the FC should follow to perform its duties.

Commissions on Centre–State Relations

India's fiscal federal evolution has been marked by recommendations from a number of commissions and committees. These have been listed below.

Administrative Reforms Commission, 1969

The Administrative Reforms Commission of 1969 held that the Indian constitution is a balanced federation with a strong Centre that is vested with adequate powers to ensure unity and integrity while providing maximum autonomy to the states. Some of its key recommendations include:

- The FC may make recommendations on principles which should govern the distribution of plan grants to states.
- The timely appointment of the FC recommendations may be such that the forthcoming FYP may be outlined.
- A member from the Planning Commission may be appointed to the FC for effective coordination.
- The FC should include two persons: 1) with experience of financial administration at the Centre and 2) with experience of financial administration in the states.

- The unit of the Plan Finance Division of the Ministry of Finance should be strengthened.[125]

Rajamannar Committee, 1971

The Rajamannar Committee of 1971 was constituted by the government of Tamil Nadu to examine the relationship between the Centre and the states to secure the utmost autonomy for the states. It recommended that the bases for the devolution of revenues on the states be broadened to include corporation tax, custom and export duties and tax on capital value of assets in the divisible pool. This Committee also observed that the Centre's plan projects depended on the recommendations of the Planning Commission. Therefore, the FC cannot operate in the same field.[126]

Sarkaria Commission, 1983

The Sarkaria Commission of 1983 was constituted to examine and review the working of the arrangements between the Centre and the states regarding their respective powers, functions and responsibilities. Some of its more important recommendations included:

- Corporate tax should be made shareable with states.
- Certain levies should be liberalized and loan procedures and foreign exchange entitlements should be in favour of the states.
- Municipal bonds should be tax exempt.

---

[125]'The Administrative Reforms Commission (Secretariat): Recommendations & Conclusions of Administrative Reforms Commission', Department of Administrative Reforms and Public Grievances, Government of India, https://bit.ly/3KiEq3P. Accessed on 28 April 2022.

[126]'Report of the Centre–State Relations Inquiry Committee', Tamil Digital Library: Government of Tamil Nadu, 1971, https://bit.ly/37T2nS9. Accessed on 28 April 2022.

- CSS should be strictly limited.

Under Article 263 of the Constitution, it is stated, 'Provisions with respect to an inter State Council If any any [*sic*] time it appears to the President that the public interests would be served by the establishment of a Council [...].'[127]

The Sarkaria Commission, thus, recommended an Inter-State Council, which was established as a permanent body on 28 May 1990 by a presidential order. Its objective is to discuss or investigate subjects of common interest as well as disputes among states.

Punchhi Commission, 2007

The Punchhi Commission on Centre–state relations was constituted under the chairmanship of Justice Madan Mohan Punchhi, former Chief Justice of India, in April 2007. This Commission was tasked to look into the new issues in Centre–state relations, keeping in mind the changes in polity and economy since the Sarkaria Commission over two decades before. The Commission submitted its report in March 2010. Some of its major recommendations included:

- The emergency provisions under Articles 355 and 356 should be amended to protect the interests of the states.
- A National Integration Council, much like the Department of Homeland Security (DHS) in the US, should be set up for matters of internal security.
- The Centre should consult states before introducing bills on items in the Concurrent List through the Inter-State Council.
- Guidelines should be put in place for the appointment of CMs.

[127]'Central Government Act: Article 263 in the Constitution of India 1949', Indian Kanoon, https://bit.ly/3Oauvk4. Accessed on 28 April 2022.

- Guidelines should be put in place for the appointment and removal of governors.

A Legacy of Trust

Before I highlight the recommendations of the 15th FC, it is imperative that we understand the composition and major recommendations of the first 14 FCs.

The First FC, under the chairmanship of K.C. Neogy, used the Census data of 1951 to determine the basis of the horizontal distribution of income tax among states as 20 per cent for the relative collection of the states and 80 per cent for their population. The share of Union excise duties was determined as 40 per cent of the net proceeds on tobacco, matches and vegetable oil to the states. On vertical devolution, the states' share of income taxes was 55 per cent.

The First FC granted sums under Article 273 of the Constitution as grants-in-aid of the revenues each year for the states of Assam, Bihar, Odisha and West Bengal in lieu of assignment of any share of the export duty on jute and jute products. Additionally, it also awarded revenue gap grants and grants for the purpose of expanding primary education.

Table 1: Weight of devolution by the First FC

Criteria	*Weight of (in percentage)*	
	Income tax	*Union excise duty*
Population (1951)	80	100
Relative collection of the states	20	–
Total	100	100

Source: 'Finance Commissions: A Legacy of Trust', Finance Commission India, https://bit.ly/3MMAv0X. Accessed on 4 May 2022.

Table 2: Quantum of transfers by the First FC

S. No.	*Particulars*	*INR Crore*
A	Share in central taxes	335
1	Grants under Article 273	16
2	Grants under the substantive portion of Article 275	25
3	Primary Education Grant	9
B	Total grants	50

Source: 'Finance Commissions: A Legacy of Trust', Finance Commission India, https://bit.ly/3MMAv0X. Accessed on 4 May 2022.

Between 1957 and 1962, the chairman of the Second FC was K. Santhanam. During this time, the vertical share of Union excise duties was lowered to 25 per cent, but the shareable pool was expanded to include excise on tobacco, matches, vegetable oil, sugar, tea, coffee, paper and vegetable non-essential oils. In its horizontal distribution, the Second FC gave 10 per cent weight for the relative collection of the states and 90 per cent based on the population Census of 1951. The 10 per cent weight was unspecified, although the report of the Second FC mentioned some adjustment factors to benefit the relatively less populated states.

The Commission, in consultation with the Planning Commission, made recommendations regarding loans made to state governments, which had to be implemented through executive action. These loans were for the rehabilitation of displaced persons, commercial enterprises, industrial housing and electricity undertaking, interest-free loans and loans against the collection of small savings.

Table 3: Weight of devolution by the Second FC

Criteria	*Weight of (in percentage)*	
	Income tax	*Union excise duty*
Population (1951)	90	90
Relative collection of the states	10	—
Other unspecified adjustments	—	10
Total	100	100

Source: 'Finance Commissions: A Legacy of Trust', Finance Commission India, https://bit.ly/3MMAv0X. Accessed on 4 May 2022.

Table 4: Quantum of transfers by the Second FC

S. No.	*Particulars*	*INR Crore*
A	Share in central taxes	852
1	Grants under Article 273	9
2	Grants under Article 275	188
B	Total grants	197

Source: 'Finance Commissions: A Legacy of Trust', Finance Commission India, https://bit.ly/3MMAv0X. Accessed on 4 May 2022.

The Third FC was chaired by Ashok Kumar Chanda from 1962 to 1966. The vertical share of Union excise duties was reduced to 20 per cent, though the shareable pool was expanded to include all the items on which Union excises were being levied. The horizontal distribution was at 80 per cent based on population (Census of 1951) and 20 per cent based on collection. Apart from population as a factor of horizontal distribution, they also considered relative financial weakness of the states, disparities in the level of development and the percentage of Scheduled Caste (SC) and Scheduled Tribe (ST) population.

In the Third FC's Explanatory Memorandum, there was a note of dissent on two recommendations:

- A special purpose grant should be made to certain states for improvement of communications.
- 75 per cent of the revenue component of the state plans should be included in the scheme of devolution recommended by the Commission.

The first recommendation was accepted, but the government did not consider the second recommendation. This was so because it was felt that there would be no real advantage in the states receiving assistance for their plans partly by way of statutory grants-in-aid, as recommended by the Third FC and partly on the basis of annual reviews made by the Planning Commission at the time of the framing of the annual plans. It was more desirable to take an integrated view of the entire financial picture of each state, both on revenue and capital, in relation to the state plan as a whole.

Table 5: Weight of devolution by the Third FC

Criteria	*Weight of (in percentage)*	
	Income tax	*Union excise duty*
Population (1961)	80	—
Relative collection of the states	20	—
Unspecified	—	100
Total	100	100

Source: 'Finance Commissions: A Legacy of Trust', Finance Commission India, https://bit.ly/3MMAv0X. Accessed on 4 May 2022.

Table 6: Quantum of transfers by the Third FC

S. No.	*Particulars*	*INR Crore*
A	Share in central taxes	1,067
1	Revenue deficit	244
B	Total grants	244

Source: 'Finance Commissions: A Legacy of Trust', Finance Commission India, https://bit.ly/3MMAv0X. Accessed on 4 May 2022.

The Fourth FC was chaired by P.V. Rajamannar from 1966 to 1969. The 20 per cent weight to economic backwardness included several considerations, including on per capita gross value of agricultural production, per capita value added by manufacturing, percentage of workers to the total population, percentage of enrolment in classes one to five in the age group 6–11, population per hospital bed, percentage of rural population to total population and percentage of population of SCs and STs of total population. All this was considered using the Census of 1961.

The grant made available on the basis of the recommendations of the Railway Convention Committee Grants, in lieu of taxes on railway fare, was recommended to be distributed to the states.

Table 7: Weight of devolution by the Fourth FC

Criteria	*Weight of (in percentage)*	
	Income tax	*Union excise duty*
Population (1961)	80	80
Relative collection of the states	20	—
Backwardness	—	20
Total	100	100

Source: 'Finance Commissions: A Legacy of Trust', Finance Commission India, https://bit.ly/3MMAv0X. Accessed on 4 May 2022.

Table 8: Quantum of transfers by the Fourth FC

S. No.	*Particulars*	*INR Crore*
A	Share in central taxes	1,323
1	Revenue deficit	422
B	Total grants	422

Source: 'Finance Commissions: A Legacy of Trust', Finance Commission India, https://bit.ly/3MMAv0X. Accessed on 4 May 2022.

The Fifth FC was chaired by Mahavir Tyagi from 1969 to 1974. The Fifth FC kept the vertical devolution the same. However, it changed the formula for horizontal devolution: 90 per cent weight was to be accorded based on population and 10 per cent based on relative collection of the states. The criterion for the distribution of Union excise duties was recommended at 80 per cent based on population, 6.67 per cent based on backwardness and 13.33 per cent based on income distance. The Fifth FC was the first to use the criterion of income distance. Backwardness was calculated based on the following parameters: ST population, factory workers per lakh population, net irrigated area per cultivator, length of railways and surfaces, shortfall in the number of schoolgoing children to those of schoolgoing age and the number of hospital beds. The Census of 1961 was used to determine the aforementioned criteria.

The grants to be made available to the states in lieu of tax under the repealed Railway Passenger Fares Act, 1957, were recommended to be distributed among the states in a specified proportion. This grant was distributed to the states on the basis of the statistics of gauge-wise route lengths of railways in each state and the passenger earnings from non-suburban traffic for each zonal railway.

Table 9: Weight of devolution by the Fifth FC

Criteria	*Weight of (in percentage)*	
	Income tax	*Union excise duty*
Population (1961)	90	80
Relative collection of the states	10	—
Backwardness	—	6.67
Distance per capita income	—	13.33
Total	100	100

Source: 'Finance Commissions: A Legacy of Trust', Finance Commission India, https://bit.ly/3MMAv0X. Accessed on 4 May 2022.

Table 10: Quantum of transfers by the Fifth FC

S. No	*Particulars*	*INR Crore*
A	Share in central taxes	3,628
1	Revenue deficit	638
B	Total grants	638

Source: 'Finance Commissions: A Legacy of Trust', Finance Commission India, https://bit.ly/3MMAv0X. Accessed on 4 May 2022.

K. Brahmananda Reddy chaired the Sixth FC from 1974 to 1979. The horizontal devolution remained the same at 80 per cent based on population and 20 per cent based on the revenues collected. The distribution of excise duties was revised to 75 per cent based on the population and 25 per cent based on backwardness. The Sixth FC used an unadjusted version of the distance criterion. This resulted in the highest per capita income state not getting any share of the 25 per cent proceeds of the Union excise collection. All the FCs from the Sixth FC to 14th FC used the data from the Census of 1971.

The Sixth FC also assessed the norms for improving the standard of administration and social services, such as the police, jails, education and public health in backward states. It also did not favour the establishment of a national fund for financing the relief expenditure of the states affected by natural calamities. Instead, it made suggestions for such a fund to be regarded in consultation with the Planning Commission.

Table 11: Weight of devolution by the Sixth FC

Criteria	*Weight of (in percentage)*	
	Income tax	*Union excise duty*
Population (1971)	90	75
Relative collection of the states	10	—
Distance per capita income	—	25
Total	100	100

Source: 'Finance Commissions: A Legacy of Trust', Finance Commission India, https://bit.ly/3MMAv0X. Accessed on 4 May 2022.

Table 12: Quantum of transfers by the Sixth FC

S. No.	*Particulars*	*INR Crore*
A	Share in central taxes	7,099
1	Revenue deficit	2,510
B	Total grants	2,510

Source: 'Finance Commissions: A Legacy of Trust', Finance Commission India, https://bit.ly/3MMAv0X. Accessed on 4 May 2022.

The Seventh FC was chaired by J.M. Shelat from 1979 to 1984. The vertical devolution proceeds from excise duties, which had been fixed at 20 per cent, were raised to 40 per cent. The horizontal devolution remained the same at 90 per cent based on population and 10 per cent on relative collection. It was recommended that the share of excise duties be distributed by giving equal weightage to four factors: population, the inverse of per capita state domestic product, the poverty ratio and a revenue equalization formula. The poverty criterion was constructed by taking the share of people below the poverty line from each state in the aggregate of all the people below the poverty line. The revenue equalization formula was constructed by measuring the distance of the revenue potential of each state from the highest potential estimated among all the states. The distance was multiplied by the respective population of the state and the share of this product was obtained from the aggregate of all such products.

Regarding debt relief, the Seventh FC suggested the following:

- There should be a consolidation of small savings loans in perpetuity.
- There should be a consolidation of the rest of the central loans into one loan for each state. A portion of the loan so consolidated may be written off for each state.
- A further portion of the loans so consolidated may be recovered over 15 to 30 annual instalments paid yearly.
- The interest rate charged should be between 4.75 per cent and 5 per cent.

Table 13: Weight of devolution by the Seventh FC

Criteria	*Weight of (in percentage)*	
	Income tax	*Union excise duty*
Population (1971)	90	25
Relative collection of the states	10	–
Inverse of the per capita state domestic product	–	25
Population below poverty line	–	25
Revenue equalization	–	25
Total	100	100

Source: 'Finance Commissions: A Legacy of Trust', Finance Commission India, https://bit.ly/3MMAv0X. Accessed on 4 May 2022.

Table 14: Quantum of transfers by the Seventh FC

S. No.	*Particulars*	*INR Crore*
A	Share in central taxes	19,233
1	Revenue gap	1,173
2	Upgradation grant	437
B	Total grants	1,610

Source: 'Finance Commissions: A Legacy of Trust', Finance Commission India, https://bit.ly/3MMAv0X. Accessed on 4 May 2022.

The Eighth FC was chaired by Y.B. Chavan from 1984 to 1989. The vertical devolution of the net proceeds of excise duties increased from 40 per cent to 45 per cent. Out of this 45 per cent, 5 per cent was kept aside to be distributed on the basis of post-devolution assessed non-plan revenue deficit of the states. The horizontal devolution criteria had changed, with

22.5 per cent based on population, 22.5 per cent based on inverse of per capita income multiplied by population, 45 per cent based on distance of per capita income and 10 per cent based on relative collection.

The Eighth FC was requested to submit its report to the President by 31 October 1983. However, at the request of the Eighth FC, its term was extended up to 29 February 1984 and then further to 30 April 1984. In view of the delay in the submission of the report, the Eighth FC submitted an interim report covering the year 1984–85 on 14 November 1983, so that the recommendations contained in the interim report could be considered prior to the presentation of the Budget for 1984–85. The recommendations made by the Eighth FC were accepted by the government and a memorandum on the action taken was tabled on 9 December 1983.

Table 15: Weight of devolution by the Eighth FC

Criteria	*Weight of (in percentage)*	
	Income tax	*Union excise duty*
Population (1971)	22.5	25
Inverse of the per capita income multiplied by population	22.5	25
Distance of per capita income	45	50
Relative collection of the states	10	–
Total	100	100

Source: 'Finance Commissions: A Legacy of Trust', Finance Commission India, https://bit.ly/3MMAv0X. Accessed on 4 May 2022.

Table 16: Quantum of transfers by the Eighth FC

S. No.	*Particulars*	*INR Crore*
A	Share in central taxes	35,683
1	Revenue account deficit	2,200
2	Grants for upgradation of services	914
3	Special problems	53
4	Financing of relief expenditure	602
B	Total grants	3,769

Source: 'Finance Commissions: A Legacy of Trust', Finance Commission India, https://bit.ly/3MMAv0X. Accessed on 4 May 2022.

The Ninth FC was chaired by N.K.P. Salve from 1989 to 1995. The states' share of the excise remained at 45 per cent, a certain portion of which was kept aside for devolution on the basis of a deficit criterion. The criteria on horizontal distribution of income tax were revised: 10 per cent on the contribution of income tax, 45 per cent on the distance per capita income, 22.5 per cent based on population, 11.25 on backwardness and 11.25 on the inverse of per capita income multiplied by the population. The Ninth FC submitted its report in two parts: first, for the period of 1989–90, and second, for the period of 1990–95.

The Ninth FC recommended that the RBI work out a formula for the amortization of the market borrowings of the states. From 1990 to 1991, the direct Union loans for the states' plans were to have a maturity period of 20 years with 50 per cent of the loans enjoying a grace period of five years. The loans given to the federating states for drought relief during 1986–89 that were outstanding as of 31 March 1989 were to be waived. The loans advanced to the states during this period and outstanding as of 31 March 1990 were recommended to be consolidated and rescheduled to 15 years in the case of all states.

Table 17: Weight of devolution by the Ninth FC

Criteria	*Weight of (in percentage)*	
	Income tax	*Union excise duty*
Contribution (income tax)	10	—
Distance of per capita income	45	33.5
Population (1971)	22.5	25
Composite index of backwardness	11.25	12.5
Inverse of per capita income multiplied by the population	11.25	—
Income adjusted total population	—	12.5
Non-plan deficits	—	16.5
Total	100	100

Source: 'Finance Commissions: A Legacy of Trust', Finance Commission India, https://bit.ly/3MMAv0X. Accessed on 4 May 2022.

Table 18: Quantum of transfers by the Ninth FC

S. No.	*Particulars*	*INR Crore*
A	Share in central taxes	87,882
1	Financing of relief expenditure (a+b)	3,137
a	Calamity Relief Fund	3,015
b	Relief fund to victims of Bhopal Gas tragedy	122
2	Revenue deficit grants	15,017
B	Total grants	18,154

Source: 'Finance Commissions: A Legacy of Trust', Finance Commission India, https://bit.ly/3MMAv0X. Accessed on 4 May 2022.

The 10th FC was chaired by K.C. Pant from 1995 to 2000. The share from the net proceeds of excise duties was raised to 47.5 per cent to compensate for the reduced share in income tax. The 10th FC did not change the weightages recommended by the Ninth FC on horizontal devolution. However, it recommended two schemes. The first was based on the conventional sharing of income tax and Union excise duties and the second on the shareable pool. It also recommended the following grants:

- upgradation grants worth ₹1,360 crore and ₹1,250 crore to solve special problems of the states;
- grants-in-aid of about ₹7,583 crore to cover the deficits on revenue accounts;
- ₹6,304.27 crore for financing calamity relief for all the states; and
- grants worth ₹5,381 crore for local bodies.

Like the Ninth FC, the 10th FC was specifically mandated to assess the entire debt position of the states and not merely for Union loans. It was also asked to recommend measures for reducing the fiscal deficit. Accordingly, the 10th FC recommended the following relief and corrective measures:

- a scheme of general debt relief for all states linked to their fiscal performance;
- specific relief for three states with fiscal stress—Odisha, Bihar and Uttar Pradesh;
- special loans for Punjab to fight militancy and insurgency; and
- a total relief of ₹44 crore for special category states.

The 10th FC was also the first one to recommend the provision of grants to the third tier of the government or the PRIs, following the 73rd and 74th Amendments to the Constitution, which was accepted by the government. These grants were recommended to be treated as part of the plans of the state governments, earmarked to be transferred to local bodies. Hereafter, the issue of the third tier invariably became an integral part of the ToRs of all the subsequent FCs.

Table 19: Weight of devolution by the 10th FC

Criteria	*Weight of (in percentage)*	
	Income tax	*Union excise duty*
Population (1971)	20	20
Distance of per capita income	60	60
Area adjusted	5	5
Index of infrastructure	5	5
Tax efforts	10	10
Total	100	100

Source: 'Finance Commissions: A Legacy of Trust', Finance Commission India, https://bit.ly/3MMAv0X. Accessed on 4 May 2022.

Table 20: Quantum of transfers by the 10th FC

S. No.	*Particulars*	*INR Crore*
A	Share in central taxes	206,343
1	Upgradation and Special Problem Grants	2,610
2	Financing of relief expenditure	4,728
3	Local bodies grants	5,381
4	Revenue deficit grants	7,583
B	Total grants	20,302

Source: 'Finance Commissions: A Legacy of Trust', Finance Commission India, https://bit.ly/3MMAv0X. Accessed on 4 May 2022.

The 11th FC was chaired by A.M. Khusro from 2000 to 2005. Following the 80th Amendment of the Constitution, the pattern for sharing of Union taxes with the states fundamentally changed. Under the amended Article 270, all the taxes included in the Union List (except the duties and taxes referred to in Articles 268, 269 and 269-A, surcharges and any cess levied for specific purpose under an Act of Parliament) are shareable with the states. The amendment came into effect on 9 June 2000. It was implemented with the recommendations of the 11th FC. The net proceeds from Union taxes and duties were fixed at 29.5 per cent. On horizontal devolution, the weightages accorded were as follows: 62.5 per cent based on the income distance method, 10 per cent on the population Census of 1971, 7.5 per cent on area, 7.5 per cent on the index of infrastructure, 7.5 per cent on fiscal discipline and 5 per cent on tax effort.

The 11th FC submitted its report on 7 July 2000. It was asked, on the President's order, to 'draw a monitorable fiscal reforms programme aimed at reduction of revenue deficit of the States and to recommend the manner in which the grants to States to cover the assessed deficit in their non-plan revenue account may be linked to progress in implementing the programme.'[128] Therefore, in addition to the main report, it had also submitted two interim reports on 15 January 2000 and 30 August 2000.

[128]'Explanatory Memorandum as to the action taken on the recommendations made by the Eleventh Finance Commission in its Interim Report submitted to the President on January 15, 2000', Finance Commission India, https://bit.ly/3EgTkXe. Accessed on 14 April 2022.

Table 21: Weight of devolution by the 11th FC

Criteria	*Weight of (in percentage)*
Income distance method	62.5
Population (1971)	10
Area	7.5
Index of infrastructure	7.5
Fiscal discipline	7.5
Tax effort	5
Total	100

Source: 'Finance Commissions: A Legacy of Trust', Finance Commission India, https://bit.ly/3MMAv0X. Accessed on 4 May 2022.

Table 22: Quantum of transfers by the 11th FC

S. No.	*Particulars*	*INR Crore*
A	Share in central taxes	376,318
1	Non-plan revenue deficit	35,359
2	Local bodies	10,000
3	Relief expenditure	8,256
4	Upgradation and special problems	4,973
B	Total grants	58,588

Source: 'Finance Commissions: A Legacy of Trust', Finance Commission India, https://bit.ly/3MMAv0X. Accessed on 4 May 2022.

The 12th FC was chaired by C. Rangarajan from 2005 to 2010. The share of states in the total shareable Union taxes was fixed at 30.5 per cent. The formula for horizontal devolution was as follows: 50 per cent on income distance, 25 per cent on the population Census of 1971, 10 per cent on area, 7.5 per cent on tax effort and 7.5 on fiscal discipline. The total grant awarded to the states for 2005–10 for local bodies was ₹25,000 crore. Further, a grant of ₹5,887 crore was recommended for health equalization.

The 12th FC had recommended grants-in-aid for several sectors, including education, health, maintenance of roads, bridges and public buildings, maintenance of forests and heritage conservation, all of which were accepted by the government.

Additionally, the 12th FC recommended that the scheme of fiscal reform facility may be replaced by a scheme of debt relief over the period of 2005–10. The government accepted this recommendation, subject to the condition that the debt relief would be admissible on the state enacting the FRL, and would be effective prospectively from the year in which the legislation was enacted. Thus, the state-level FRBM was enacted for all states between 2002 and 2007, except for Sikkim and West Bengal, which enacted it in 2010.

Table 23: Weight of devolution by the 12th FC

Criteria	*Weight of (in percentage)*
Income distance	50
Population (1971)	25
Area	10
Fiscal discipline	7.5
Tax effort	7.5
Total	100

Source: 'Finance Commissions: A Legacy of Trust', Finance Commission India, https://bit.ly/3MMAv0X. Accessed on 4 May 2022.

Table 24: Quantum of transfers by the 12th FC

S. No.	*Particulars*	*INR Crore*
A	Share in central taxes	613,112
1	Non-plan revenue deficit	56,856
2	Local bodies	25,000
3	Calamity relief	16,000
4	Roads and bridges	15,000
5	Education	10,172
6	State specific	7,100
7	Health sector	5,887
8	Buildings	5,000
9	Forests	1,000
10	Heritage conservation	625
B	Total grants	142,640

Source: 'Finance Commissions: A Legacy of Trust', Finance Commission India, https://bit.ly/3MMAv0X. Accessed on 4 May 2022.

The 13th FC was chaired by Dr Vijay L. Kelkar from 2010 to 2015. The share of states in the net proceeds of the shareable Union taxes was set at 32 per cent. The formula for horizontal devolution was changed: 47.5 per cent based on the fiscal capacity distance, 25 per cent on the population Census of 1971, 17.5 per cent on fiscal discipline and 10 per cent on area. The 13th FC recommended 14 different grants, aggregating to ₹258,581 crore, which included grants for local bodies, revenue deficit and disaster relief, to mention a few.

Table 25: Weight of devolution by the 13th FC

Criteria	Weight of (in percentage)
Fiscal capacity distance	47.5
Population (1971)	25
Fiscal discipline	17.5
Area	10
Total	100

Source: 'Finance Commissions: A Legacy of Trust', Finance Commission India, https://bit.ly/3MMAv0X. Accessed on 4 May 2022.

Table 26: Quantum of transfers by the 13th FC

S. No.	*Particulars*	*INR Crore*
A	Share in central taxes	1,448,096
1	Local bodies	87,519
2	Non-plan revenue deficit	51,800
3	State specific	27,945
4	Disaster relief	26,373
5	Elementary education	24,068
6	Roads and bridges	19,930
7	Justice delivery	5,000
8	Water sector management	5,000
9	Forest	5,000
10	Unique Identification (UID)	2,989
11	Performance incentive	1,500
12	District Innovation Fund	616
13	Statistical system	616
14	Employee and pension database	225
B	Total grants	258,581

Source: 'Finance Commissions: A Legacy of Trust', Finance Commission India, https://bit.ly/3MMAv0X. Accessed on 4 May 2022.

The 14th FC was chaired by Y.V. Reddy from 2015 to 2020. The vertical devolution of taxes was increased from 32 per cent to 42 per cent. The formula for horizontal devolution was: 50 per cent based on income distance, 17.5 per cent based on the population Census of 1971, 15 per cent on demographic change based on the new population Census of 2011 and 7.5 per cent on forest cover. In assessing the states' needs, the 14th FC did not go by the plan and non-plan distinctions, but considered the entire revenue expenditure. It, thus, recommended ₹194,820 crore as revenue deficit grants.

The 14th FC was given special ToRs for 'cooperative federalism' to achieve national goals. CSS were envisaged in the areas of health, education, agriculture and rural development, etc. However, the rigidity of these schemes did not allow them to meet local requirements. Thus, the states asked for greater autonomy in designing the implementation of these CSS. In this context, the Union Government, under the recommendations of the 14th FC, decided to devolve a much higher share of 42 per cent of the Union net tax receipts to the states. This allowed the states higher autonomy to finance and design their CSS.

Table 27: Weight of devolution by the 14th FC

Criteria	*Weight of (in percentage)*
Income distance	50
Population (1971)	17.5
Area	15
Demographic change (population 2011)	10
Forest cover	7.5
Total	100

Source: 'Finance Commissions: A Legacy of Trust', Finance Commission India, https://bit.ly/3MMAv0X. Accessed on 4 May 2022.

Table 28: Quantum of transfers by the 14th FC

S. No.	*Particulars*	*INR Crore*
A	Share in central taxes	3,948,188
1	Local bodies	287,436
2	Revenue deficit grant	194,820
3	Disaster relief	55,097
B	Total grants	537,353

Source: 'Finance Commissions: A Legacy of Trust', Finance Commission India, https://bit.ly/3MMAv0X. Accessed on 4 May 2022.

Finance Commission in COVID Times

The 15th FC was constituted by the President under Article 280 of the Constitution on 27 November 2017. I was privileged to be the chairman of the 15th FC, which comprised four distinguished members. The title of the report 'Finance Commission in COVID Times', submitted to the President for the period 2021–26, itself speaks of the onerous task the 15th FC had in hand when the pandemic had significantly impacted the economy and shrunk the overall pie of resources. The Union Government accepted most of the recommendations on 1 February 2021, in its action taken report in Parliament.

In a slight variation from past practice, the 15th FC produced two reports based on its ToR. The interim report for the year 2020–21 was titled, 'Report for the Year 2020–21'. The term of the 15th FC was extended to submit its report by October 2021 for a five-year period. Reckoning with the interim report, the recommendations were designed to cover a six-year period from 2020 to 2026.

This report was organized in four volumes:

- Volume I and II, like the previous reports, contain the main report and the accompanying annexes.

- Volume III is devoted to the Union Government and examines key departments in greater depth, with the medium-term challenges and the road map ahead.
- Volume IV is entirely devoted to the states. The 15th FC analysed the finances of each state in great depth and came up with state-specific considerations to address each state's key challenges.

The main report has 117 recommendations. Out of these, 108 action-oriented recommendations have been included in another publication called 'Salient Recommendations.'[129] In volumes III and IV, the 15th FC has suggested numerous reforms for the Union ministries and state governments, respectively.

In the lead up to the constitution of the 15th FC, there was an asymmetry of expectations. It was felt that the 14th FC had been overgenerous in not opting for an incremental increase in the share of tax devolution, in favour of the states. This had been the practice in the past, but this share sharply increased from 32 to 42 per cent. Simultaneously, it was explained that, given the abolition of the Planning Commission, the resources assigned to the states through that conduit had ceased. It was also felt that since many of the CSS were in the domain of the states and could be rationalized substantially, the higher untied funds to the states would reinforce federal autonomy but not necessarily give significantly higher resources to the states. On the other hand, the states felt that since the expected enhanced financial resources from the recommendations of the 14th FC had a natural practice, the devolution of 42 per cent needed to increase.

[129]'Salient Recommendations of the Fifteenth Finance Commission's 2021–26 Report', *Gist of Fifteenth Finance Commission Report along with Action Taken Report on Its Recommendations*, September 2021, Government of Tamil Nadu, https://bit.ly/3N7pQ1d. Accessed on 4 May 2022.

In a lighter vein, the 15th FC faced the classic dilemma which all FCs face—that the needs of the Union had increased substantially and there were good reasons to reduce the vertical devolution. Hardly any state government that we visited believed that a sharp upward increase would be appropriate. I am mentioning this only because I would like other FCs, which were constituted in the background, to be aware of the somewhat unusual circumstance of incremental changes in the percentage of vertical devolution that the 15th FC faced.

The second broad feature was the report's very wide-ranging ToR. The Constitution, under Article 280(2)(c), states, 'any other matter referred to the Commission by the President in the interests of sound finance.'[130]

Based on this, successive FCs have been given increasingly broader ToRs. For the 15th FC, the terms were particularly wide-ranging since it was asked to recommend performance incentives for the states in many areas.

Another somewhat unique feature was a subsequent amendment to the ToR, which asked the 15th FC to examine the rationale for a non-lapsable fund for defence and internal security. In the context of these broad features, the 15th FC's core recommendations have been listed below.

Vertical Devolution

To maintain the predictability and stability of resources, especially during the pandemic, the 15th FC recommended maintaining the vertical devolution at 41 per cent—same as in the report for 2020–21. It maintained the level of 42 per cent of the divisible pool recommended by the 14th FC. However, the 15th FC made the adjustment of about 1 per cent due to the changed status of the erstwhile state of Jammu and Kashmir into

---

[130]'Central Government Act: Article 280 in the Constitution of India 1949', Indian Kanoon, https://bit.ly/37iSxbW. Accessed on 15 April 2022.

the new union territories of Ladakh and Jammu and Kashmir.

In the 15th FC's assessment, gross tax revenues for a five-year period were expected to be ₹135.2 lakh crore. Out of that, the divisible pool (after deducting cesses, surcharges and the cost of collection) was estimated to be ₹103 lakh crore. The states' share, at 41 per cent of the divisible pool, came to ₹42.2 lakh crore for 2021–26. Including the total grants worth ₹10.33 lakh crore and the tax devolution of ₹42.2 lakh crore, aggregate transfers to states were estimated to remain at around 50.9 per cent of the divisible pool during 2021–26.

The total FC transfers (devolution + grants) constitute about 34 per cent of the estimated gross revenue receipts of the Union, leaving adequate fiscal space for the Union to meet its resource requirements and spending obligations on national development priorities.

Horizontal Devolution

Based on the principles of need, equity and performance, the overall devolution formula is as follows.

Table 29: Weight of devolution by the 15th FC

Criteria	*Weight (in percentage)*
Population	15
Area	15
Forest and ecology	10
Income distance	45
Tax and fiscal efforts	2.5
Demographic performance	12.5
Total	100

Source: 'Finance Commission in COVID Times: Report for 2021–26, Vol. 1', Finance Commission India, https://bit.ly/3OWFLkl. Accessed on 4 May 2022.

On horizontal devolution, while the 15th FC agreed that the Census 2011 population data better represented the needs of the states, to be fair to the states, and reward the ones that had done better on the demographic front, a 12.5 per cent weight was assigned to the demographic performance criterion. Additionally, it reintroduced the tax effort criterion to reward fiscal performance.

Revenue Deficit Grants

Based on uniform norms of assessing the revenues and expenditures of the states and the Union, the Commission recommended total revenue deficit grants of ₹294,514 crore to 17 states over our award period.

Local Governments

The total size of the grant to local governments was recommended to be ₹436,361 crore for the period 2021–26. Of these total grants, ₹8,000 crore were performance-based grants for the incubation of new cities and ₹450 crore were for shared municipal services. A sum of ₹236,805 crore was earmarked for rural local bodies, ₹121,055 crore for ULBs and ₹70,051 crore for health grants through local governments.

ULBs were categorized into two groups based on population, and different norms were used for the flow of grants to each, based on their specific needs and aspirations. Basic grants were proposed only for cities or towns with a population of less than a million. For million-plus cities, 100 per cent of the grants were performance-linked through the Million-Plus Cities Challenge Fund (MCF).

Health

The 15th FC recommended that health spending by states be increased to more than 8 per cent of their budget by 2022.

Given the interstate disparity in the availability of medical doctors, it was essential to constitute an All India Medical and Health Service, as is envisaged under Section 2A of the All-India Services Act, 1951. The total grants-in-aid support to the health sector over the award period worked out to ₹106,606 crore, which is 10.3 per cent of the total grants-in-aid recommended by the 15th FC. The grants for the health sector will be unconditional.

The 15th FC also recommended health grants aggregating to ₹70,051 crore for urban HWCs, building-less sub-centres, public health centres (PHCs), CHCs, block-level public health units, support for the diagnostic infrastructure of primary healthcare activities and conversion of rural sub-centres and PHCs to HWCs. These grants are to be released to the local governments. From the remaining grant of ₹31,755 crore for the health sector (total of ₹106,606 crore minus ₹70,051 crore for local bodies and ₹4,800 crore for state-specific grants), the 15th FC recommended using ₹15,265 crore for critical care hospitals. This included ₹13,367 crore for general states and ₹1,898 crore for North Eastern Hill (NEH) states. The 15th FC recommended ₹13,296 crore for training the allied healthcare workforce. Out of this, ₹1,986 crore are to be for NEH states and ₹11,310 crore for general states.

Performance Incentives and Grants

The 15th FC recommended grants of ₹4,800 crore (₹1,200 crore per year) from 2022–23 to 2025–26 for incentivizing states to enhance educational outcomes. A grant of ₹6,143 crore was recommended for online learning and development of professional courses (medical and engineering) in regional languages (matribhasha) for higher education in India.

The 15th FC recommended that ₹45,000 crore be kept as a performance-based incentive for all states for carrying out agricultural reforms including:

- amending their land-related laws on the lines of NITI Aayog's model law;
- maintaining and augmenting their groundwater stock;
- growing their agricultural exports; and
- producing oilseeds, pulses and wood and wood-based products.

On state-specific grants, ₹49,599 crore were recommended during our award period for social needs, administrative governance and related infrastructure, conservation and sustainable use of water, drainage and sanitation, preserving culture and historical monuments, high-cost physical infrastructure and tourism.

Table 30: Grants recommended by the 15th FC

S. No.	*Grant components*	*2021–26 (INR crore)*
1	Revenue deficit grants	294,514
2	Local governments grants	436,361
3	Disaster management grants	122,601
4	Sector-specific grants	129,987
i	Sectoral grants for health	31,755
ii	School education	4,800
iii	Higher education	6,143
iv	Implementation of agricultural reforms	45,000
v	Maintenance of Pradhan Mantri Gram Sadak Yojana roads	27,539
vi	Judiciary	10,425
vii	Statistics	1,175
viii	Aspirational districts and blocks	3,150

S. No.	Grant components	2021–26 (INR crore)
5	State-specific	49,599
	Total	1,033,062

Source: 'Finance Commission in COVID Times: Report for 2021–26, Vol. 1', Finance Commission India, https://bit.ly/3OWFLkl. Accessed on 4 May 2022.

Defence and Internal Security

Considering the extant strategic requirements for national defence in the global context, the 15th FC recalibrated the relative shares of Union and states in gross revenue receipts by reducing our grants component by 1 per cent. This will enable the Union to set aside resources for the special funding mechanism that the 15th FC has proposed. The 15th FC recommended that the Union Government may constitute a dedicated non-lapsable fund, Modernisation Fund for Defence and Internal Security (MFDIS) in the Public Account of India. The total indicative size of the proposed MFDIS over the period 2021–26 is ₹238,354 crore.

Fiscal Consolidation

The 15th FC provided a range for the fiscal deficit and debt paths of both the Union and states. For the states, it provided a net borrowing limit of 4 per cent of the GSDP in 2021–22, which tapers off by the terminal year to 3 per cent. For the Union, being responsible for macro-stabilization, the 15th FC recommended an elevated borrowing path. It also recommended additional borrowing room to states based on performance in power sector reforms.

On the CSS, the 15th FC recommended that a threshold amount of annual appropriation be fixed, below which the funding for a CSS may be stopped. Below the stipulated threshold, the administrating department should justify the need for the continuation of the scheme. As the life cycle of ongoing schemes has been made co-terminus with the cycle of FCs, the third-party evaluation of all CSSs should be completed within a stipulated time frame. The flow of monitoring information should be regular and should include credible information on output and outcome indicators.

The 15th FC, in view of the prevailing uncertainties as well as the contemporary realities and challenges, recognized the need for majorly restructuring the FRBM Act. A timetable for defining and achieving debt sustainability may be examined by a high-powered intergovernmental group, which could craft the new FRBM framework and oversee its implementation. It is important that the Union and state governments amend their FRBM acts, based on the recommendations of the group, to ensure that their legislations are consistent with the fiscal sustainability framework that has been put in place. This group could also be tasked with overseeing the implementation of the 15th FC's diverse recommendations.

State governments may also explore the formation of independent public debt management cells, which will chart their borrowing programmes efficiently.

Budget of 2022–23

The Union Budget of 2022–23 and the Economic Survey of 2021–22 have brought out the central transfers for the current fiscal year, which have been listed in Table 31.

The figures highlight that the transfers remain in the region of 29.6 per cent, notwithstanding the stability in the accepted recommendation of 41 per cent–42 per cent, if adjusted for union territories, by the 14th and 15th FCs. These have not made a decisive difference because the share of the divisible pool, namely, net tax revenue, discounting cess and surcharge, has remained unaltered. The issue of cess and surcharge has been extensively covered in this chapter and the recent Budget has made no difference.

Table 31: Revenue receipts of tax revenue (in INR crore)

	Actuals 2020–21	*Budget estimates* 2021–22	*Revised estimates* 2021–22	*Budget estimated* 2022–23
Gross tax revenue	2,027,101.95	2,217,059.27	2,516,059.27	2,757,820.13
Corporation tax	457,718.97	547,000	635,000	720,000
Taxes on income	487,143.71	561,000	615,000	700,000
Wealth tax	11.85	—	—	—
Goods and services tax	548,777.34	630,000	675,000	780,000
Customs	134,750.39	136,000	189,000	213,000
Union excise duties	391,749	335,000	394,000	335,000
Service tax	1,614.84	1,000	1,000	2,000
Taxes of union territories	5,336.34	7,059.27	7,059.27	7,820.13
A. Centre's net tax revenue	1,426,287.08	1,545,396.53	1,765,144.65	1,934,770.66
Devolution to the states	594,996.76	665,562.74	744,784.62	816,649.47

Source: 'Receipt Budget, 2022–2023', India Budget, https://bit.ly/3KHOyDu. Accessed on 4 May 2022.

Legacy Issues, New Challenges

Vertical Devolution

In the context of vertical devolution, the need to balance the requirements of the Union with those of the state remains problematic. A rigorous analysis of the expenditure outcomes of each of the central ministries has eluded successive commissions. In a sense, the FC is not the expenditure commission. The rationale for the constitution of a permanent expenditure commission is that, without its analysis of a mechanical correlation between outlays and outcomes contained in the annual statement of the FM, the need for the rigour in evaluating the outcomes of public expenditure will not be met in a continuous and timely manner. In a sense, all FCs tend to take the expenditure of the Union as a given, with some suggestions on reprioritization without rigour or scrutiny. This will remain problematic without other institutional arrangements.

Connected with this, is the issue of the increasing reach of the new CSS and the Union Government's expenditure and the rationale for it. This has larger implications, some of which have been commented upon in a different chapter regarding the constitutional amendments needed.

Another issue that has become increasingly portentous is the non-divisible nature of cesses and surcharges. Following the 80th Constitutional Amendment of Article 270 in 2000, while the divisible pool has been broadened to include all central taxes, it specifically excludes cesses and surcharges. The relevant constitutional provision reads,

> 270. (1) All taxes and duties referred to in the Union List, except the duties and taxes referred to in articles 268 and 269, respectively, surcharge on taxes and duties referred to in article 271 and any cess levied for specific

> purposes under any law made by Parliament shall be levied and collected by the Government of India and shall be distributed between the Union and the States...[131]

Over a period of time, cess and surcharge as a portion of the divisible pool have been creeping up to reach 19.9 per cent of the divisible pool in 2021, as demonstrated in Table 32.

For understandable reasons, the states believed that keeping them out of the divisible pool substantially undercut the recommendations of the 15th FC. It should not be the case that what is given by one hand is taken away by the other. There have been repeated suggestions that there should be a ceiling on cess and surcharge as a percentage of the divisible pool. Alternatively, if this is considered too prescriptive, a portion of the cess and surcharge, say, around 30 per cent, should be shared with the states. At any rate, this is not a matter within the purview of the FC per se. Any such arrangement, either by way of a prescriptive ceiling or a sharing formula, would need an amendment of the Constitution. Pending such an amendment, this requires a larger debate and a consensus, which involves both the Centre and states. One way could be for such consultations and arrangements to be made part of the functions of the intergovernmental group, which we have suggested, or for it to become a part of the ToR of the next FC to hold consultations between the Union and states for arriving at a mutually acceptable arrangement regarding cesses and surcharges.

[131]'Article 270: Taxes levied and distributed between the Union and the States', Constitution of India, https://bit.ly/3uGCM7J. Accessed on 15 April 2022.

Table 32: Behaviour of cess and surcharge (in INR crore)

	2011–12	*2012–13*	*2013–14*	*2014–15*	*2015–16*	*2016–17*	*2017–18*	*2018–19*	*2019–20 (RE)*	*2020–21 (BE)*
Direct taxes	2,913	48,862	63,883	81,543	40,468	58,840	53,433	145,802	155,817	175,807
Indirect taxes (excluding GST)	63,394	72,545	77,387	86,417	137,482	172,224	150,529	172,312	182,665	195,460
GST compensation cess							62,612	95,081	98,327	110,500
Total cesses and surcharges	92,537	121,407	141,270	167,960	177,950	231,064	266,574	413,195	436,809	481,767
Total cess and surcharge as percentage of gross tax revenue	10.4	11.7	12.4	13.5	12.2	13.5	13.9	19.9	20.2	19.9
GST compensation cess as percentage of gross tax revenue							3.3	4.6	4.5	4.6

Source: 'Finance Commission in COVID Times: Report for 2021–26, Vol. 1', Finance Commission India, https://bit.ly/3OWFLkl. Accessed on 4 May 2022.

Horizontal Devolution

The issue of norms for determining the horizontal devolution needs wider debate. Ever since the inception of the FC, population and issues of poverty and equity have featured in one way or the other in every FC's award.

On the issue of population, the controversy around the Census data, which the FC is advised to use while making its recommendations, continues. From a common-sense perspective, since the population is not only invariably used but also reflects the concept of needs, it should be based on the most recent Census data available in the public domain. The past practice in this regard has not been uniform. Prior to the 15th FC, for nearly 40 years, the 1971 Census data was used, which had lost contemporary relevance. This issue ties back to the broader issue of our award policy encouraging, incentivizing and rewarding demographic management. While the latest data suggests that India, as a whole, may be on the threshold of a replacement rate, the issue of balancing the contemporary population Census data with population stabilization policies would engage public attention. Those who have managed their demography responsibly would have done so by multiple measures including girl child education, gender equality and awareness for the use of family planning methods, to mention a few. So, while there is an overriding rationale for using the latest Census data for population, the need to balance and reward improved demographic management with the current population will remain debatable.

The broader issue of political empowerment embedded in the controversy of the delimitation of constituencies, which has been frozen till 2026, will be equally troublesome. Of course, political empowerment must be distinguished from the allocation of financial resources. While there is merit in the need to recognize population in making financial allocations, the issue of political empowerment needs separate consideration. The two are not necessarily congruous or symmetric.

On the issue of geographical area, there has been little or no controversy. The boundaries of states are fixed and can only be altered through a legislative process. Recognizing the basic fact that states with a larger geography need enhanced resources is hardly debatable. The question of what weight should be assigned to each state must be left to the judgement of successive FCs.

Connected with the concept of needs is also the issue of forest area. Prior to the 14th FC, the specific needs of states that have a sizable forest area did not receive any specific recognition. The states that have a sizable forest area, particularly the Himalayan and Northeast states, have argued that the maintenance of these forests and the ecosystem surrounding them requires financial resources, and entails harder externalities for the country as a whole. They are not necessarily benefitted by either the forest produce or river systems. The 15th FC recognized this by according a higher weightage of 10 per cent to forest states, not only because we saw merit in their contention but also since they act as a carbon sink, which enables our conformity to environmental norms.

The issue of equity emanates from a moral compulsion. It has been recognized over the decades that in states where poverty numbers are high, the per capita income remains significantly below national averages. These states need additional resources to improve social and physical infrastructure to approximate national averages. While this has not been contested per se, it has certainly raised the debate of duration. For instance, some of the more advanced states believe that they receive a very insignificant proportion of the total revenues that are generated in their states and there should be a time period or a limit beyond which they should not be cross-subsidizing the poor development records of states where poverty numbers are still high. It is no accident that these also happen to be states where demographic management has been weaker with a high population. So, while the issue of equity has an unquestionable moral compulsion, it brings up the issue of balancing and rewarding better governance in another form. The weightage given to the per capita income or the distance of states with lowest per capita income in relation to the states where the per capita income is the highest has been the methodology used by the successive FCs. The weightage remains a matter of debate.

On the issue of performance, apart from recognizing improved demographic management, tax effort has also been recognized by successive FCs, since the 12th FC. Rewarding tax effort in terms of improved compliance norms deserves recognition. The weightage accorded will inevitably vary over time. The above approach balances the criteria of needs, equity and performance.

There can be a debate on whether some additional norms need to be considered by future FCs. These could relate to new emerging challenges like environmental compulsions beyond mere forests, improved agricultural and livelihood practices, successfully harnessing emerging technologies in multiple ways and patterns of economic activity.

The Third Tier

Ever since the enactment of the 73rd and 74th Constitutional Amendments in 1992, the needs of the third tier have invariably featured in the ToRs of the subsequent FCs. Recognizing this, the third tier has been granted varied amounts of funds. While the 14th FC had allotted ₹2.86 lakh crore to the third tier, the 15th FC, as explained earlier, decided to make a very substantial increase by recommending a 40 per cent increase, amounting to ₹4.36 lakh crore. A few broad issues are embedded in these grants, namely, whose responsibility is it, after the Constitutional Amendment, to take care of the needs of the third tier of the government? This must be seen in the context of Article 243 of the Constitution. If this constitutional provision is read strictly, the FC is not obligated to give direct awards, except to suggest modalities to increase the Consolidated Fund of the State. In practice, this has not happened. The issue has been extensively dealt with in a separate chapter in this book pertaining to the third tier.

Revenue Deficit Grants

The issue of the revenue deficit grants under Article 275 of the Constitution remains an engaging one. Right from its inception, successive FCs have resorted to recognitions under Article 275. These remain unconditional grants to reinforce the general resources of the states. These general resources are calculated on the basis of norms, both on likely revenue and the expenditure projected by the states and after careful scrutiny of the FC. An appropriate amount—appropriate in the judgment of the FC—is given to the states, which has often been described as a gap-filling method. In the past, these have been unconditional, seen as almost a right of the states. The problem is that while a percentage of devolution is given to the states, that percentage—which is fixed by the FC—is viewed, for understandable reasons, as a right of the states, and is outside the Consolidated Fund. All grants under the revenue deficit grants come from the Consolidated Fund of India. Grants, by definition, are not rights but discretionary. Therefore, should they remain unconditional? While the nature and quantum of the grants depend on the discretion of the FC and the decision of accepting this is contained in the Action Taken Report, no restrictions have ever been placed on the revenue deficit grants. What happens is the norms, based on which the revenues and expenditures of the states are assessed by the FC, are flouted by the states through fiscal profligacy or tardy revenue measures in one form or the other. Nonetheless, these resources remain available. The issue of conditionality, or of revenue deficit grants, remains a dilemma for the FC.

Action Taken Report

Under Article 281 of the Constitution, it is stipulated that:

> Recommendations of the Finance Commission The President shall cause every recommendation made by the Finance Commission under the provisions of this Constitution together with an explanatory memorandum as to the action taken thereon to be laid before each House of Parliament Miscellaneous Financial Provisions[.]

This constitutional obligation has been adhered to fully and every report of the FC has been invariably accompanied by an Action Taken Report (ATR). The broader issue of whether these recommendations should be binding or purely recommendatory is a subject of wider debate, but in accordance with the existing constitutional provision, they are, indeed, recommendatory. In practice, however, the recommendations of the FCs have been treated as awards and accepted by the government in office. This is true in respect of the basic awards, which involves the vertical and the horizontal distribution of the divisible resources as well as those given under Article 275 of the Constitution. This has also meant that, following the constitutional amendment, the recommendations regarding the third tier have also been accepted by the government. This is equally true of the recommendations regarding disaster management.

Consistent with the same practice, for the 15th FC, in the ATR placed in Parliament, the government accepted the following basic recommendations.

- 41 per cent of the net proceeds of taxes to be shared with the states.
- All revenue deficit grants given in Article 275 of the Constitution as well as grants given to ULBs and the provision regarding disaster management.
- Regarding sector-specific grants, the ATR says, 'Government will give due consideration to sectors identified by the Commission while formulating and implementing existing and new Centrally Sponsored and Central Sector Schemes.'
- Regarding state-specific grants, the ATR says, 'Keeping in view the untied resources with the State Governments and the fiscal commitments of the Central Government, due consideration will be given to the above recommendation.'
- The broad recommendations for a no lapsable fund for the defence sector has been accepted in principle but sources of funding and modalities will be considered in due course.
- The fiscal roadmap given by the FC was broadly accepted including enhanced borrowing ceilings for the states.

As is the normal practice, other recommendations made by the commission will be considered in due course. However, this is an area of weakness because many recommendations made by earlier FCs have remained under consideration without decisions or action being formally taken. It is from this perspective that the 15th FC had recommended the constitution of an intergovernmental group.[132]

To some extent, the need for monitoring fiscal compliance both by the Centre and the states leaves an autonomous entity like a fiscal council, which has been dealt with in an earlier chapter. No doubt, there has been an increasing tendency for the ToR of successive FCs to be enlarged under the constitutional provision of Article 280 (2)(c). The President is, therefore, obligated, in the interest of sound finance, to make recommendations in regard to vertical and horizontal devolution as well as grants under Article 275 of the Constitution.

GST Council

The role and function of the FC and the GST Council is an evolving one. The GST Council is, under the Constitution, a permanent institution and the FC is not. The GST Council, within its purview, determines the rates of indirect taxes, which impact both the revenues of the Union and states. The FCs can only second-guess the decisions likely to be taken by the GST Council for the entire period of their awards. The issue of decisions by the GST Council, which substantially alters the basis of the FC's judgment, has no recourse mechanism. Wider debate is, therefore, necessary on the relationship between the GST Council and the FC.

---

[132] In view of the uncertainty that prevails at the state that we have done our analysis, as well as the contemporary realities and challenges, we recognise that the FRBM Act needs a major restructuring and recommend that the time-table for defining and achieving debt sustainability may be examined by a High-powered Inter-governmental Group.

'Finance Commission in COVID Times: Report for 2021–26, Vol. 1', Finance Commission India, p. 376, https://bit.ly/3OWFLkl. Accessed on 6 June 2022.

Fiscal Norms

On fiscal norms, FCs have invariably been asked to examine and propose the expected fiscal trajectory. The Union Government is governed by the obligations of the FRBM Act, 2003, as amended by the FRBM Committee's Report in 2017. The 15th FC made two changes: first, it gave a band rather than a fixed point on the fiscal trajectory; and second, it made recommendations for the states as well. Each individual state was considered separately. The broader issues on macroeconomic stability and appropriate fiscal trajectory have been examined in a separate chapter in this book.

The final issue, which will remain a continuing challenge for the FC, is its discontinuation. Should the FC be a permanent institution, which many have argued for, based on examples in other countries, particularly Australia, South Africa and even Canada? Institutions in India have an endemic history of becoming self-perpetuating. There are credible arguments to leave it as it is rather than making it a more permanent institution. Another connected issue is whether the awards of the FC should span a period of, let us say, one or two years—or account for other structural changes—rather than the current period of five years. The issue of a recourse mechanism for the FC is debatable.

FCs are a critical component of maintaining Centre–state relations. The states are important stakeholders in the FCs' deliberations. As a consultative mechanism between the Centre and the states, a body of this nature needs to be credible and acceptable to the central and state governments. This ties back to the broader issue of a credible consultative mechanism for Centre–state relations, on which there must be a wider consensus.

Since the FC is not a permanent body—it winds up after giving its recommendations to the President—there is no continuing link for dialogue with the states, much less any recourse to correct the award of the FC depending on the evolving economic circumstances during the period of the award. The earlier feature of the Planning Commission, which has now been abolished, used to provide a consultative forum—although their mandate could never alter the awards of the FC—as accepted by Parliament. The Sarkaria Commission's recommendation for setting up an Inter-State Council has also not proved to be a viable dynamic entity. NITI Aayog is the country's premiere intellectual think tank, which is not expected to perform the functions of either the FC or the Planning Commission. In this context, there is a need to consider a more permanent consultative mechanism for continuing dialogue on financial and related issues between the Centre and the states.

ACKNOWLEDGEMENTS

These essays have been written over a period of three years or so. They are based both on personal experience as well as lectures and presentations made in a number of forums and institutions. Putting this ensemble in a coherent book has involved painstaking effort which I would like to acknowledge.

I would also like to acknowledge the unstinting support I received from the FC and others who were engaged in the FRBM Review Committee. The access to the rich websites of these bodies, which are now in public domain, was helpful in shaping our understanding. No doubt, the facilitator of this book has been my executive assistant, Esther Ruolngul, who has unfailingly worked long hours to transcribe my thoughts and, thereafter, put in enormous effort into checking the accuracy of, and sources for, the conclusions reached. This greatly facilitated the diligence process of the publishers. I also received valuable inputs from Kandarp Patel, who worked in the 15th FC, as well as from Prachi Mishra and Jessica Seddon, who helped me on multiple issues. I am grateful both to my private secretary, A.C. Mehta, and research assistant, Aniket Singh. I express my gratitude to the publishers for their due diligence and forbearance in bringing out this publication within a short span.

The five chapters that I have written for this book derive a great deal from my work experiences over the years. I am indebted to several individuals and institutions whose association and interaction enabled me to develop the ideas and themes. In preparing the chapters, on several aspects, I received valuable inputs from Amit Khare, Anita Karwal, Ramesh Chand, Kamal Kishore, Krishna S. Vatsa, Atul Kotwal, Vishal Sharma and Aditi Thakker. Ram Mohan and Ramji Lal, who work in my office, have assisted in the secretarial work. I thank all of them. Any error or omission remains my responsibility.

ANNEXURE

To access the annexure of this book, please scan the QR code given below.

INDEX